Til Åse,
med beste hilsen
fra
Morten

Palgrave Studies in European Union Politics

Edited by: **Michelle Egan**, American University, USA
Neill Nugent, Manchester Metropolitan University, UK
William Paterson, University of Birmingham, UK

Editorial Board: **Christopher Hill**, Cambridge, UK
Simon Hix, London School of Economics, UK
Mark Pollack, Temple University, USA
Kalypso Nicolaïdis, Oxford, UK
Morten Egeberg, University of Oslo, Norway
Amy Verdun, University of Victoria, Canada

Palgrave Macmillan is delighted to announce the launch of a new book series on the European Union. Following on the sustained success of the acclaimed *European Union Series*, which essentially publishes research-based textbooks, *Palgrave Studies in European Union Politics* will publish research-driven monographs.

The remit of the series is broadly defined, both in terms of subject and academic discipline. All topics of significance concerning the nature and operation of the European Union potentially fall within the scope of the series. The series is multidisciplinary to reflect the growing importance of the EU as a political and social phenomenon. We will welcome submissions from the areas of political studies, international relations, political economy, public and social policy and sociology.

Titles include:

Morten Egeberg *(editor)*
MULTILEVEL UNION ADMINISTRATION
The Transformation of Executive Politics in Europe

Heather Grabbe
THE EU'S TRANSFORMATIVE POWER

Lauren M. McLaren
IDENTITY, INTERESTS AND ATTITUDES TO EUROPEAN INTEGRATION

Justus Schönlau
DRAFTING THE EU CHARTER
Rights, Legitimacy and Process

Katie Verlin Laatikainen and Karen E. Smith *(editors)*
THE EUROPEAN UNION AND THE UNITED NATIONS

Forthcoming titles in the series include:

Ian Bache and Andrew Jordan *(editors)*
THE EUROPEANIZATION OF BRITISH POLITICS

Palgrave Studies in European Union Politics
Series Standing Order ISBN 1-4039-9511-7 (hardback) and ISBN 1-4039-9512-5 (paperback)

You can receive future titles in this series as they are published by placing a standing order. Please contact your bookseller or, in case of difficulty, write to us at the address below with your name and address, the title of the series and one of the ISBNs quoted above.

Customer Services Department, Macmillan Distribution Ltd, Houndmills, Basingstoke, Hampshire RG21 6XS, England

Multilevel Union Administration

The Transformation of Executive Politics in Europe

Edited by

Morten Egeberg
Director of ARENA – *Centre for European Studies*
and
Professor of Political Science,
University of Oslo, Norway

First published 2006 by
PALGRAVE MACMILLAN
Houndmills, Basingstoke, Hampshire RG21 6XS and
175 Fifth Avenue, New York, N.Y. 10010
Companies and representatives throughout the world

PALGRAVE MACMILLAN is the global academic imprint of the Palgrave
Macmillan division of St. Martin's Press, LLC and of Palgrave Macmillan Ltd.
Macmillan® is a registered trademark in the United States, United Kingdom
and other countries. Palgrave is a registered trademark in the European Union
and other countries.

ISBN-13: 978-1-4039-9765-4   hardback
ISBN-10: 1-4039-9765-9   hardback

This book is printed on paper suitable for recycling and made from fully
managed and sustained forest sources.

A catalogue record for this book is available from the British Library.

A catalog record for this book is available from the Library of Congress.

10   9   8   7   6   5   4   3   2   1
15   14   13   12   11   10   09   08   07   06

Printed and bound in Great Britain by
Antony Rowe Ltd, Chippenham and Eastbourne

Contents

v

List of Tables

List of Figures

Preface

A key argument in this book is that the executive branch of government in Europe is being transformed in a profound way. It is not obvious that such a change is taking place. Although studies find considerable *policy* convergence across Europe, they also reveal remarkable *institutional* robustness at the national level. Also, the extent to which executive bodies at the EU level have emancipated themselves from national governments and taken on a life of their own seems highly contested in the literature. However, the studies presented in this book seem to indicate that particular organizational features and institutional dynamics of the European Commission tend to make it more autonomous of national governments in practice, although not necessarily more influential. Politics at the Commission appear to have become more like politics as we know them from national executives.

At the international level, the peculiar development of executive bodies (that is, the Commission and EU agencies) which are separated from councils of ministers seems, according to studies presented in this book, to trigger significant centrifugal forces within national governments. One cannot expect such forces to be generated by classical international organizations in which councils of ministers and their secretariats take care of all executive tasks. Thus, although national authorities as such may have changed only marginally due to European integration, new *relationships* between institutions nevertheless have appeared. National agencies emerge in this book as constituent parts of *two* administrations: on the one hand they continue to serve national ministries, on the other they take part in the formulation and implementation of EU policies in close cooperation with the Commission or EU-level agencies, relatively independently from their respective ministries. Thus, we argue that a genuine *Union* administration that spans levels of governance is in the making.

This book gradually emerged as a result of cooperation with several younger scholars who have all been, or are, affiliated to ARENA – Centre for European Studies at the University of Oslo in one way or another. The result, I hope, therefore reflects an integrated project in the real meaning of the word. My gratitude is first and foremost to the contributors: Dario, Frode, Gitte, Günther, Jarle, Maria, Trygve, Ulf and Øivind, with whom it has been a pleasure to cooperate. I would also like to thank Johan P. Olsen whose supportive *and* highly critical remarks have been important. ARENA, by providing human, economic and technical resources has made this project possible. I am grateful to the rest of the academic staff and to the administrative personnel in this respect. In particular, I want to thank Øivind Bratberg for his quite extraordinary dedication as regards editorial and administrative support. Thanks also to the EU-financed Connex-Network of Excellence which has provided arenas for presentation and discussion of some of the draft chapters. Three of the chapters are revised journal articles: a previous version of Chapter 5 appeared in *West European Politics* 2003, 26 (3): 19–40. A previous version of Chapter 2 came out in *Comparative European Politics* 2005, 3 (1): 102–17 and, finally, a previous version of Chapter 4 was published in the *Journal of European Public Policy* 2006, 13 (1): 1–15. I thank the publishers Routledge and Palgrave Macmillan for accepting this without hesitation. I also would like to thank the staff at Palgrave Macmillan for their advice and support in the production of the book. Last, but not least, I am grateful to my wife Inger for her enduring tolerance and generosity.

MORTEN EGEBERG

Notes on the Contributors

Dario Barbieri is a researcher at L. Bocconi University in Milan, Italy. He was a PhD student at ARENA – Centre for European Studies at the University of Oslo, Norway, between February and June 2004. His research interests are public management and supranational institutions.

Morten Egeberg is Director of ARENA – Centre for European Studies and a Professor of Political Science at the University of Oslo, Norway. He has published several books, chapters and articles in international journals on governance and public administration at the national as well as the EU level.

Maria Martens is a PhD student at ARENA – Centre for European Studies at the University of Oslo, Norway. Her research interests are multilevel governance in the environmental policy area and the role of agencies at various levels.

Gitte Hyttel Nørgård holds a Master's degree in political science from the University of South Denmark, Odense. In 2003–04 she was affiliated to ARENA – Centre for European Studies at the University of Oslo, Norway, as a research assistant.

Günther F. Schaefer was a Professor of Public Administration and Public Policy at the European Institute of Public Administration (EIPA) in Maastricht, the Netherlands. One of his main research interests was EU committees. He is now retired.

Øivind Støle holds a Cand.Polit. (Master) degree in Political Science from the University of Oslo, Norway. In 2003–04 he was affiliated to ARENA – Centre for European Studies at the University of Oslo as a research assistant.

Ulf Sverdrup is a Senior Researcher at ARENA – Centre for European Studies at the University of Oslo, Norway, and has been a Jean Monnet Fellow at the European University Institute in Florence. He has published several articles in edited books and international journals on multilevel administration, implementation of EU policies and EU treaty reform.

Jarle Trondal is Director of the Centre for European Studies at Agder University College in Kristiansand, Norway. As a PhD student he was affiliated to ARENA. He has published several articles in edited books and international journals on multilevel public administration, EU committees and higher education.

Trygve Ugland is an Assistant Professor of Political Studies at Bishop's University, Canada. He was partly affiliated to ARENA during his doctoral studies. He has published several articles in international journals on public policy, particularly on food safety policy.

Frode Veggeland is a Senior Researcher at Norwegian Agricultural Economics Research Institute in Oslo, Norway. He was partly affiliated to ARENA during his doctoral studies in political science. He has published several articles in international journals on trade, environment and health.

List of Abbreviations

AGCM	Italian Antitrust Authority
APAT	Italian Environment Agency
BSE	Bovine Spongiform Encephalopathy
CC	Comitology Committee
CCA	Consultative Committee of Appointments
CFSP	Common Foreign and Security Policy
COSAC	Conference of Committees Specialized in EU Affairs
CWP	Council Working Parties
DG	Directorate General
EAS	External Action Service
EC	Commission Expert Committee
ECB	European Central Bank
ECJ	European Court of Justice
ECN	European Competition Network
ECSC	European Coal and Steel Community
EDA	European Defence Agency
EEA	European Environment Agency *or* European Economic Area
EEC	European Economic Community
EFSA	European Food Safety Authority
EFTA	European Free Trade Association
EIONET	European Environment Information and Observation Network
EIPA	European Institute of Public Administration
EMU	Economic and Monetary Union
EP	European Parliament
EPSO	European Communities Personnel Selection Office
ERG	European Regulators Group
ESA	European Standardized Accounts
ESCB	European System of Central Banks
ESDP	European Security and Defence Policy
ESS	European Statistical System
Etrios	European Training and Research Institute for Official Statistics
FVO	Food and Veterinary Office
IGO	International Governmental Organization
IMF	International Monetary Fund
IMPEL	The European Union Network for the Implementation and Enforcement of Environmental Law

IRG	Independent Regulators Group
ITTA	Danish IT and Telecom Agency
NFP	National Focal Point
NPM	New Public Management
NSI	National Statistical Institute
OECD	Organization for Economic Cooperation and Development
OEEC	Organization for European Economic Cooperation
OVPIC	Office of Veterinary and Phytosanitary Inspection and Control
SEA	Single European Act
SG	Secretariat General
SPS	Sanitary and Phytosanitary
TES	Training of European Statisticians
UN	United Nations
WTO	World Trade Organization

1
Europe's Executive Branch of Government in the Melting Pot: an Overview

Morten Egeberg

Introduction[1]

National governments have for more than a hundred years had to deal with a multitude of international governmental organizations (IGOs). In this respect governments have striven for coordination in order to be able to present their national positions as coherently as possible on the international scene. They have also been supposed to implement carefully what has been agreed upon in these forums. The development of the European Union (EU) and its predecessors has without doubt added considerably to these tasks: its extraordinarily broad and expanding policy agenda has significantly challenged the ability of national governments to act consistently on the European scene (Kassim et al. 2000), and the huge amount of EU-generated legislation to be implemented has put national administrations, although to varying degrees, under unprecedented pressure (Knill 2001; Sverdrup 2004).

In this book, however, we argue that the EU does not only add considerably to already existing patterns of multilevel governance, but that it in addition makes a *unique* difference to executive organization and politics in Europe. The uniqueness first of all relates to the existence of the European Commission (Commission), which is the only multipurpose executive body at the international level that is organizationally separated from councils of ministers. Given that this institution also has the potential to act relatively independently as an executive, this means that the executive branch of EU member states has a new and higher layer of executive organization to which to relate. Second, we argue that the peculiar functional division of labour that exists between the Commission and the Union Council (Council) triggers unique centrifugal forces at the very heart of national governments. The Commission is in need of expertise

1

for drafting new policy proposals and it depends on reliable partners for ensuring that EU decisions are properly implemented. Both might be found among national (regulatory) agencies that over the last years have increasingly been organized at arm's length from their respective ministries. This book reveals that the Commission has become increasingly 'normalized', in the sense that it at present embodies many of the organizational and behavioural patterns that are highly typical of executives as we know them from national settings. This 'normalization' also includes its boundary-spanning activities in relation to particular parts of administrations at the level beneath, which could mean that sub-territorial cores (here: national ministries) are partly circumvented. Thus, we might see a genuine multilevel *Union administration* emerging. Such developments would indicate what we will denote as a more profound transformation of executive politics within the EU.

The birth of a supranational executive

If the Commission really is as pivotal as is argued in this book we have to ask how it came about in the first place. Although WWII clearly demonstrated that the inherited political order in Europe had been unable to preserve international peace, it did not follow from this that new forms of international organization would automatically be invented or established. In fact, both the Organization for European Economic Cooperation (OEEC) and the Council of Europe were arranged as conventional IGOs, although the latter incorporated an indirectly elected parliamentary assembly. Arguably, significant institutional innovation did not take place before the organizational design of the European Coal and Steel Community (ECSC) was unveiled in 1950 (Egeberg, Chapter 2). The most crucial point, advocated by Jean Monnet, adviser to the French Foreign Minister Schuman, was the need for an executive body that could act independently of national governments and bring supranational input into the policy process in a systematic manner. The proposal for a High Authority was accepted by the five other founding countries, but only after a Council of Ministers had been added, subsequent to Dutch claims. Monnet had originally dismissed the Council, probably on the grounds that he saw it as belonging to 'the old order' (Duchêne 1994: 241). The recent war, mounting problems in the Ruhr area and the narrowness of the policy sector involved may all have contributed to getting the new supranational executive approved (Dinan 2004). The potential for radical institutional reform, such as the transfer of power to the supranational level, seems badly understood in much of the literature. Profound systemic crises, such as WWII, provide windows of opportunity for innovative entrepreneurs, windows that under normal circumstances are simply not available (Egeberg, Chapter 2).

Arguably, the four key institutions of today's EU, namely the Union Council (Council), the Commission, the European Court of Justice (ECJ) and the European Parliament (EP) were all already in place in 1952. Without in any sense trivializing the range of institutional adaptations that have taken place in the meantime, this indicates a remarkable path dependence as regards institutional development. In fact, the ECSC, Euratom and the European Economic Community (EEC) shared the same institutional framework although each had their own executive body. These executive bodies were, however, structured according to the same principles and cooperated and shared joint services in such fields as statistics, information and law (Hallstein 1962: 19–20). Interestingly, greater caution on behalf of member governments as regards the powers of the commissions was observed at the time when the Euratom and the EEC treaties were negotiated (Hallstein 1962: 20). This may suggest that had a commission first been proposed when more time had elapsed since the war and when governments were faced with an almost open-ended policy agenda (compared to that of the ECSC), it might never have been born. However, in 1955 the template for a supranational executive was already in place and only minor modifications were imposed on it.

Consolidating a supranational executive

Organizational boundaries do matter (Egeberg 2003a). So, establishing a permanent bureaucracy with its own political leadership separate from the Council and its secretariat does have consequences: it leads to the development of institutional interests on behalf of the Commission and, thus, to inter-institutional politics (Egeberg, chapters 2 and 3). However, although important, we should not assign too much weight to organizational boundaries alone. IGO secretariats may also become powerful in relation to their political masters, although within the limits set by a common organizational framework (Reinalda and Verbeek 2004; Trondal et al. 2005). Formally independent units may, on the other hand, be permeated by external actors and be without much real influence. Thus, in order to be able to ascertain the extent to which such a new type of body will manage to act relatively independently in practice we will have to take into consideration not only that it has been formally erected as a separate entity but also how it is organized and staffed and, eventually, how it actually works (Egeberg, chapters 3 and 4).

Given the inherited Westphalian state order the most crucial question is of course whether a separate supranational executive can succeed in gaining sufficient autonomy from national governments. Ernst Haas, in his *The Uniting of Europe*, concludes the chapter on the ECSC's High Authority by stating that 'the bulk of High Authority practices marks a radical departure from decision making techniques in conventional international organisation – even when it falls far short of federal practice' (Haas 1958/2004: 484). At the same time, however, he indicates that 'the ultimate influence, direct or indirect, on High Authority decisions is the national governments acting singly or in concert through the Council of Ministers' (Haas 1958/2004: 479). Also Duchêne (1994: 241) reports that High Authority relations with the Council of Ministers, the body which in Monnet's eyes belonged to the old order in the new, were sticky. The EEC Commission has also been portrayed as a house in which member states allocated portfolios among commissioners primarily on the basis of perceived national interests. A certain consistency as regards such distributions even provoked talk about the establishment of national fiefdoms at the Commission (Dinan 2004: 85–6). In 1960 President de Gaulle seems to have wanted the Rome treaties to be revised to subordinate the Commission to the Council of Ministers (Duchêne 1994: 319). And President Pompidou in 1971 sketched out a new role for the Council of Ministers, that of a future European government, reducing the Commission's role to that of a technical auxiliary (Neunreither 1972: 233).[2]

In contrast to those who portray the Commission as permeated by national interests at all levels (for example, Peterson 1999; Menon 2003) I argue in this book that the Commission seems rather to have enhanced its autonomy vis-à-vis national governments over the years. (Whether the Commission has become more or less successful in promoting its interests in various arenas is another story.) Such a development can be traced by looking at organizational and recruitment procedures and at how the Commission actually works at different points in time (Egeberg, chapters 3 and 4). For example, at an early stage, the Commission services had to rely to a considerable degree on personnel seconded from member state administrations. At present most posts are permanent, and life-long careers at the Commission are quite common. From what we know from studies of bureaucracies in general, it is easy to imagine what such a change might have meant for officials' loyalties (Egeberg 2003a). Rules established in order to prevent national clusters of officials developing may be equally important. A long-term trend seems to be that the Commission services have gradually enhanced their control of recruitment and appointment decisions (Peterson 1971). New procedures for appointing top officials seem so far to have contributed further to reducing the amount of interference by governments or commissioners in such processes (Egeberg,

Chapter 3). At the political level commissioners' cabinets (private offices) have to be multinational in composition thus diluting their previous roles as exclusive access points and enclaves for particular nationalities. Treaty revisions have also empowered the President of the Commission as regards the distribution of portfolios, both at the inception of a new college and during its term of office.

Equally important in marking clearly the boundaries around an organization could be the choice of specialization principles within the entity. Arranging the Commission according to the territorial composition of the EU could easily mean internalizing intergovernmental patterns of decision-making. However, instead, the sectoral and functional principles prevail, meaning that attention tends to be focused primarily along sectoral and functional lines rather than geographical ones. The departmental affiliation of both officials and commissioners therefore stands out as particularly important for understanding their actual decision behaviour (Egeberg, chapters 3 and 4). This is not to say, though, that nationality does not matter: we know for example that officials may facilitate access to the Commission for their compatriots and that commissioners are on the alert as regards issues that might turn out to be of particular importance for their country of origin (Egeberg, chapters 3 and 4).

A growing party politicization of the College of Commissioners may also complement or even displace potential cleavages along national lines. The College has increasingly been composed of political heavyweights and one might assume they are carrying with them more clear-cut party-political identities. And the EP has not only the right to dismiss the College as a collective but has also got a stronger role as regards the composition of the College and in daily policy-making vis-à-vis the Commission (Egeberg, chapters 3 and 4). As regards the Barroso Commission, it may be the first time that EP party groups have organized themselves into an official opposition to a Commission team.[3]

One or several EU executives?

The European Council, in addition to being an upper house for solving problems that cannot be solved in the Council, has been said to have executive functions as regards its broad agenda-setting role. However, the European Council is not an executive in the sense that it usually works out concrete policy proposals or has the responsibility for implementing EU policies. The Council, on the other hand, is clearly assigned executive tasks in relation to the Common Foreign and Security Policy (CFSP) and the European Security and Defence Policy (ESDP). It was, in addition, allocated similar functions within the area of justice and home affairs. The Amsterdam Treaty communitarized parts of this area, although criminal matters remained in the third pillar. In criminal matters the Commission also obtained a right of initiative, although a shared one (Ucarer 2003).

Executive functions in the area of foreign and security policy.   CFSP is characterized by cooperation as well as competition between the Commission and the Council. Although the leadership belongs to the shared position of High Representative of the CFSP and secretary general of the Council, the external relations Commissioner disposes of the money, most of the manpower (including the 128 delegations around the world) and most of the instruments. According to Cameron and Spence (2004: 125) the Commission has considerable autonomous control of the first pillar instruments, which make up 90 per cent of the foreign policy toolbox at the EU's disposal. The Convention on the Future of Europe and the 2004 Rome Treaty opened the way for work to begin on a common foreign service for the EU (the External Action Service (EAS)). The Constitutional Treaty establishes an EU foreign minister as a separate executive institution outside the Council and the Commission. The new post has been described as 'double-hatted' in the sense that the person in charge will be a vice-president of the Commission and at the same time will chair the Foreign Policy Council. As far as 'external relations' and coordination with other external activities are concerned, the foreign minister is to be subject to ordinary Commission procedures in his or her capacity as a vice-president. When it comes to his or her role in the CFSP the incumbent is supposed to act as a more independent executive institution, although mandated by the Council. The Commission, in its communication to the Convention, not surprisingly argued for the entire post to be completely integrated in the Commission.[4]

This in-between solution can be interpreted as a classical compromise between supranationalists and intergovernmentalists. The compromise nevertheless seems to indicate that the EU's foreign policy chief will move closer to the Commission, and perhaps equally importantly, this executive function will for the first time be *separated* from the Council. If this is implemented, weekly meetings and coordination tasks will mean that the foreign minister will probably have to spend much more time and energy in the Commission than in the Council. This may, in the long run, tip the balance in favour of the Commission. There might also be a built-in dynamic in this direction in the choice of the term 'foreign minister', because 'ministers' usually constitute a collective body at the top of a multipurpose executive. The new foreign minister apparatus and diplomatic corps will probably be composed of staff from the Council secretariat, the Commission's external services and national diplomats. If a common external service is to become a reality this would indeed create enormous pressure for down-sizing national foreign services (Batora 2005). The practical work on setting up the new organization started in 2004 under the supervision of the Council's foreign policy chief and the president of the Commission.[5] However, following the popular rejection of the Constitutional Treaty in France and the Netherlands in 2005, the work seems to have been put on ice.[6]

'Agencification' at the EU level. During the 1990s a range of new EU-level agencies were established. The main function of some of these, such as the European Environment Agency (Barbieri, Chapter 11), is to gather information in order to support EU policy-making and implementation across the Union. Others are entrusted with the responsibility to prepare decisions to be made by the Commission, as is the case for the European Agency for the Evaluation of Medicinal Products. Others are assigned implementation tasks such as assisting the Commission in the management of EU programmes. In highly specialized areas such as trademarks or plant variety rights, or more recently aviation safety, such agencies come close to independent regulatory authorities, since they are empowered to issue binding individual decisions (Dehousse 2002).

The arguments behind EU-level 'agencification' are remarkably similar to those that have been advanced in relation to the establishment of agencies at the national level. Commission overload and accusations of inadequate control with implementation seem to be important reasons for delegation. Another is to ensure continuity and impartiality as regards (individual) regulatory decisions by organizing such decision-making in bodies at arm's length from the respective ministries (Majone 1996; Everson et al. 1999). An increasingly party politicized Commission could make such reforms even more topical (Majone 2002).

In many respects most agencies are clearly connected to the Commission: they work closely with the Commission, the Commission may have the organizational or budgetary responsibility for the agency and agency directors are usually appointed on a proposal from the Commission (Everson et al. 1999; Almer and Rotkirch 2004). As might be expected, though, given the character of the areas concerned, the European Defence Agency (for the development of defence capabilities) is supposed to work under Council authority and the police cooperation unit 'Europol' has to operate under 'European laws' (Constitutional Treaty, Article III-276). However, most agencies can be perceived as being situated somewhere between the Commission and the Council. Typically, there is a strong representation by the member states and a more limited representation by the Commission in the composition of supervisory boards (Almer and Rotkirch 2004: 58). Since some agencies may be seen as partly a functional alternative to comitology (Dehousse 1997b) this 'double-headedness' makes sense: it reflects the legislator's willingness to sit in and monitor delegated law-making activities. More generally, the 'in-between status' mirrors a non-parliamentarian, 'power-separated' polity. As in the US, agencies are part of the power struggle between executive and legislative branches (Shapiro 1997). Since the legislator cannot hold executive politicians fully accountable, it is instead eager to have some direct influence over regulatory agencies. A parliamentarized EU would not solve this problem since the other legislative chamber, the Council, would not be part of such an arrangement.

Connecting to national administrations

The role of EU-level committees.   Our studies of EU-level committees gave us the first indication that national administrations might be, at least partly, playing two different roles; one as the traditional 'servant' of national ministers and one as a part of a Union administration, for example by being a contributor to policy formulation at the Commission. Although national officials attending Commission expert committees, Council working parties and comitology committees all share a strong identification with their respective policy sectors, they differ from each other as regards the weight they assign to the role of a national representative at the EU level: while those participating in Council and comitology committees most typically perceive themselves as representing their respective governments, those on Commission groups tend to assume more multifaceted and expert-oriented roles (Egeberg, Schaefer and Trondal, Chapter 5). Those emanating from national agencies outside ministries emphasize their independence from national governments even more clearly (Trondal 2001: 210). Compared to Council and comitology participation, those attending Commission expert committees are also considerably less likely to be coordinated or mandated by foreign ministries or other central authorities (Egeberg, Schaefer and Trondal, Chapter 5). Thus, a new institutional 'cleavage' might become discernable, indicating that parts of national administrations on certain occasions function as parts of a Community administration while on other occasions they fulfil their traditional obligations as servants of national political authorities. In relation to the EU the latter role is most clearly assumed in the Council setting, but also in comitology committees in which the legislative process continues at a more detailed level.

Double-hatted national agencies. Compared to Commission expert committees in which national officials are supposed to act as independent experts – and in fact do so to a considerable degree – issue-specific networks consisting of national agencies and the Commission or an EU-level agency as a kind of hub can be interpreted as a further step toward the development of a genuine multilevel Union administration (Figure 1.1). By using agencies instead of individuals as 'building blocks', more regularity and a higher level of institutionalization will probably be imposed on the administrative system. Being responsible for policy preparation as well as implementation, the Commission is certainly in need of stable partners, not least as regards the implementation stage. Having to rely entirely on national governments for implementation means that implementation practices become highly contingent, not only upon national administrative traditions but also on shifting political winds at the national level (Knill 2001). In order to enhance the degree of consistency and harmonization

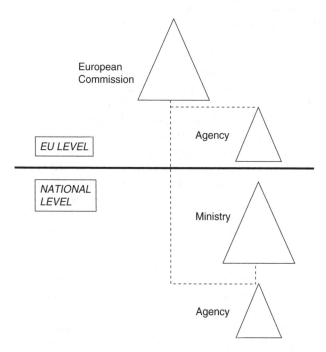

European Commission

EU LEVEL

Agency

NATIONAL LEVEL

Ministry

Agency

Figure 1.1   The 'double-hatted' national agency in a multilevel Union administration

across the Union the Commission would benefit from being able to interact directly with parts of national administrations that enjoy a certain leeway for independent action. These might be found among national agencies that, due to, *inter alia*, 'New Public Management' reforms or EU directives, have been established at arm's length from ministries in order to apply regulatory statutes in an impartial manner. Studies have shown that such semi-detached bodies are in fact considerably less sensitive to political inputs than ministerial departments (Egeberg 2003a).

In this book we present studies of five different policy fields which all show some signs of national agencies serving two masters. In all of these – the competition area (Støle, Chapter 6; Barbieri, Chapter 11), telecom sector (Nørgård, Chapter 10), food safety area (Ugland and Veggeland, Chapter 9), environmental field (Martens, Chapter 8; Barbieri, Chapter 11) and statistical area (Sverdrup, Chapter 7) – national agencies simultaneously constitute parts of national governments while also being involved in European networks in which the Commission or an EU-level agency often makes up the hub. Several observations are consistent across policy sectors: most typically, that as integral parts of national governments, national agencies assist their respective ministries at Council and comitology meetings. In these settings there is usually no doubt about who is the leader of the delegation or who is entitled to instruct and in fact does instruct those attending; it is the ministry. Also, when EU directives are to be transposed into national legislation, national agencies often do much of the preparatory work, with which they are familiar from other legislative processes. Here again they seem to be relatively attentive to what the ministry wants. On all these occasions, though, it is the agencies that possess most of the necessary expertise.

When it comes to putting the transposed legislation into practice, however, the role of national agencies seems to shift remarkably. At this stage they may operate in close cooperation with their respective directorates in the Commission and their respective 'sister agencies' in other member states, often through networks. This means that national agencies may end up having to defend decisions that are in conflict with the intentions of their own governments. For example, while the Swedish government supported the attempted merger of Volvo and Scania, and even lobbied for its acceptance in Brussels, the Swedish competition authority advised against the merger (Støle, Chapter 6). Such clashes of course also occur at the national level quite independently of the EU; they are inherently linked to fragmented states. What is probably new is that the national agency, in a way, acts on behalf of a *second* master or centre, or at least on behalf of a transnational network of agencies in which the EU executive may constitute a node. The Commission may itself have initiated the creation of such a network, as in the telecom sector (Nørgård, Chapter 10; see also Gornitzka 2005). However, the EU executive has also successfully linked into existing networks that may have been relatively independent (Eberlein and Grande 2005: 101–2) but for which it has gradually taken over the coordinating functions, as seems to be the case for the implementation network of pollution authorities (Martens, Chapter 8). Like national ministries, the Commission might be perceived by national experts as a potential threat to their independence (Ugland and Veggeland, Chapter 9). In addition to playing a crucial role at the implementation stage, agency networks may also contribute in the policy formulation phase at the Commission. Our case studies show that ministries are usually informed about network activities. However, they tend to abstain from steering network activities, for example by appointing and instructing participants. Interestingly, there are indications that such interference is deemed inappropriate, at least by the agency personnel themselves.

Two of our case studies can be seen as critical to the argument in that they both deal with member states whose governments exemplify strong hierarchical features. The Danish administrative tradition has built on relatively large 'integrated ministries' although 'agencification' has also occurred. In addition, Denmark is well known for tight coordination procedures in EU affairs (Nørgård, Chapter 10). It might therefore seem less likely for Danish agencies to be 'captured' by transnational webs. The same argument can be advanced as regards Italy whose reputation for a particularly hierarchically-oriented bureaucracy should make double-hatted agencies less probable here too (Barbieri, Chapter 11). If agencies even under these circumstances are 'absorbed' by transnational networks of the kind we have described, 'double-hattedness' proves to be more than a mere theoretical construction. Nørgård's study (Chapter 10) clearly shows that the Danish telecom agency operates in network activities with little ministry interference. This room for manoeuvre is, however, based on a considerable amount of trust between the two institutions concerned. Trust at the same level does not seem to exist in the Italian case (Barbieri, Chapter 11). Even if the national environment agency is allowed to participate in the European Environment Agency's network (EIONET), its representatives are appointed and mandated by the ministry. Also the Italian competition authority may be subject to close supervision in 'political' matters. However, the strong leadership role of DG Competition in this area seems to strengthen the agency's actual autonomy from its ministry. This relative autonomy may also be due to its organizational location between the government and the parliament.

Finally, if an EU foreign minister with executive functions separated from the Council becomes a reality, we can foresee that this organization too, like the Commission, might come to need national partners for policy formulation purposes as well as implementation. Thus, agencies under foreign ministries could become contributors to the preparation of EU foreign policy in the same way that agencies belonging to other ministries now partly serve the Commission. As regards implementation of EU foreign policy, member states' embassies abroad could also wear two hats in the future; one expressing their traditional role as part of a national diplomatic service and the other symbolizing their partnership in an EU foreign service.

Double-hatted regional governments.   A key point in the multilevel governance literature is that EU institutions provide opportunity structures that induce sub-national governments and societal actors to circumvent their respective national governments and connect directly to the supranational level in order to pursue their goals (Marks et al. 1996; Ansell 2000; Jachtenfuchs and Kohler-Koch 2004). Regions in particular have been focused on in this respect. However, considered as potential parts of a community administration the number of regions (about 250) in itself discounts the establishment of regular interaction with the Commission on a system-wide basis. This means that as far as the EU policy formulation phase is concerned, the options left for regional governments that want to have a say are to go through their respective national governments or through their own interest organizations; to lobby individually or to be represented by the Committee of the Regions which the Constitutional Treaty defines as an 'advisory body' in line with the Economic and Social Committee. As regards implementation of EU regional policy, those regions for which a particular programme is to be put in place may come to develop closer and more direct links with the Commission during the programme period. However, Commission–region relations may be tense and national governments have been reluctant to cede much decision-making power to such partnership arrangements (Bauer 2002).

Theorizing the transformation of executive politics

How can we then account for the behavioural patterns and changes outlined above, characterized by Commission autonomization, sectorization, party politicization and the 'capturing' of national agencies? Our main analytical tools are drawn from organization and institutional theory (Egeberg 2003a, 2004, chapters 2, 3 and 4; Olsen 1992; March and Olsen

2005). Accordingly, the organizational setting provides goals and role expectations as well as mechanisms – such as cognitive frames, incentives and norms of appropriateness – that may ensure compliance with these expectations. Thus, in order to understand and explain patterns of executive politics we emphasize organizational and institutional factors such as ways of specialization, various procedures, demography and culture. Such independent variables are considered at two levels: the EU level and the national level. We are well aware that organizational and institutional factors will only be able to tell us part of the truth: the processes under study are obviously too complex to be covered by a single theoretical perspective. Our choice has been analytical parsimony, and to see how far this approach takes us rather than developing a more complex and perhaps more realistic model that may be less comprehensible.

In fact, an organizational and institutional approach has probably little to offer as regards the establishment of the key institution dealt with; namely the High Authority – later the Commission. As argued above, the most crucial step in our story is probably the establishment of an executive body separated from the ministers' council. It is tempting to see this formative event as best explained by a 'big bang'. Earlier profound transformations of European politics had occurred subsequent to catastrophic wars such as the Thirty Years' War and the Napoleonic wars, which like WWII, provided exceptional windows of opportunity that clever entrepreneurs knew how to exploit (Egeberg, Chapter 2). Having been established with certain organizational resources, the new executive body triggered an institutional dynamics that gradually demarcated its role in relation to the Council. This was partly done by installing, over time, procedures for organizing and staffing that served to shelter the institution. In addition, sectoral and functional specialization seems to have largely displaced territorial politics at the Commission (Egeberg, chapters 3 and 4). Quite reasonably, given the historical background, the struggle for institutional integrity has primarily been fought against the Council and member governments. The current turf battles over the control of the EU's foreign service and European agencies testify to this historical path. The increasing party politicization of the Commission is probably primarily a result of the institutional dynamics of the European Parliament, but it is also connected to the changing demography at the Commission's helm (Egeberg, Chapter 4).

The peculiar functional division of labour between the Council and the Commission at the international level is thought to trigger the centrifugal forces within national governments that lead to 'double-hatted' agencies (Egeberg, Chapter 2). From an organizational perspective this phenomenon is unlikely to be generated by classical IGOs, even if extensive administrative networking takes place around them. The reason is that in the latter case the 'threads' are assumed to be (re-)collected within a government-dominated body, that is an IGO. It is otherwise with the Commission: as an institution eager to establish itself as a supranational political executive separated from the Council of Ministers it tends to look for partners other than ministries. Arguably, however, the institutional architecture at the EU level is a necessary but not a sufficient condition for the emergence of the type of multilevel administrative relationships described in this book. Such a development is also seen as highly contingent upon particular organizational and institutional features at the national level. In general, we expect national governments that are clearly fragmented and vertically specialized into ministries on the one hand and agencies on the other to be most vulnerable to 'agency capture' by the Commission. By the same token, agencies that are subject to strong coordination mechanisms, as in the Danish case (Nørgård, Chapter 10), or to hierarchical state traditions, as in the Italian case (Barbieri, Chapter 11), are expected to be more difficult to 'recouple'.[7] Union enlargement may represent a particular challenge in this respect due to the fact that regulators in the new member states are often still close to national governments.[8]

Integration of a set of parts may come about in two qualitatively different ways. First, the parts may become tightly connected as relatively coherent wholes. This is what we expect to happen when nation-states collaborate, even intensively, in IGOs: the prevailing territorial principle of specialization found in IGOs does not seriously challenge the nation-state system. Second, integration might imply reorganization of the parts themselves, something which most of us would perceive to be a more profound kind of system change. This is what can be expected given the peculiar institutional architecture of the EU at the international level (Egeberg, Chapter 2). Due to the way in which the various key institutions are organized internally and as a result of the functional division of labour between them, patterns of cooperation and conflict that cut *across* national boundaries can also be expected to emerge – along ideological (partisan), sectoral and institutional (for example Commission vs. Council) lines. Important scope conditions for such a development to take place are found at the national level: while it is pretty hard to imagine totalitarian states being 'absorbed' in such a manner, fragmented states (with detached agencies, central banks and courts) and pluralist civil societies (with voluntary associations and political parties) are much more open for 'recoupling', precisely because they are loosely coupled systems. Basically, similar scope conditions were at work in the era of European state-making (Tilly 1975).

Haas (1958/2004) and Schmitter (1970) were already focusing on potential transnational coalitions, in particular of interest groups and political
parties. We have emphasized transnational networks of executive bodies
that tend to extend the Commission–Council divide into the very heart of
central state machineries. Such a development could be a significant indication of important changes in the European order: integrated polities
have in common that the executive at the centre possesses or disposes over
agencies at the level beneath which are at least partly decoupled from the
political core at that same level. This even holds for Germany in which
implementation is held to be in the hands of the regional (*Länder*) governments; in fact, administrative networks across levels quite similar to those
being analysed in this book have been observed (Benz and Bogumil 2002).[9]

Conclusion

The Commission has often been characterized as a hybrid organization,
hard to classify in ordinary institutional terms. This volume reveals that
the Commission has become increasingly 'normalized', in the sense that
it at present embodies many of the organizational and behavioural patterns that are highly typical of executives in the national setting: executive politics is in general more often politics among sectoral portfolios
(ministries) than contestation along territorial lines, and the leadership
is intrinsically political. 'Agencification' at the EU level adds to this normalization. The executive branch also normally spans levels of governance
so that the central body has its own offices at lower levels, or, alternatively,
connects directly to lower-level agencies and thus partly bypasses the
'territorial core' of the constituent areas. The networked administrative
system portrayed in this book, in which the Commission often constitutes
the hub, might be seen as a nascent version of a multilevel executive which
integrates sub-territories, not as coherent wholes but rather as loosely
coupled systems.

Although an increasing number of studies deal with the Commission
and its relationships with national administrations, the topic is still heavily
under-theorized. This volume's authors share a theoretical framework
which informs all the contributions in a consistent way. First, politics at the
Commission is interpreted as reflecting, although not in a deterministic
sense, organizational and institutional features present at different points
in time. Second, the emerging partnerships between the Commission, EU
agencies and national regulatory authorities could hardly develop without
the peculiar institutional architecture of the Union, in particular the functional specialization between the Council and the Commission. Finally,

the prospects for such partnerships to grow are also seen as conditioned by organizational and institutional patterns at the national level. For example, strong and hegemonic state traditions will probably hamper such multilevel networking. Although we have seen several indications of an emerging multilevel Union administration, such a development might be hampered or even reversed. The relationship between certain institutional features and particular patterns of executive politics is, like most relationships, probably conditioned. Union enlargement may bring in historical experiences and political cultures that may change the conditions significantly. Also, since institutional and organizational factors seem to play such a crucial role in the process of transformation of executive politics, it follows that the process might at least be partly reversed by deliberate redesign of the institutional environment at one or more levels of governance.

Acknowledgements

I am grateful to Johan P. Olsen and Jarle Trondal, and to participants at the CONNEX conference in Oslo 27–28 May 2005, for their valuable comments on a previous version of this chapter.

Notes

1. In order not to overburden this chapter with references where possible I only refer to the chapter in which a broader topic is covered. The chapters themselves contain detailed lists of references.
2. The process of shaping a federal executive that could act separately from the Federal Council (*Bundesrat*) in the new German federation of 1871 may deserve to be mentioned briefly here. The *Bundesrat*, composed of representatives of the constituent states, seems at first to have been supposed to act both as the German government and as the upper house of the legislature. It was some time before separate ministries were established. At the outset, Bismarck designed the Chancellorship as a branch of the Prussian Foreign Office, with the assistance of a few officials to manage the *Zollverein* and the Post Office (Taylor 1945/2001: 134–5).
3. *European Voice*, 3–9 March 2005.
4. COM (2002) 728 final.
5. *European Voice*, 2–8 December 2004.
6. *European Voice*, 9–15 June 2005.
7. Ugland (2002) applies a similar logic as regards the potential for integrating *policy* components.
8. The director general of the Commission's DG Infso to *European Voice*, 10–17 November 2004.
9. Also confirmed by Werner Jann, Professor of Public Administration at Potsdam University.

2
The Institutional Architecture of the EU and the Transformation of European Politics

Morten Egeberg

Introduction

If deep change is indeed taking place in the European political order, how would we detect it? And how could it be explained? These are the two important questions dealt with in this chapter. It starts by addressing the indicator problem: what could be a fruitful yardstick for ascertaining qualitative alterations to a political system basically composed of nation-states? I suggest that the extent to which cleavages cut *across* national borders could be one attractive way of gauging system change. After thus having clarified the dependent variable, I then, in two successive steps, outline how changes in the structure of conflict at the European level might be accounted for. While Marks and Steenbergen (2004) hypothesize that political contestation at the European level is connected to that in domestic arenas, I argue here that the patterns of cooperation and conflict found at the European level are highly dependent on the institutional architecture found at that same level. However, if EU-level institutions do really matter in this respect, we have to (and this is the second step) ask how this institutional structure has itself come about. This second step, of course, opens up an enormous research agenda that has already been widely addressed. Thus, in this chapter the last theme will only be relatively superficially touched upon. The message is, however, that when we are dealing with profound institutional change, such as significant authority transfer from nation-states to a supranational level, and particularly so when such change is intended, the prevalent rational choice explanations, including liberal intergovernmentalism, may face problems.

Thus, the main purpose of this chapter is twofold: first, to introduce an indicator of profound change in the European political order – this

17

marker is the extent to which a multidimensional structure of conflict can be observed – and, second, to account in part for this structure by looking at the way in which EU institutions are organized. My concern here is to illustrate the assumed relationship between particular institutional features and patterns of conflict. Further empirical research is certainly needed in order to substantiate the postulated relationships. The notion is not, however, that the institutional architecture of the EU determines political behaviour, only that it makes some patterns more likely than others.

If profound transformation – how to see it?

Our point of departure is the state system in Europe more or less inherited from the Peace of Westphalia (1648). One key feature of this political order was that politics at the European level was organized as politics between sovereign states. The real sovereignty of various states might have been highly questionable at different points in time; however, patterns of cooperation and conflict at the European level seem to have mainly coincided with state borders. Thus, political life has been either domestic or interstate in character.

The recent turn in EU research toward the Europeanization of the nation-state (Olsen 2002b) recognized that to come to grips with significant changes in the existing state order meant investigating the way in which European integration manifested itself at the national level. It was seen as insufficient to study the creation of EU-level institutions and EU policy-making without taking into account how these actually affect countries. Thus, it was necessary to look for impacts on national institutions, politics, policies and identities, and at whether these demonstrated converging or diverging trends across nation-states (Olsen 2002b). Although this research focus no doubt represented a major step forward, it might nevertheless have encountered problems in revealing profound changes (if they have occurred). After all, high levels of institutional and policy convergence across countries could be seen as compatible with the state-centred system outlined above. For hundreds of years, government officials in Europe have learnt from each other and been exposed to trans-border diffusion of institutional arrangements and policy solutions. And multitudes of international governmental organizations (IGOs) have worked over the years for more harmonization and standardization within different policy fields without seriously challenging the 'politics between sovereign states' paradigm. One could of course argue that the Union Council is qualitatively different since it allows qualified majority voting. However, the Council has been deeply consensual in its habits,

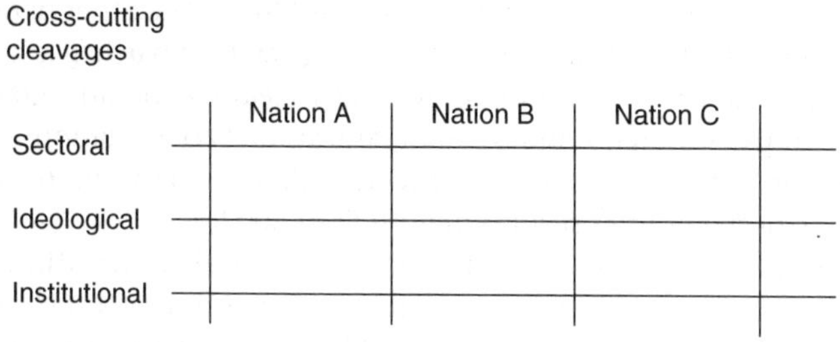

Cross-cutting
cleavages

	Nation A	Nation B	Nation C
Sectoral			
Ideological			
Institutional			

Figure 2.1   A multidimensional conflict structure

and great efforts have been made to accommodate the individual dissenter (Hayes-Renshaw and Wallace 1997: 275). It has also been pointed out that too little attention has been devoted to how European integration affects politics (for example patterns of conflict) at different levels of governance (Mair 2004).

I suggest here that we can discuss deep transformation to the extent that a primarily unidimensional, territorially-based conflict structure at the European level is now complemented by patterns of cooperation and conflict that cut across national borders (Figure 2.1). A mixture of territorial, sectoral, functional, ideological or inter-institutional conflicts would constitute a multidimensional political space at the European level, parallel to what we see at the domestic level and thus very different from what we traditionally have seen at the international level. It is worth mentioning that both the multilevel governance literature (Kohler-Koch 1996b; Hooghe and Marks 2001) and transnational relations scholars (Risse 2002b) have for some time indicated that international institutions may provide opportunity structures that encourage transnational coalitions among non-governmental organizations (NGOs). However, one could argue that only the emergence of more systematic and persistent non-territorial lines of cooperation and conflict represents a real challenge to the highly institutionalized pattern of 'politics between sovereign states'.

The institutional explanation

How can cleavage patterns be accounted for? Lipset and Rokkan (1967) saw structures of conflict at the national level as a result of macro developments such as the national and industrial revolutions. Their explanation was partly institutional in the sense that, for example, the national revolution also engendered state structures that evoked tensions along the centre–periphery dimension. The emergence of sectoral and functional conflicts subsequent to the industrial revolution, on the other hand, can probably not be that clearly related to the growth of particular government organizations. By the end of the 1920s, cleavages became gradually 'frozen' in party systems and other organizational constellations (Lipset and Rokkan 1967). Even in the present era of Europeanization, the robustness of national politics seems salient (Olsen 2002b).

The idea in this chapter is that, although political contestation at the European level may be connected to that in domestic arenas (Marks and Steenbergen 2004), a full account of EU-level cleavages can only be achieved by considering the institutional architecture at that same level. Institutions as organized entities discriminate between conflicts; they 'channel conflict' and do not treat all conflicts impartially (Egeberg 2003a). Thus, institutions organize some conflicts into politics and some conflicts out of it (Schattschneider 1975). The notion is not that institutions as a rule 'invent' conflicts; however, institutions may systematically activate some latent cleavages while routinely ignoring others. For example, certain ideological and sectoral conflicts are already present at the domestic level. By widening the political space and by organizing themselves in a particular manner, EU institutions might make it reasonable for groups to align transnationally. Like the previous nationalization process, today's Europeanization entails institution-building that evokes tensions along a centre–periphery dimension.

While institutions that are specialized according to geographical criteria tend to encourage cooperation and conflict along territorial lines, institutions arranged by non-territorial criteria are expected to foster cleavages *across* geographical units (Egeberg 2003a). Thus, in purely organizational terms, significant transformation (and integration) of a system based on sectoral components could be achieved by installing an organizational layer at the top, specialized according to geography; while deep integration of a system built on territorial components, as in the EU case, would presuppose some system-wide institutions structured by non-territorial criteria (Egeberg 2004). The classic IGO has been arranged according to territory so that key decision-makers have formally represented the constituent governments (Figure 2.2).

Thus, an IGO's structure underpins rather than challenges a state-centred order characterized by a unidimensional conflict pattern along territorial lines at the international level. Arguably, the congress and concert system that developed subsequent to the Vienna Congress of 1814–15 contributed to civilizing the European state system (Schroeder 1994; Holsti 2004). However, IGOs don't seem to have been able to 'tame' nation-states significantly; it might be indicative that there is apparently no relationship

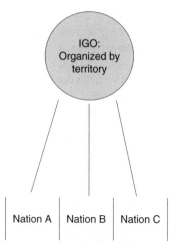

Figure 2.2 The IGO and territorial cleavages

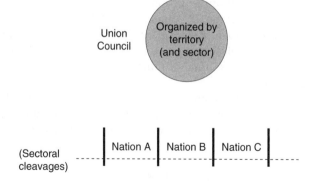

Figure 2.3 The Council and the related cleavages

between their existence and the extent to which nation-states have been involved in wars (Singer and Wallace 1970). The Council of the EU shares the basic features of an IGO, although it allows much more qualified majority voting to take place at the ministerial level than any IGO (Figure 2.3). Studies show that differences between nation-states prevail, particularly along a north–south dimension (Thomson et al. 2004). However, participants at all levels of the Council tend to complement their primarily national allegiances with a considerable sense of responsibility for reaching collective decisions (Hayes-Renshaw and Wallace 1997; Lewis 2002; and see Egeberg et al., Chapter 5).

The Council, like several IGOs, also complements its primarily geo-graphical arrangement by running sectorally and functionally specialized ministerial councils and working parties. Thus, although the institutional set-up of the Council is supposed to be primarily conducive to the 'politics between nations' pattern, the Council's dual structure also enables sectoral identities that cut across nationalities (Egeberg et al., Chapter 5). In add-ition, ministers may, at times, speak for the party-political family from which they are drawn (Hayes-Renshaw and Wallace 1997: 6), and align along a left–right dimension (Mattila 2004).

Having gained more power over time, the other legislative branch of the EU polity, the European Parliament (EP), increasingly provides an inter-esting arena for European party families. The EP embodies organizational features that tend to focus attention on non-national lines of cleavage (Figure 2.4). For example, the Parliament's physical arrangement seats members according to European party family rather than by nationality. Economic incentives make it rational for party groups to align trans-nationally. Studies do in fact show that although EP party groups behave less cohesively than groups in member state legislatures, they are more cohesive than parties in the US Congress (Hix 1998; Raunio 2002). Voting behaviour in the EP mainly coincides with a left–right dimension (Hix 2001). To these ideological (partisan) dimensions the EP's system of stand-ing committees adds a sectoral or functional dimension to the conflict pattern (Neuhold 2001).

The European Commission, the most authentically executive body in the EU polity, also divides its work primarily according to non-territorial criteria, although the procedure for appointing commissioners and the

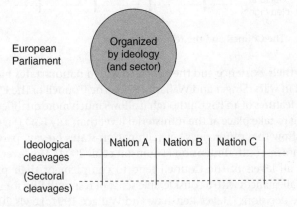

Figure 2.4   The European Parliament and the related cleavages

geographical quota system for recruiting personnel to the services may point in the opposite direction (Figure 2.5). The essentially sectoral and functional directorate general (DG) structure probably explains why patterns of cooperation and conflict at the Commission so often seem to follow sectoral rather than territorial lines (Egeberg 2004). The Commission's structure in this respect may be highly conducive to connecting compatible parts of national sector administrations (Trondal and Veggeland 2003; Egeberg et al., Chapter 5). This kind of sectorally or functionally-based administrative network across levels of governance is certainly not peculiar to the EU, but can also be found, for example, in the OECD. In IGOs (and in the EU Council), however, such sectorization is counter-balanced by the fact that these institutions are primarily organized according to territory. This 'corrective' is absent at the Commission.

It is not surprising that the segmented organization of the Commission also tends to encourage the participation of sectoral interest groups, particularly of those organized at the European level (Kohler-Koch 1997). Interestingly, students of international non-governmental organizations (INGOs) in general have found that such groups, although significant in the agenda-setting phase, have been far less important at decision-making stages. At these stages, they have needed to work through governments and IGOs more directly, and this has obviously proved harder (Risse 2002b: 265). However, from an organizational point of view, the structure of the Commission is more compatible with the tasks and interests of non-territorial associations than is that of IGOs; thus, it might facilitate interaction between them and the Commission. Finally, in addition to the sectoral bias, we should start looking for instances where Commissioners assume party political roles as well. An ever closer relationship between

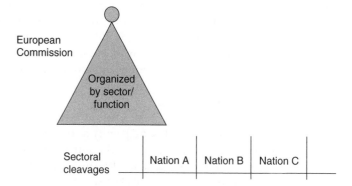

Figure 2.5   The Commission and the related cleavages

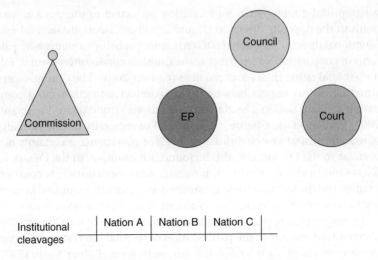

Figure 2.6   The institutional differentiation and the related cleavages

the Commission and the EP, as well as an increasing proportion of political heavyweights in the College over time, indicates why we should do
this (Egeberg, Chapter 3).

The complex institutional architecture at the EU level, with a considerable degree of functional specialization among the different institutions, in
itself injects institutional cleavages into the system (Figure 2.6). Institutions tend to impose particular world views, ways of thinking, expectations
and allegiances on their members, and more so under some organizational
conditions than others (March and Olsen 1989; Checkel 2001; Egeberg
2003a). Thus, people of different nationalities belonging to the same
institution may come to share important attitudes that are not necessarily
shared by those affiliated with other institutions. Tensions between, for
example, executive and legislative bodies are well known from national
politics as well. In addition, the division of work among EU bodies insti-
tutionalizes a 'centralization-decentralization' dimension in the sense
that the Commission is often perceived as an engine of integration, while
the Council embodies national control.

Now, one could argue that although inter-institutional conflicts, cutting across nationalities, do occur rather frequently at the EU level, this
kind of 'turf battle' nevertheless takes place on the surface and does not
really penetrate the lower levels of governance. It may be easier to understand that ideological (partisan) and sectoral cleavages at the EU level are
observable across levels of governance since they can be mediated through

national political parties and interest groups. There are signs, however, that conflicts between EU institutions might run deeper. The Commission could be interested in dealing more directly with parts of national administrations, both for policy development and for implementation purposes, thus further institutionalizing a genuine multilevel Union administration. Arguably, the 'agencification' process that has taken place in most member states over the last years – meaning that regulatory tasks have been hived off from ministerial departments and allocated to semi-independent bodies – has cleared the way for making them 'double-hatted'; that is, these bodies are supposed to serve both national governments and the Commission (Egeberg, Chapter 3). By connecting national agencies in issue-specific administrative networks, partly bypassing national governments (ministries), the Commission would, in a sense, actually extend its organization down through the levels without formally erecting its own offices. One could perhaps say that while the Council links up national governments, the Commission in this way effectively links up national 'sub-governments'.

Similarly, in order to help safeguard the uniform application of Community law, cooperative relationships have developed between the European Court of Justice (ECJ) and courts in the member states. Important in this respect is the procedure which enables national courts to refer to the ECJ questions of EU law that they must decide before giving judgement (Arnull 2003). Also illustrative of the direct relationships between equivalent institutions at the two levels, bypassing national governments, is the European System of Central Banks (ESCB) in which national central banks constitute 'branches' of the European Central Bank (ECB) (Verdun 2003: 314). For example, while the German government has heavily criticized the Stability Pact, the German Central Bank has openly defended it (*Aftenposten*, 18 November 2003). Finally, consider the EP which recognizes national parliaments and the Conference of (parliament) Committees Specialized in EU Affairs (COSAC) as consultative bodies (Mittag and Wessels 2003: 433).

Correlates of multidimensional institutions and politics

Multiple channels of interest representation.   As with IGOs, one can perceive the Council of the EU as an arena in which interests related to people's countries of residence are pursued. Sectoral concerns, and even partisan interests, might also be articulated in the Council. However, it is probably right to say that territorially related concerns are prevalent in this setting. Although people's country affiliations undoubtedly generate particular interests in a lot of cases – for example, as regards EU transport policy (on traffic congestion, need for infrastructure and so on) – citizens may, nevertheless, have significant ideological (partisan) concerns at the same time. Transport policy, for example, tends to provoke disputes over the role of the public sector. The EP provides a forum primarily for accommodating these kinds of considerations, although sectoral and geographical concerns are not absent. Further, people's affiliations to various industries and professions may evoke common transnational interests. Again considering EU transport policy, those working in one transport sector may perceive their interests as divergent from those of people employed within another mode of transport. EU-level interest groups and their access to compatible parts of EU institutions, particularly in the Commission, might have a potential for channelling these kinds of interests. Finally, the mere existence of EU-level institutions could be seen as an expression of the fact that people have interests simply by virtue of living in this part of Europe.

Redistribution of political power.   First, conferring upon EU institutions the right to make policies that have a direct impact at the domestic level may, in itself, profoundly reshape established local power relationships. 'Europeanization' is an example of what Schattschneider (1975) would have called 'socialization of conflict', that is the act of expanding the scope of the political space by changing the locus of power and thus involving more participants. According to Schattschneider (1975: 11), 'socialization' in this meaning of the word 'inevitably breaks up local power monopolies and old sectional power complexes'. Second, every shift in the location of a line of cleavage 'produces a new set of winners and losers and a new kind of result' (Schattschneider 1975: 61). For example, in the EU setting, upgrading the role of the EP also enhances the importance of the ideological (partisan) dimension in relation to territorial (international) politics. Thus, the question of how power is distributed among member states has to be complemented by an awareness of the relative strength of the party families at the EP. Multiple cross-cutting cleavages at the EU level will inevitably redistribute political power in the system in a highly complex manner.

Prevention of deep cleavages along one axis.   The argument goes that a system is in fact held together by its inner conflicts, provided that these conflicts cross-cut each other. On the other hand, a society which is split along just one line of cleavage or has cumulative, coinciding lines reinforcing each other, may be in danger of being torn by violence or falling to pieces

(Ross 1920; Coser 1956). This argument supports our notion that a complex institutional architecture at the EU level that paves the way for a multidimensional conflict structure at the same level represents a qualitative step in the direction of deeper system integration and transformation.

Explaining institutional change

Given that EU institutions *are* important for explaining the emergence of new patterns of political cooperation and conflict at the European level, how can we account for the development of these institutions themselves? It is indeed an intriguing question why actors (for example national governments) which are powerful under certain institutional conditions (for example the Westphalian state order) might come to agree to institutional reforms that actually diminish their power in the system. Intergovernmentalism based on rational choice theory and a functional approach will encounter problems in trying to provide an adequate account of this. According to these perspectives, EU institutions are deliberately designed in order to reduce transaction costs related to collective problem-solving. Thus, control clearly remains with the original institution-builders (Moravcsik 1998; Schimmelfennig 2004). Taking these theories as our point of departure, power *redistribution* can only be explained by adding historical institutionalism or principal–agent theory. The historical variant of rational choice institutionalism argues that, as an unintended consequence of institutional design, institutions might take on a life of their own and start to drift away from what was originally planned (Pierson 1996). In a similar vein, principal–agent analysts contend that information asymmetry and incentive systems in the 'agent-institution' could lead to the principal's loss of control (Pollack 2004).

The problem, however, is that as far as the European project is concerned, the intention at its very inception was to transfer power to the supranational level, that is to restrict, not delegate, some of the control exercised by the constituent governments (Burgess 2004). How could the founding countries agree to this? In the works of institutionalists who in general emphasize the robustness and 'stickiness' of institutions, we also find ideas about the conditions under which radical change nevertheless might take place. Serious 'performance crises' and shocks could constitute such change catalysts (March and Olsen 1989). In that respect, WWII represented a system breakdown on an unprecedented scale in the European political order. Arguably, this catastrophe opened an enormous window of opportunity for entrepreneurial leadership. Jean Monnet, adviser to the French foreign minister Robert Schuman, had been, among other things, a deputy secretary general at the League of Nations and had therefore experienced at close quarters the failure of intergovernmental organizations to prevent wars. He seems to have invented the most innovative body in the new institutional set-up: the High Authority (later the Commission), which he presented as 'Europe's first government', and he also saw the need for a court (Duchêne 1994: 235).

According to Monnet's biographer (Duchêne 1994: 210–11), it was the French minister Andre Philip who proposed a common assembly in order to meet the charge of technocracy, and it was the chief Dutch negotiator Dirk Spierenburg who insisted that a council of ministers had to be installed in order to counterbalance the High Authority. Interestingly, deep systemic crises in conjunction with systems' inability to 'deliver' peace and order have been seen as the catalyst for earlier key processes of political transformation in Europe. The Thirty Years' War as well as the Napoleonic wars have been interpreted similarly (Schroeder 1994).

It is quite remarkable that the four core institutions of the current EU were in fact in place from the very start in 1952, although nascent. It follows that ideas about the role of path dependency, institutional robustness and incremental changes will be pivotal in order to reach a more comprehensive understanding of the formation of the EU's institutional architecture (March and Olsen 1989; Pierson 1996; Sverdrup 2002; Olsen 2002a). In addition, various external or contingent events seem, at different points in time, to have triggered new major initiatives or made certain institutional solutions more feasible. Duchêne (1994: 291–2, 299) mentions the importance of the Suez crisis in 1956 for both the EEC and the Euratom negotiations. Later events such as the war in Bosnia or the spread of mad cow disease seem to have made a difference (Veggeland 2000; Sverdrup 2002; Olsen 2002a). Theoretically, these observations draw on a garbage-can model of decision-making in organizations. Such a model emphasizes the influence of events taking place simultaneously with the choice process in focus (March and Olsen 1976). The notion is that decisions result from an 'ecology' of decision processes. Finally, the development of EU institutions might be seen as partly imitative of organizational forms already deemed legitimate at the national level (McNamara 2001), thus drawing on theories of the impact of institutional (normative) environments (Meyer and Rowan 1977).

Figure 2.7 treats the EU's institutional architecture as the dependent variable, and considers the explanatory factors discussed above. In addition, the figure aims at showing that the current institutional structure of the EU may itself help to explain changes in that same structure. The idea is that as this institutional structure over time has grown more 'mature'

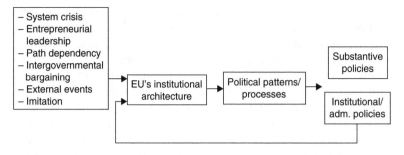

Figure 2.7 Explaining change in the institutional architecture of the EU

and 'dense', it increasingly has to be reckoned with as an independent factor when changes in this same structure are to be accounted for. As shown, then, not only various substantive policies can be seen to reflect the complex institutional configuration outlined in this chapter, but also the Union's institutional and administrative policies. The Convention on the Future of Europe might make an illustrative example: both the Convention's actual pattern of participation and its clearly deliberative elements can be interpreted as mirroring the EU's multi-faceted institutional arrangement (Eriksen et al. 2004).

Conclusion

According to March (1999: 134–5), the social science literature in general recognizes three primary criteria for gauging the integration of a set of parts. These criteria are the degree of interdependence, structural connectedness and consistency (coordination) between the parts. Applied to the state system, one could conceive of IGO density as one simple indicator of integration between states: IGOs may reflect interdependence between the member countries, they connect the participants structurally and coordinate their activities in order to establish consistency in certain policy areas. The integration criterion proposed in this chapter is meant to be able to indicate more profound system transformation, since it presupposes a certain reorganization of the parts themselves. Cleavages cutting across national boundaries imply that European integration in this deep sense goes hand in hand with a certain disintegration at the national level; disintegration not only of national political systems, but also of the state apparatuses themselves.

The EU's complex institutional architecture, with its institutional differentiation as well as the internal set-up of each institution, has in this chapter been seen as the key factor behind cross-cutting cleavages at the EU level. It is hard to see how just these lines of conflict could be activated transnationally without particular institutions 'making them relevant', so to speak. It should, however, be pointed out clearly that the aim of this chapter has been to illustrate the role of EU institutions in this respect. Only further research can create the basis for drawing firm conclusions. Moreover, this chapter has argued that a complex institutional configuration and the corresponding cross-cutting cleavages have some very important correlates. These are multiple channels of interest representation, redistribution of political power and the prevention of deep cleavages along one axis.

Finally, if the existing EU institutions really are so pivotal, how do they come about? This is a theme already given a lot of attention in the literature. This chapter argues that in order to explain profound, and partly intentional, institutional change, the prevalent intergovernmentalist interpretation and other rational choice explanations need to be significantly complemented by other approaches. These other approaches encompass ideas about the role of systemic crises and breakdowns, external and contingent events and the role of imitation of already legitimized organizational forms. Although system crisis, entrepreneurial leadership, path dependency, intergovernmental bargaining, external events and imitation all have a role to play, I hypothesize that, over time, a more developed institutional structure at the EU level will increasingly tend to reproduce itself.

Acknowledgements

I thank Svein Andersen, Jonathan Aus, Jeffrey Checkel, Åse Gornitzka, Johan P. Olsen, Martha Snodgrass, Ulf Sverdrup and three anonymous referees for their comments on an earlier version of this chapter.

3
Balancing Autonomy and Accountability: Enduring Tensions in the European Commission's Development

Morten Egeberg

Introduction

The existence of the European Commission is arguably the most peculiar component in the institutional architecture of the European Union (EU). While councils, parliamentary assemblies and courts may be found in governance structures at the international level as well, a separate executive body like the Commission is not in place anywhere else. The Commission and its predecessor, the High Authority of the European Coal and Steel Community (ECSC), were deliberately designed as engines of integration. They were to inject genuine *European* interests into the policy-making processes of the Community. To be able to fulfil this task, they had to be organized independently of the Council and the member governments, and have their own political leadership: the College of Commissioners.

However, organizing autonomous institutions within a political setting immediately raises questions about accountability and legitimacy. A certain degree of independence may be acceptable if the organization is clearly mandated, as may be the case for some administrative agencies. They may be allowed to handle individual cases according to a given law without interference, as well as their own personnel affairs. Autonomy may also be tolerable if the institution builds its activity solely on agreed-upon values or scholarly knowledge. If none of these conditions is fulfilled, justifying their independence becomes more problematic (Olsen 2004). Concerning the Commission, it is primarily its role as promoter of the so-called general and common European interest that has legitimized its independence. Autonomy may also have been deemed acceptable in areas in which the task has been to reach a logically correct decision by interpreting given rules or by applying expert knowledge, as in the competition field. However, as policy initiator in a polity with an increasingly comprehensive political agenda, it may have become more difficult over time to legitimize policy proposals by claiming that they would serve the public weal. Arguably, therefore, the most salient historical tension in organizing the Commission has been the balancing between autonomization, on the one hand, and territorialization (that is, co-opting or installing national components in the structure) on the other. The reason for considering territorialization as the alternative route of legitimization is of course the fact that power was transferred from the nation-states in the first place. However, other possible routes to increased legitimacy in a highly politicized context are conceivable; namely sectorization (that is, co-opting or installing sectoral or functional components in the structure) and party politicization (that is, making commissioners more politically accountable to the European Parliament). While territorialization obviously may bring the Commission closer to a kind of intergovernmental arrangement, autonomization – as well as sectorization and politicization – would all work to *transcend* intergovernmental patterns of cooperation and conflict. They would instead re-direct such patterns along inter-institutional, sectoral or ideological lines.

In this chapter I will not go into the processes through which the Commission has been organized and reorganized along the dimensions outlined above. Rather, focus is directed on the relationship between certain organizational devices on the one hand and actual decision-making within the Commission on the other; to what extent do more or less 'autonomous' decisions or emphasis on national, sectoral or partisan concerns reflect the organizational structure and demography within which decision-making takes place? I proceed from here, first, by further elaborating on the theoretical argument, then by discussing autonomization, territorialization, sectorization and party politicization through organizational means. Empirically, I build to a considerable extent on secondary sources, supplemented by original interview data on Commission recruitment and appointment decisions to assess the degree of autonomy in what is, for most organizations, a crucial field.

How organization directs and redirects patterns of conflict: the theoretical argument

Organizational structures are arrangements of roles and norms that impose certain expectations and obligations on the incumbents of a particular organization (Scott 1981). For example, an organizational chart visualizes who is expected to do what, and how different tasks should relate to each other. Thus, the structure broadly defines the interests and goals that are to be pursued. People are assigned specialized agendas, increasingly so the lower the hierarchical level at which they find themselves. One might assert that allocation of tasks responds perfectly well to human cognitive capacities (Augier and March 2001). According to Simon (1965), these capacities are limited and entail 'bounded rationality' in organizational decision-making. Under such conditions, only those interests and concerns that are clearly embodied in the organizational structure will have any fair chance of getting adequate attention in the policy-making process. In addition to the organizational structure, the demography and physical arrangement of an organization may, under certain circumstances, affect its actual decision-making processes (Pfeffer 1982). If, for example, officials with an identical background, let us say in terms of geography, cluster in a particular organizational division, it is more likely that this particular demographic attribute could make a difference in their decision-making behaviour (Selden 1997).

According to Gulick (1937) there are four fundamental ways in which tasks may be distributed horizontally among units, namely in relation to territory (geography), purpose (sector), function (process), or clientele served. If, for example, an organization is internally specialized according to the geographical area served, it is expected to induce spatial perspectives and encourage policy-makers to pay attention primarily to particular territorial concerns. In this case, the structure reflects the territorial composition of the system and focuses attention along territorial lines of cleavage. Organizations based on a purpose principle, on the other hand, are supposed to foster sectoral horizons among decision-makers and policy standardization across territorial units. Specialization by function, meanwhile, implies dividing work according to the means (or kind of process) by which one wants to achieve one's goals. Typically, such a structure contains a legal, technical, economical or budget division. An organization structured according to the clientele served may, for instance, have units for children, youth or elderly people.

An important point is that the choice of principle of specialization tends to anchor a particular pattern of cooperation and conflict in the organization and, simultaneously, to displace other patterns. Thus, institutions do not treat all conflicts impartially; they organize some conflicts into politics and some conflicts out of it (Schattschneider 1975). This seems to hold not only in theory, but also when it comes to actual decision behaviour (Egeberg 2003a). It is therefore no accident that the central governments of nation-states, which often build on historically-rooted regions, arrange their ministerial structure according to sector rather than geography. This has furthered integration of the regional parts by refocusing conflict away from territorial lines in favour of sectoral lines, and has probably enhanced central governments' independence from the regions. By the same token, erecting geographically-based ministries, as, for example, the Scottish and Welsh Offices in the British central government, may indicate that processes of territorial disintegration are taking place. Taylor (1990: 49) reports that Metternich, without realizing the consequences, actually proposed to divide the centralized chancellery of the Habsburg Monarchy into four departments according to geographical (national) criteria. The proposal was, however, never put into effect; Metternich may in the end have sensed what implications it could have held for the unity of the empire. In an EU context, one could argue that while the territorially-based Council structure (like international governmental organizations) primarily reflects and sustains the inherited nation-state system, the specialization principles embedded in the Commission and the European Parliament tend to refocus attention along other lines of cleavage. Arguably, only these non-territorial principles of specialization are conducive to profound integration and transformation of a state-centric international system (Egeberg 2001, 2004).

Most ways of specialization may create serious external dependencies for an organization. These dependencies may, however, also become important sources of legitimization. For example, dividing work by geography increases the likelihood that members of a particular organizational unit start to identify with 'their' territory (Egeberg 2003a); at the same time, such an arrangement may bring legitimacy to an organization that finds itself in an environment dominated by actors that represent particular geographical areas. By changing the principle of specialization, existing dependencies may be reduced, but only to be replaced by new dependencies (and new potential sources of legitimacy). The process principle may represent an exception since this way of arranging work doesn't clearly link up to important societal cleavages. Given that adequate legitimacy is achievable, organizing by process could therefore be highly conducive to gaining autonomy. Inserting procedures that safeguard institutional autonomy in important areas such as recruitment policy may also serve to strengthen such a development.

Co-opting or installing territorial, sectoral or party political components into an organization's structure challenges its actual autonomy. However, this may be a necessary trade-off in order to raise external support or ensure accountability in a political environment. Although losing overall autonomy, an organization may nevertheless increase its independence in relation to particular external actors by deliberately choosing a particular principle of specialization. For instance, an organization could arrange its tasks by sector in order to 'escape' territorial politics. In practice, important institutions obviously have to balance several dimensions simultaneously. For example, the long-term goal of the Commission may have been to autonomize itself, legitimized as it was by addressing the EU's 'general interest'. Nevertheless, the Commission has adapted to external constraints by adopting territorial (national), sectoral and, as will probably be more evident in the future, party political components into its structure.

Autonomization vs territorialization

From its inception, the Commission was meant to be able to act independently of national governments. Since one of its main tasks was to take care of the common European interest – as it could be derived from the treaties – an autonomous and impartial role in the policy process might be legitimized. This construction seems to parallel to some extent the executive's role in the French republican state tradition (Elgie 2003: 149). The Commission's independence was clearly expressed in its formal structure, which forbids commissioners as well as officials from taking instructions from outside the organization. To stress this, the first president of the High Authority, Jean Monnet, originally wanted a college of only five members – simply to underline the fact that commissioners were not to represent particular countries (Duchêne 1994: 240). The Commission has on several occasions, most recently in its proposal to the Convention on the Future of Europe, emphasized the need for an independent and impartial body whose mission should be to serve the general interest of the Union.[1]

However, from the very start, it became fairly clear that running the Commission was indeed a balancing act between autonomy and dependence on the member states (Christiansen 1997; Lequesne 2000). From the point of view of the member states, a Commission with potential to become a genuine political actor and entrepreneur could not be allowed to act solely according to its own will, even if this will were defined as the community interest. The appointment procedure of the College – according to which member states nominate 'their' commissioner – and the national quota system – according to which the recruitment of officials should reflect the population size of the member countries – can be seen in this light. Member states' strong reluctance to give up their representation in the College, as demonstrated during the Convention on the Future of

Europe, clearly illustrates this point.[2] Seen from the inside, a Commission that adopted an increasingly complex political agenda couldn't rely entirely on legitimacy derived from pursuing the common good in an impartial way. Additional legitimacy could be provided by co-opting key affected parties such as national administrations, for example by including them in policy preparatory committees.

Thus, from the beginning, there have been organizational components that have underpinned autonomization while others have supported territorialization. Studies seem to indicate that commissioners, although more or less sensitive to the concerns of their country of origin, cannot in general be seen as representatives of 'their' governments (Nugent 2001: 115; Egeberg, Chapter 4). The same can be said of Commission officials: although they may serve as points of access for their compatriots (Michelmann 1978), and their attitudes on broad issues like capitalism and supranationalism may be linked to their nationality (Hooghe 2001), their actual behaviour is probably best accounted for by considering their bureaucratic role (Egeberg 1996; Nugent 2001). This seems to hold even for 'national experts' who are seconded from their governments to serve at the Commission for a limited number of years (Trondal 2006). Consistent with this, an overwhelming majority of national officials participating in Commission and Council committees considers Commission officials to act mainly independently of particular national interests (Egeberg, Schaefer and Trondal, Chapter 5).

Moreover, there is reason to believe that the Commission has gained *more* autonomy from national governments over time, at the political as well as the administrative level. Concerning the College level, the Amsterdam Treaty assigned somewhat more leeway to the Commission President-elect as regards the selection of commissioners, and this leeway has been widened in the Constitutional Treaty. After Amsterdam the president also acquired the final say in how portfolios are allocated and even the right to reshuffle the team during the Commission's five-year term of office by redistributing dossiers, thus making it difficult to attach particular national flags to particular directorates general. Also, the president is authorized to dismiss individual commissioners. The Prodi Commission, furthermore, made cabinets more multinational in composition.[3] This has probably changed the role of entities previously portrayed as national enclaves (Michelmann 1978), or as being apparently sensitive to national interests (Spence 1994: 107–8; Cini 1996: 111–15).

Developmental trends and reform efforts pertaining to the services over the years all point in the same direction: territorial components in the organization have continuously been weakened. In previous decades the community administration had to rely heavily on national civil servants on short-term contracts (Coombes 1970), while currently a large majority are employed on a permanent basis (Page 1997). While the Commission is supposed to maintain a broad geographical balance, nationality has been declared no longer to be the determinant in appointing a new person to a specific post.[4] Two small case studies on recruitment of Commission personnel may serve to illustrate the autonomization thesis.[5]

Appointing top officials at the Commission. Personnel policy at the Commission has from the very start been a highly contentious issue. In particular, control over the career system and the appointment of senior officials have been seen as questions inherently linked to the grand debate on a federal vs an intergovernmental Europe (Coombes 1970). To federalists, an *independent* career civil service was regarded as an essential prerequisite to the evolution of a federal executive. Previously, American federalists had argued along similar lines (Olsen 2003). To intergovernmentalists, on the other hand, the notion of a self-contained, zealous body of 'Eurocrats' was not particularly inviting. Thus, those who shared General de Gaulle's conception of the future development of the Community argued that the Commission should consist of officials seconded from national administrations (Coombes 1970: 121). As a compromise, the Commission services developed into a career system with an increasing proportion of permanent posts – which, over time, came to be dominant – while, at the same time, member states shared senior posts among themselves under a sort of quota system (Coombes 1970: 157–8). This practice almost reached the stage where national governments were claiming certain posts as being theirs by right (Cini 1996: 126).[6]

As part of a more comprehensive administrative reform package launched by the Prodi Commission, new rules of procedure for appointing top officials have been introduced in order to internalize the recruitment process, although more informal steps in this direction had already been taken a long time ago (Coombes 1970: 158; Peterson 1971). How these new formal norms work in practice can be seen as a litmus test of what can be achieved through organizational design in this crucial area. The new formal procedure for appointing directors general (A1), deputy directors general and directors (A2) is presented in Appendix 3.1. In case of a vacancy, the post has to be published either internally (compulsory) or externally (optional). Internal and external candidates alike must submit their applications on standard application forms. The Directorate General for Personnel and Administration (DG ADMIN), in cooperation with private consultants if desired, is to carry out a systematic technical evaluation of the applications, thus verifying that candidates meet the requirements of the vacant post. These technical evaluations are then to be submitted to a so-called *rapporteur*. The *rapporteur*, designated from a pool of top Commission officials by the secretary general, shall assist in the process of identifying the best candidates. He or she is responsible for following an appointment from its initial publication to the final decision by the Commission.[7] Thus, a *rapporteur's* tasks are to consult the recruiting commissioner on the required profile of candidates, and to prepare (with the assistance of DG ADMIN and, when appropriate, external consultants) a presentation of accepted candidatures to the Consultative Committee of Appointments (CCA) (see below), followed by a recommendation indicating which candidates should be interviewed by the CCA. The *rapporteur's* assessment must take into account not only the specialist skills of applicants (although this is primary), but also the need to maintain a broad geographical balance, and measures to encourage the promotion of women. In doing his or her evaluation, the *rapporteur* is obliged to consult the recruiting commissioner.[8]

The principal mandate of the CCA is to advise the College on appointments at the A1 and A2 levels. The CCA is to act as an interviewing and evaluation board, which recommends a shortlist of candidates to the commissioners who in turn are responsible for the final decisions on appointments. The committee is chaired by the secretary general of the Commission and has the following members: (i) the director general for DG ADMIN, (ii) the permanent *rapporteur*,[9] (iii) the *rapporteur* in charge of the appointment under consideration, (iv) the director general of the recruiting DG (for appointments of deputy directors general and directors within the DG), (v) the head of the cabinet of the ADMIN Commissioner, and (vi) the head of the cabinet of the Commission president (for the appointments of directors general). The committee shall seek to reach a consensus. If necessary, a vote may be taken at the request of a member; in such cases, a decision requires a simple majority of members present. In the event of a tie in the voting, the chair shall have the casting vote.[10] On the basis of the CCA's shortlist, the recruiting commissioner shall decide, in agreement with the ADMIN commissioner and the president (for directors general only), which candidate is to be appointed. The commissioner is also entitled to appoint a candidate not originally shortlisted by the CCA, or to decide to repeat the entire application process if none of the applicants is deemed acceptable.

According to the formal procedure outlined above, member state governments or their permanent representations in Brussels have no formal points of access to the recruitment process. In spite of this barrier, they could of course try to intervene informally at different stages in order to push 'their' candidates forward; however, such contacts with Commission officials (the *rapporteurs*) do not seem to take place (source: interviews). Alternatively, government officials could approach 'their' respective commissioners or cabinet members; however, the extent to which this actually occurs is not known. Commissioners and cabinet members do have multiple points of access to appointment processes. It is the commissioners, in cooperation with top officials, who actually create vacancies in the first place (interview). Moreover, the commissioner in question also clearly has an influence regarding whether or not to publish a post externally (interview). During the last couple of years, vacant posts have increasingly been subjected to public advertisements,[11] although there is a clear policy statement that 'priority will continue to be given to internal candidates'.[12] The intention is 'to grow a service' (interview).

The pre-selection phase, in which DG ADMIN verifies whether applicants meet the requirements of the vacant post, is a 'hands-off' phase for commissioners and cabinet members (interviews). At the next stage, the *rapporteur* consults the recruiting commissioner before submitting to the CCA his or her recommendation as to whom they should interview, but there is not much involvement of commissioners or cabinets evident here either. The recruiting director general, or *rapporteur*, is the 'king of interviewing' (interviews). Concerning appointments of directors general, rules already preclude the possibility of having a compatriot of the sitting commissioner as a director general. If a commissioner becomes involved it is rarely in order to pursue national or partisan interests; rather, such interference usually reflects concerns for his or her portfolio (interview).

CCA proceedings normally take the form of consensus-seeking. Cabinet members play no particular role, do not try to steer the process and are not particularly influential (interviews). If voting takes place, Commission officials may form comfortable majorities in relation to cabinet members: 4–2 in the case of A1 appointments, and 5–1 for A2 appointments. The final critical question is of course whether or not the recruiting commissioner accepts the shortlist provided by the CCA. Normally, the shortlist is taken: approximately 95 per cent of those interviewed by the commissioner are from the list (interview). However, if the commissioner chooses to interview applicants who have not been shortlisted, this doesn't necessarily mean they will be appointed. During a three-and-a-half year period only one applicant seems to have been recruited without having first being shortlisted by the CCA (interviews). It seems to be deemed inappropriate to ignore the proposed list, as well as highly risky (interview).

The most striking lesson to be drawn from this small case study is that the tendency to attach national flags to top posts at the Commission seems to have been significantly reduced, and that the strict geographical quota system formerly practised has been almost completely abandoned. It appears as if the recruitment of senior personnel has not only become relatively insulated from pressure from national governments, but from the political level of the Commission as well. Governments may still express concern that their respective countries are inadequately 'represented', however, they seem to be without noticeable influence on individual appointments (interview). Not surprisingly, the same tendency can be observed as regards appointments of heads of unit. Formerly, national governments and cabinets intervened frequently even at this level; now, head of unit appointments are only exceptionally referred to a level that brings in cabinet members (interview).

Commission officials themselves ascribe the actual internalization (into the services) of senior official recruitment to the so-called 'objectivization' of the process (interview), which means the adoption of a transparent procedure and clearly specified requirements that have to be met. For example, in order to safeguard merit-based recruitment, external candidates have to meet strict criteria specified solely for them to pass the 'technical' pre-selection assessment made by DG ADMIN. They should have 'at least 15 years' professional experience in a post of responsibility, the last five years of which must have been in a senior post highly relevant to the one advertised.[13] The services' enhanced control of the appointment process may also be due to a change of organizational roles installed through the new procedure. The permanent *rapporteur* is a full-timer wholly dedicated to this task, while the other *rapporteurs* are senior officials with special responsibilities in the area. Thus, the new rules of procedure generate more focused attention and capacity to deal with top appointments at the administrative level.

It was EU enlargement, estimated to bring in ten A1 and forty-two A2 officials from the accession countries, that sparked the procedural reform discussed above. Concerns about the future professional quality of the services seem to have at least partially motivated the change (interview). The Commission's announcement of the same vacant positions in *all* the accession countries in order to create a broader competition is highly indicative of a less rigid quota system (interviews). The new rules of procedure were adopted solely on the basis of a Commission decision, and thus without being submitted to the Parliament or the Council (interview).

Establishing the European Communities Personnel Selection Office (EPSO). In July 2002 the European Parliament, the Council, the Commission, the Court of Justice, the Court of Auditors, the Economic and Social

Committee, the Committee of the Regions and the European Ombudsman together erected a common inter-institutional body entrusted with the means of selecting officials and other civil servants. The new organization was given the task of drawing up reserve lists from candidates in open competitions in line with the needs indicated by each institution.[14] Thus, the *concours* (competitive exam) formerly arranged by each institution for hiring new recruits will in the future be arranged as a joint venture. From the common reserve lists the institutions then have to pick their respective newcomers. Only in exceptional cases, and with the agreement of the EPSO, may institutions hold their own open competitions to meet specific needs for highly specialized staff.[15]

EPSO has its own executive board composed of the secretaries general of the eight collaborating institutions (interview). This kind of agencification should in theory insulate the organization's activities from potential pressure from EU-level politicians as well as from national governments. On the other hand, an inter-institutional joint committee with the EU-level trade unions that organize officials in the eight cooperating institutions might somewhat constrain its autonomy. This joint committee is consulted by EPSO, for example on draft selection procedures. However, 'EPSO decides' (interview). In fact, the unions seem to have been generally supportive of the new recruitment regime that EPSO represents (interview), as they have consistently pushed for a Europeanized and internalized personnel system (Coombes 1970: 163; Peterson 1971).

Since EPSO is still a young organization, there are relatively few experiences so far that measure its actual independence from external pressure. However, in preparation for enlargement, EPSO made a decision that might have been politically difficult to reach at the Commission (interview). In order to overcome several practical problems as well as to save money, EPSO decided that candidates taking part in the common *concours* to be arranged for each accession country would have to choose between English, French and German when taking their pre-selection tests. The language issue is a very sensitive one and could easily have become politicized, not least since the former Commission Vice-President in charge of administration (Neil Kinnock) had praised a multilinguistic service and expressed concerns about a potential reduction in the number of languages to be used (interview). Politicization would easily have been fuelled by the protests that were conveyed from both accession and member governments (interview).

In preparing for enlargement the Commission presented 'indicative figures', not quotas, for staff to be drawn from each of the accession countries and to be employed in the planning process during a seven-year transition period.[16] Although national governments would not be expected to try to influence individual recruitment decisions at or below the A8 level, it is nevertheless likely that the way in which this flexible quota system is actually implemented by the hiring institutions would be of considerable interest. Arguably, the encapsulation of the recruitment process that EPSO provides has removed the political access points that governments might have used in this respect. The Commission has also considered the option of running specific competitions for middle managers 'in cooperation with EPSO'.[17] This manner of recruitment would probably internalize appointment decisions at the medium level to an even greater extent.

Sectorization

Organizational devices such as the increased discretionary power conferred upon the president, the required multinational staffing of cabinets, more permanent administrative posts, as well as new rules of procedure for the appointment of senior officials and EPSO seem to have enhanced the actual autonomy of the Commission at the expense of national governments. However, while territorialization has lost ground to autonomization, sectorization may simultaneously have challenged the autonomization process. Since the Commission divides its work primarily according to the purpose or sector principle, it attracts in turn similarly structured societal interest groups (Kohler-Koch 1997). These organizations find clearer points of access to such structures than they would to structures arranged according to geography. At the same time, policy-makers in a sectorized bureaucracy may come to see co-optation or involvement of societal groups within their issue area as a route to legitimization of policy proposals (Andersen and Eliassen 2001). According to the Commission's white paper on governance, 'with better involvement comes greater responsibility'.[18] Thus, understandably, the Commission has in fact encouraged the formation of EU-level interest organizations (Mazey and Richardson 1996).

While sectorization, like territorialization, may threaten institutional autonomy, sectorization displaces territorialization. The Commission might (in theory) have been organized primarily by territory so that each of the directorates general (DGs) corresponded to a particular member state. Each geographically-based DG could have been composed of officials seconded from the national administration of the country served by that particular DG. Each commissioner might have been in charge of the DG that was to serve the country from which he or she had been nominated. However, things are in fact arranged quite differently. Although there certainly are, as mentioned, some territorial components in the structure of the Commission, most are non-territorial: the division of labour among DGs reflects different sectors or functions rather than geographical areas. Most posts are permanent and filled – according to merit, with a view to geographical balance – by the Commission services themselves. Units and cabinets are staffed multinationally to avoid national clusters or enclaves (Egeberg 2004). On this basis it makes sense that empirical studies so often portray decision-making at the Commission as politics between sectoral portfolios (or DGs) rather than between nations (Coombes 1970: 203; Cram 1994; Cini 2000; Hooghe 2000; Mörth 2000).

Party politicization

It has been argued above that the Commission, at the political as well as the administrative level, has, over time, enhanced its autonomy in important respects in relation to national governments. One could, however, similarly assert that the College as a body has become more dependent on the European Parliament (EP). From the very inception of the ECSC, as forerunner of the EP the Assembly has had the power to dismiss the whole of the College, though not individual commissioners. The Maastricht Treaty codified the right of the EP to be consulted before the president of the Commission could be appointed and also that the College should be subject to a vote of approval by the EP. On 13 January 1999 the EP adopted as a resolution a report by its Committee on Institutional Affairs advocating a stronger link between the results of the European election and the nomination of the College of Commissioners and its programme for the parliamentary term. The Constitutional Treaty largely supports this resolution by stating that the European Council, when proposing its candidate for president of the Commission, should take into account the elections to the European Parliament. According to the Constitution, the candidate would be *elected* by the EP, not only 'approved' (Article I-26). While it remains to be seen whether the Constitution materializes fully, as shown, some small steps towards a parliamentary system have already been taken. And in searching for a candidate to succeed Mr Prodi as Commission president, the actors seemed to behave as if the parliamentary principle had already come into force. Highly compatible with such a development would be the growing proportion of commissioners with ministerial experience, often at a senior level (MacMullen 2000). The fact that commissioners participate at their respective European political party meetings might be interpreted as a significant expression of the relevance of their partisan role.[19]

Party politicization would threaten autonomization processes at the Commission. However, as with sectorization, party politicization would displace territorialization: it would bring to the fore ideological lines of conflict and cooperation rather than politics between nations. It represents an alternative route to legitimization of the institution and its policy proposals.

Decoupling the political and administrative levels

From an organizational theory point of view, one way of handling the tensions associated with the Commission's development is to separate more clearly the political and administrative levels. Autonomization of the services could be legitimized on the grounds that they should be capable of impartially implementing, or monitoring the implementation of, common policies, and of providing reliable knowledge and 'Europeanized' policy expertise for the College of Commissioners. The College, on the other hand, obviously a genuine political body, could derive its legitimacy from being accountable to external bodies such as the directly elected EP or, as the Commission has proposed, to the EP as well as to the European Council.[20]

In fact, an emerging dual structure could be discerned at an early stage of the Commission's history. Monnet himself seems to have preferred a small, informal and integrated Commission (Duchêne 1994: 240). However, soon after his departure, a larger gap opened between the High Authority's members and its officials than he had planned. The services developed into more of a bureaucracy along French lines (Nugent 2001: 22). A clearer distinction between the roles of the two levels developed, indicated by growing differences in their recruitment patterns (MacMullen 2000). As we have seen, in conjunction with this development, the services gained more control over their recruitment and appointment processes, a feature indicating a more British or Scandinavian type of administration. Thus, while politicization of civil service careers seems to have increased in most Western countries in the early twenty-first century (Rouban 2003: 316), the opposite trend has been observed at the Commission. Moreover, the Prodi Commission spelled out how cabinets' 'policy creep' should be stopped. They should be down-sized and multinationally composed. They are to assist commissioners in particular in policy areas outside their portfolios, but should avoid interfering in departmental management.[21]

National agencies at the Commission's service?

Certain recent reform initiatives launched by the Commission could be interpreted as efforts to autonomize not only its own services, but parts of national administrative structures involved in serving the community as well. From the Commission's point of view, having to rely on national governments for implementation of EU policies makes community policies vulnerable to distortion. Studies show that implementing through national governments exposes common policies to considerable influence from national politics and administrative traditions (Goetz 2001; Heritier et al. 2001; Knill 2001; Olsen 2003; Sverdrup 2004). In order to push standardization of administrative practice across countries a bit further, some directives have contained specific requirements as to how national agencies should be set up (such as in the fields of communication and transport), with the underlying assumption of a close relationship between structure and actual implementation behaviour.

The autonomy of the community administration would, almost by necessity, be enhanced if the Commission could run its own agencies at the national level. This is, however, entirely unrealistic and not even an objective for the Commission, which prefers to focus on policy development.[22] As an alternative to Commission-run agencies, the idea has been launched of a networked administrative system, according to which the Commission could partly 'dispose of' national agencies.[23] Through New Public Management-inspired reforms, encouraged by the OECD as well as the EU, most regulatory tasks have already been hived off from national ministries to semi-detached bodies, a process referred to as 'agencification' (Kickert and Beck Jørgensen 1995; Christensen and Lægreid 2001). This kind of administrative infrastructure provides an opportunity for running 'double-hatted' regulatory agencies at the national level. Such agencies may serve two principals simultaneously. They constitute on the one hand an integral part of the national bureaucracy as originally intended. On the other hand, however, due to their relative independence they may also be well placed to serve as part of the community administration, through policy development as well as implementation. It would be impossible for a ministerial department to play the kind of dual role allotted to autonomous agencies.

The Commission, therefore, would constitute the hub of a network, where its partners would be national agencies working in the same policy area, such as telecom.[24] This kind of structure would represent a type of semi-autonomization of a multilevel community administration which could be highly conducive to enhanced policy convergence in the Union.

Studies of expert committees at the Commission and Council working parties have already indicated an emerging decomposition of national central governments: national officials do in fact play different roles in the two settings. Those in Commission groups, often originating from government agencies, are relatively seldom mandated by central coordinating bodies, such as foreign ministries, to behave in a certain manner. Thus, they have considerable leeway to contribute to *European* policy development, often on a highly sectoral basis. Those on Council committees on the other hand, typically originating from ministries, are usually instructed by their home office and tend to perceive themselves primarily as government representatives (Egeberg, Schaefer and Trondal, Chapter 5; Trondal and Veggeland 2003).

Conclusion

From its very inception the High Authority, later the Commission, was meant to act independently from member governments. The body was indeed an institutional innovation, pointing beyond a purely intergovernmental order. Its legitimacy as an autonomous organization was to be derived from its role as an injector of the general European interest into the policy process. This author's interpretation is that the Commission has, in important respects, gradually strengthened its independence from member states. The introduction of new organizational procedures, both at the political and administrative levels, has pushed autonomization further. The two small case studies presented in this chapter illustrate this trend. Although the lessons that can be drawn from these two reforms are still limited, they both point towards enhanced internalization of recruitment and appointment decisions. By allocating and earmarking administrative resources to appointing top officials and by 'objectivizing' the rules of procedure, the highly contentious practice of attaching national flags to particular posts seems to have been further reduced. Also, through the inter-institutional, 'agencified' EPSO, which runs the *concours* for newcomers, a barrier has been erected against external pressure, for example, on how the quota system will be practised in the future.

Since the agenda of the Commission has become increasingly comprehensive and multifaceted, it has probably also become harder to legitimize its independence and policy proposals by referring to what is in the general interest. One could interpret the efforts to involve civil society, and particularly European-level sectoral interest groups, as a way of compensating for the diminished role of territorial components in the Commission's structure in this respect. Internal and external sectorization threaten autonomization processes, but also tend to displace territorialization. Politics at the Commission is, in general, better described as politics between sectoral or functional portfolios than between nation-states.

Another, additional, route to legitimacy and accountability is represented by a closer relationship to the European electorate. So far, the small steps that have been taken point more in the direction of a kind of parliamentary system than towards a directly elected Commission president. Like sectorization, party politicization might hamper autonomization processes; it may, however, at the same time counteract territorialization by bringing in ideologically-based transnational coalitions. The Commission's proposal to make itself accountable also to the European Council could be interpreted as a way of reintroducing the territorial dimension. However, making the College – or individual commissioners, for that matter – partly accountable to the European Council as a body is very different from an intergovernmental arrangement. The latter case would mean that each commissioner was made accountable to the government that had appointed him or her.

Important institutions usually have to cope with competing demands, values and principles, often simultaneously. A certain organizational de-coupling may simplify the balancing act. Regarding the Commission, a clearer demarcation of the political and administrative components seems gradually to have occurred. For example, the new rules of procedure for the appointment of senior officials are in practice not only insulating such processes from national governments but from commissioners and their cabinets as well. This separation makes it possible to maximize, so to speak, along at least two dimensions at the same time. The political component can be made accountable and thus less autonomous through territorialization, sectorization or party politicization. The services, on the other hand, can be autonomized up to a certain point, legitimized by their role as impartial implementer and provider of reliable knowledge and Europeanized policy expertise for the political leadership. The development of EU-level regulatory agencies and 'double-hatted', semi-detached national agencies, both working in close cooperation with the Commission services, might be interpreted as the first real signs of building a genuine multilevel Union administration.

The inherent tensions in the Commission's development make it difficult to assess what the most important implications may be for the European integration process. However, the lesson to be drawn from this analysis seems to be that the way the Commission has been organized contributes to changing the pattern of conflict and cooperation in European politics from a primarily intergovernmental pattern to a multidimensional cleavage

structure. Such a change can be seen as an essential feature of system transformation (Egeberg 2004). Most notably, having become an actor in its
own right through autonomization, the Commission has complemented a
decision system primarily composed of states and intergovernmental
organizations by introducing inter-institutional conflict and cooperation. By connecting up national agencies it may even challenge the
internal consistency of national governments. Sectorization means that
politics at the Commission primarily takes the form of politics between
sectoral DGs, which in turn link up with transnational sectoral groups
and compatible parts of national administrations. And, finally, the
prospects of a college appointed more according to parliamentary principles would expand the room for party politics at the EU level.

Acknowledgement

An earlier version of this chapter was presented at a conference on administrative reform at the University of Potsdam 12–13 November 2004. I
thank the participants, and in particular discussant Klaus Goetz, for their
helpful comments.

Notes

1. See *European Governance. A White Paper*, COM (2001) 428 final, p. 8, and *For the European Union. Peace, Freedom and Solidarity. Communication of the Commission on the Institutional Architecture*, COM (2002) 728 final, p. 18.
2. Cf., for example, *European Voice* 14–20 November 2002, and 22–28 May 2003.
3. *European Voice* 22–28 July 1999.
4. Press statement by Vice President Neil Kinnock, 29 September 1999.
5. Based on personal interviews with four senior Commission officials (Brussels 15–16 May 2003), among whom two were participants at meetings of the Consultative Committee on Appointments, plus documents (referred to). On 16 September 2005 an additional top official of the CCA was interviewed as a follow-up, subsequent to Union enlargement.
6. *An Administration at the Service of Half a Billion Europeans. Staff Reforms at the European Commission* (Spring 2002), p. 20.
7. Manual – Commission Top Management: the Selection, Appointment and Appraisal of Senior Commission Officials (07/11/02).
8. *An Administration at the Service of …* , p. 21.
9. A2 official at DG ADMIN with an overall responsibility for recruitment of top officials. May also serve as *rapporteur* for specific appointments.
10. Rules of procedure for the Consultative Committee on Appointments (CCA) (ADMIN-2002-00355-01-00).
11. *An Administration at the Service of …* , p. 20.
12. Manual, p. 5.
13. *An Administration at the Service of …* , p. 20.

14. *Official Journal of the European Communities*, vol. 45, L197/53; *An Administration of the Service of* ... , p. 6.
15. *Official Journal* ...
16. Meeting of Vice-President N. Kinnock with ministers responsible for public administration in the accession countries, 26 May 2003.
17. Meeting of Vice-President ...
18. *European Governance* ... , p. 15.
19. At least, this is the case for social democratic commissioners. Source: Espen Barth Eide, member of the presidency of the Party of European Socialists (PES).
20. *For the European Union* ... , p. 18.
21. *European Voice*, 22–28 July 1999.
22. *Externalization of the Management of Community Programmes – including presentation of a framework regulation for a new type of executive agency*, COM (2000) 788 final.
23. *Externalization* ... , p. 6.
24. *Externalization* ... , p. 6.

Appendix 3. 1 **Appointments of senior officials, grade A1: formal procedure**

Publication of posts

External publication — Internal publication

Applications with standardized forms

Technical evaluation of applications by DG ADMIN

Rapporteur evaluates files and recommends to Consultative Committee on Appointments (CCA) list of candidates to be interviewed

CCA interviews candidates and establishes shortlist for the 'recruiting' Commissioner

Commissioner takes final decision in agreement with the President and the Commissioner for Personnel

Commission appoints senior official

Source: Manual – Commission Top Management: the Selection, Appointment and Appraisal of Senior Commission Officials (07/11/02), p. 7.

4

The College of Commissioners: Executive Politics as Usual?

Morten Egeberg

Images of the European Commission

There are many images out there, among scholars as well as in political life, of how the European Commission (Commission) actually works. Some authors have portrayed it as being permeated by national interests at all levels (Kassim and Wright 1991; Peterson 1999; Menon 2003). Others emphasize that although commissioners' nationality certainly may have an impact on their preferences on some occasions, for the most part, commissioners approach and undertake their duties and tasks in an impartial manner (Nugent 2001: 115). Most authors, however, do not make an assessment of the relative weight assigned to national interests, Commission interests, portfolio interests or party political concerns in the College of Commissioners (Coombes 1970; Donnelly and Ritchie 1994; Ross 1995; Cini 1996; Page 1997; Hooghe 2001; Peterson 2002; Smith 2003; Peterson 2004). Thus, the College seems, in several respects, to be a 'black box' in the scholarly literature. This becomes even more evident when it is compared with other key EU institutions. Much more empirical information is available on how the Union Council and the European Parliament actually work. Studies of these institutions have revealed that while contestation along national lines seems to prevail in the Council (Thomson et al. 2004), politics in the Parliament reflects mainly a left–right dimension (Hix 2001).

The lack of clarity about the way in which those at the Commission's helm really behave can also be seen as reflected in public debate, not least in the heated argument over the composition of the College that took place at, and subsequent to, the Convention on the Future of Europe. The fact that some governments were willing to give up 'their' permanent commissioner (for example, the 'inner six'), while others were fiercely against a rotation system (for example the ten new member states), could at least be interpreted as mirroring considerable confusion about how the body actually works (see *European Voice*, 23–29 October 2003; 6–12 November, 2003).

There certainly is, therefore, an urgent need for clarification. How do commissioners actually behave at College meetings? Which roles are evoked and which cleavages are discernable? Partly inspired by scholars who have previously studied the role behaviour of ministers in national cabinets (Olsen 1980; Searing 1994), I will investigate the extent to which commissioners champion the collective interests of their institution, their particular portfolio interests, national ('constituency') concerns, or party political interests. The extent to which they pursue portfolio, national or partisan interests indicates whether conflicts within the College tend to occur along portfolio, national or partisan lines. It is equally important to try to understand and explain in theoretical terms their behaviour and the conditions under which certain ways of acting might be more frequently observed than others. One of the reasons for the overt confusion in the academic literature about how the College actually works might very well be that the topic has been heavily under-theorized up to now, thus making it hard to interpret various empirical observations in a meaningful and systematic way.

It is here suggested that our understanding may be considerably enhanced by taking into consideration the organizational setting within which commissioners are embedded. This environment imposes multiple, often competing, role expectations on them. A careful examination of the characteristic features of this setting and the types of policy that are dealt with in the College might provide some clues for sorting out the circumstances under which some roles are evoked more often than others. First, the chapter introduces the general theoretical framework and characterizes the College along key organizational (independent) variables. Indeed, the main purpose of this chapter is to theorize College behaviour. However, I also outline a method by which actual behaviour in such a setting might be observed. Some exploratory data on commissioners' behaviour (dependent variable) in the College will then be presented for illustrative purposes, and the results discussed in relation to the predictions made.

Theorizing commissioners' behaviour

If we take as our point of departure the legal rules that are meant to govern commissioners' behaviour in the College, we would expect them to make decisions solely with a view to what might be defined as being in the interest of Europe. According to Article 213 (EC Treaty), 'Members of the Commission shall, in the general interest of the Community, be completely independent in the performance of their duties', and 'they shall neither seek nor take instructions from any government or from any other body'. Liberal intergovernmentalists seem to share this view on commissioners as independent actors, although with a clearly circumscribed mandate (Moravcsik 1998). In fact, neo-functionalists, historical-institutionalists and principal-agent analysts as well could probably subscribe to the same expectation, although in their view the Commission would, due to 'locking in' mechanisms and information asymmetry, have more scope for acting according to its own will (Sandholtz and Stone Sweet 1998; Pierson 1996; Pollack 2004). Those adhering to more classical intergovernmentalism, on the other hand, will probably tend to interpret College behaviour as more 'COREPER like' behaviour (see Cini 2003b).

Seen from an organizational theory perspective, one has to 'unpack' individual actors' organizational contexts in order to account for their actual behaviour, interests and loyalties (Egeberg 2003a, 2004). There are four key organizational factors to be taken into consideration in this respect: namely organizational structure, organizational demography, organizational locus and institutionalization. An *organizational structure* is a normative (role) structure that imposes codified expectations as regards the decision behaviour of the various role incumbents. The logic of appropriateness, incentives and bounded rationality are the mechanisms that are supposed to connect role expectations and actual behaviour (March and Olsen 1989; Searing 1994; Simon 1965). Organizations that require participation on a full-time basis ('primary structures') and that provide permanent posts are more likely to significantly affect participants' interests and loyalties than organizations made up of part-timers ('secondary structures') and temporary positions.

Most organizational structures are specialized. Thus, they assign 'sub-roles' to most members, thereby inserting permanent tensions between the whole and its parts (multiple roles). In general, a positive relationship exists between a person's hierarchical rank and his or her identification with the organization as such (Egeberg and Sætren 1999). However, even among those of highest rank, loyalties are split between the organization as a whole and the parts of which they are in charge. The relative emphasis given to the two levels in this respect will depend on, among other things, the amount of organizational capacity devoted to coordination and to the person at the very top.

It also matters *how* organizations are specialized. While specialization in itself entails the emergence of particular portfolio interests, the chosen principle of specialization tends to determine the substance of these interests. For example, in organizations that are structured according to geography, decision-makers are likely to emphasize the concerns of particular territories and to focus attention along geographical cleavages, while in entities arranged by sector or function participants tend to pursue sectoral or functional interests and to perceive the world as divided primarily along sectoral or functional lines (Gulick 1937; Egeberg 2003a).

Organizational demography refers to the composition – in terms of basic attributes such as age, sex, ethnicity, nationality and education – of the social entity under study (Pfeffer 1982: 277). In addition, the former, present (for example length of service) and future careers of organizational members are included. When it comes to accounting for decision behaviour in organizations, these demographic factors interact with each other and with structural variables in a complicated manner. For example, participants' backgrounds are supposed to be more important in organizations characterized by short-term contracts than in entities with life-long career patterns, and more important within secondary structures than within primary structures. Thus, empirical studies of public bureaucracies have in general revealed rather weak relationships between officials' background and their actual decision behaviour (Meier and Nigro 1976; Lægreid and Olsen 1984). Also, a wide variety of experiences acquired outside the organization are not particularly relevant to policy disputes taking place within it. Only when a very clear 'representational linkage' exists can we expect a background factor to affect significantly a person's organizational behaviour (Selden 1997).

By *organizational locus* is meant the physical location, space and structure of an organization. Studies have revealed some independent impacts of locus on organizational members' contact patterns, coordination behaviour and identities (Pfeffer 1982: 260–71; Egeberg 2003a; Egeberg and Sætren 1999). The number of unplanned meetings between decision-makers is particularly sensitive to how the physical setting is arranged. Thus, for example, the amount of attention leaders pay to the concerns of their respective portfolios versus the organization as a whole may be partly affected by whether they are located on the premises of their departments or situated together as a leadership group.

According to Selznick (1957), *institutionalization* describes organizations that are growing increasingly complex by adding informal norms and practices, and that are becoming infused with value beyond the technical requirements of the task at hand (pp. 17–22). Thus, only the emergence of informal norms that underpin an organization's transition from being a pure instrument for somebody else to becoming a principal in itself (its process of 'autonomization') can be seen as part of an institutionalization process in a strict sense. Informal norms may accentuate role expectations codified in the organizational structure. However, such norms may also challenge this structure.

In addition to the organizational factors discussed above, the *type of policy* dealt with should be taken into consideration in order to account for the actual behaviour of decision-makers. According to Lowi (1964), 'policy determines politics'. Thus, for example, we would expect issues dealing with the role and competence of the focal institution in an overall system of governance to evoke 'organization-wide' roles, while sectoral policies would activate more particularistic roles. In a similar vein, some kinds of items on the agenda could be thought to establish a more obvious 'representational linkage' than others.

Assumptions about commissioners' behaviour

In order to make qualified assumptions about College behaviour we have to take as our starting point the values that commissioners have on the independent variables outlined above. At the outset, since commissioners find themselves at the very top of an organization that also constitutes their primary structure, we would expect them to primarily champion the collective interests of their institution. Among the factors that pull in the same direction are their collective responsibility, their cabinets which are supposed to monitor all portfolios, the president's privilege to distribute and redistribute dossiers and to ask individual commissioners to step down, and the fact that the president concentrates on coordination tasks by having the Secretariat General as his sole portfolio.

However, commissioners are in charge of specialized portfolios that probably require more time and energy than the weekly College meetings. In addition, the commissioners under study are physically located with their respective services. Therefore, in most cases, commissioners are supposed to assume narrower portfolio roles rather than an institution-wide role. Since portfolios are arranged according to sector or function, we expect portfolio interests to be equivalent to sectoral or functional interests. Had the Commission been organized by geography (as, for example, the UK central government's Scottish and Welsh offices), we would expect the concerns of particular territories to be at the forefront.

Most commissioners are also affiliated to political parties which might add to the imposition of particular role expectations. Over time, the College has been increasingly composed of political heavyweights (MacMullen 2000). The College under study (N = 20) consisted of 15 former ministers and 15 former parliamentarians. Only one member was without any known party affiliation. Commissioners occasionally affirm their political identity for a wider audience by attending meetings convened by their respective European party federations, or party groups in the European Parliament.[1] Finally, if we add the enhanced role assigned to the European Parliament as regards the appointment of College members, and, in particular, the growing importance of the results of the European elections in this respect, we could indeed expect the party role to become more salient among commissioners. However, notwithstanding these small steps in the direction of parliamentarism, under the current regime commissioners' party affiliations are supposed to be of less relevance in most decision situations.

What room is left then for the role of nationality? Like national cabinet ministers commissioners have, in a sense, territorial constituencies (Searing 1994). We can expect both to be attentive to the concerns of these territories, although neither ministers nor commissioners are allowed to take instructions from them. While national cabinets may strive informally to reach a certain geographical balance as regards their composition, in the Commission this is formalized. Thus, the role that nationality might play in the College has to be somewhat ambiguous and delicate. As has already been said, the organizational structure within which commissioners find themselves could generally be expected to decouple their decision behaviour from their origins. Also, the informal norms and culture that have developed in the College seem largely to underpin the formal arrangement in this respect: commissioners should avoid overt nationalism (Cini 1996: 111), too close relationships with member states (Donnelly and Ritchie 1994: 35) and 'COREPER-like behaviour' (Joana and Smith 2004).[2] In addition, since regulatory policy seems to be the dominant type of policy at the EU level (Majone 1991), national interests may often be hard to specify. Compared to budgetary matters, winners and losers can, in general, be less clearly identified as far as regulatory policy is concerned (Peters 1992).

On the other hand, when issues having obvious implications for a particular country are dealt with, a 'representational linkage' might nevertheless occur. In addition, since commissioners are on temporary contracts, concerns related to future career prospects could possibly interfere in a given decision situation. As regards the College under study, about half of the members might very well have a future political career at the Commission or in their country of origin (EuropeanVoice.com, 29 January 2004). However, since governments may change during commissioners' time in Brussels, being attentive to the concerns of the government which nominated them is far from any guarantee for being reappointed or appointed somewhere else.

Methodological approach

Given the relatively small number of commissioners it would hardly make sense to do a statistical analysis of this group as such. I decided instead to use key informants who were asked to report on five-point scales how frequently the four roles ('commission role', 'portfolio role', 'country role', 'party political role') were actually evoked at College meetings, without, however, unveiling the behaviour of individual commissioners. They were asked to make this assessment as regards five different types of policy that commissioners deal with: namely sectoral (regulatory) policies, budgetary matters, institutional policy, administrative policy and personnel policy. 'Institutional policy' designates Commission statements on the overall role and competence of the various EU institutions, while 'administrative policy' is mainly about internal reform. In addition, the interviewees were asked to characterize role behaviour when topics on the agenda clearly could have distributional consequences along national lines ('geographical policy'). This might sometimes be the case within all the five issue areas mentioned above, but, in addition, cohesion policy, location decisions and the like are of course subsumed into this policy category.

In order to select informants, I decided to approach top officials, all from the Secretariat General (SG), who usually sit in at College meetings. Compared to commissioners and cabinet members (who may sit in occasionally), SG officials are, arguably, more 'neutral' observers of the proceedings. The interviewees include four who cover the Prodi Commission (the focus of this study) and one from the Delors period. The interviewee from the Delors period provided background information on College behaviour. Three of the informants were very experienced Commission officials. Three had previously also served as cabinet members, and in that capacity they had also occasionally attended College meetings. I started by sending them a letter (winter/spring 2004) in which I briefly described my project. Attached to the letter followed the standardized form which presented the four roles, the frequency scales, and the various types of policy areas to be considered. After some days I phoned them and made appointments for interviewing. During the interview, the interviewee had the form in front of her or him. Thus, since variable values are numbered (1–5), there was virtually no room left for misinterpreting their answers. The level of convergence among responses turned out to be high. This suggested that the most reliable and transparent way of presenting the results would probably be to emphasize (in bold) the most 'representative' variable values directly in the form used for interviewing. Where clear divergence among responses appeared, I have chosen a value in between or simply marked out two (neighbouring) values instead of only one. This could not be done, however, without making some hard judgements. In this respect, I considered, for example, whether only one informant dissented or not, and the amount of experience from the College the 'dissident' could draw on when making her or his assessment. Those presenting interview data in a more unstandardized manner of course face similar difficulties as regards the selection and weighing of various observations. However, such problems are probably highlighted when applying the method proposed here. Related to the standardized form, I also recorded the interviewees' more broad and qualitative reflections around College behaviour. In addition, I asked the informants about the potential impacts that commissioners' past and future careers and physical location might have on their role enactment.

In spite of the fact that most of the informants are experienced people, it is no simple task to perceive and register commissioners' behaviour. Which role they actually assume at College meetings might be a highly subtle affair. In particular, since pursuing national interests is, in general, deemed inappropriate in the Commission setting (see above), commissioners could be expected to try to disguise these kinds of motives by instead taking positions that are normatively justifiable. According to Elster (1998: 104), however, when doing this, they will tend to argue for a position that differs somewhat from their ideal point since a perfect coincidence between private (national) interest and impartial argument is suspicious. Nevertheless, there is a danger of a certain under-reporting of the 'country role'.

How commissioners seem to behave in College

The College under study voted between six and ten times a year (source: interviews). Given the hundreds of items that are on the agenda each year for the weekly meetings,[3] this decisional style seems extremely consensus-oriented. We cannot, however, on the basis of voting frequency,

Table 4.1 Sectoral (regulatory) policy: how frequently the four roles are evoked in College

	Frequently				Seldom
Commission role	1	2	3	4	5
Portfolio role	1	2	3	4	5
Country role	1	2	3	4	5
Party role	1	2	3	4	5

infer that commissioners usually agree to what becomes the official Commission line, as a result of more or less extensive deliberation. We know that dissidents, instead of pushing for a vote, can be satisfied with having their disagreement recorded in confidential minutes (interview). In this study we focus on the interests that commissioners actually pursue at College meetings, and how their behaviour in this respect might be accounted for.

Since sectoral or regulatory policies are by far the most common types of policy on the College's agenda (interview), it seems natural to begin by looking at the frequency with which the various roles are evoked within this domain (Table 4.1). The consistency among the ratings given by the different informants was extremely high in this case, something that is demonstrated by the fact that it was sufficient to indicate only one value on each variable. Table 4.1 shows that the 'portfolio role' is most frequently assumed; followed by the 'commission role'. As said, due to the way in which the Commission structure is specialized, portfolio interests mean, in practice, sectoral or functional interests. Had the Commission been arranged according to territory, portfolio concerns would have been geographical. The prevalent sectoral or functional orientation of commissioners is underpinned not only by the internal organization of the Commission, but also by partly parallel structures found within key institutional interlocutors, such as the standing committees of the European Parliament and the ministerial meetings of the Council (interview).[4] In addition, the physical location of commissioners with their respective services may accentuate the 'portfolio role' somewhat to the detriment of collegiality, or the 'commission role' (interviews).

Sectoral and regulatory policies may also contain elements that entail clear distributional consequences along national lines. Within the competition policy area, for example, state aid cases might sometimes be thought to trigger a 'representational linkage' between commissioners and their countries of origin. The same could be true as regards, for instance, the priority given to various infrastructure projects in the

Table 4.2 Budgetary matters: how frequently the four roles are evoked in College

	Frequently				Seldom
Commission role	1	2	3	4	5
Portfolio role	1	2	3	4	5
Country role	1	2	3	4	5
Party role	1	2	3	4	5

Table 4.3 Institutional policy: how frequently the four roles are evoked in College

	Frequently				Seldom
Commission role	1	2	3	4	5
Portfolio role	1	2	3	4	5
Country role	1	2	3	4	5
Party role	1	2	3	4	5

transport sector. Table 4.1 shows that the 'country role' is in fact assumed, although not frequently. The 'party role' seems even more rarely enacted. Commissioners' party political affiliation can, however, sometimes be demonstrated, in particular when social policy and state aid cases are on the agenda (interviews).

As regards budget-making, or issues with clear budgetary implications, Table 4.2 indicates that the 'portfolio role' is still the role most frequently evoked in the College. However, aside from the 'commission role', the 'country role' appears relatively often within this policy field. Contributors and beneficiaries may usually be more easily identified than in the regulatory field, and this fact makes a 'representational linkage' more likely (interview). When it comes to the institutional policy area, commissioners apparently see themselves most of the time as representing the Commission as a whole (see Table 4.3). Sometimes, however, the portfolio role is also adopted within this field, for example when a commissioner wants to enhance the role of his or her policy sector within the overall constitutional architecture. It also happens, although less often, that strongly articulated government positions, as for example on the composition of the College in the Constitutional Treaty, are reflected in commissioners' behaviour (interviews).

The administrative policy field seems to share some of the basic properties of the institutional policy area (Table 4.4). However, while the 'commission role' is equally dominant, the 'country role' is even more muted. A possible

Table 4.4 Administrative policy: how frequently the four roles are evoked in College

	Frequently				Seldom
Commission role	1	2	3	4	5
Portfolio role	1	2	3	4	5
Country role	1	2	3	4	5
Party role	1	2	3	4	5

Table 4.5 Personnel policy: how frequently the four roles are evoked in College

	Frequently				Seldom
Commission role	1	2	3	4	5
Portfolio role	1	2	3	4	5
Country role	1	2	3	4	5
Party role	1	2	3	4	5

relationship between the strength of the New Public Management (NPM) movement in commissioners' home countries and their attitudes towards NPM-inspired reforms at the Commission was hinted at (interview). Occasionally, enactments of the 'party role' can also be observed when change proposals are framed within a NPM paradigm (interview).

The personnel policy area differs significantly from the rest of the administrative field (see Table 4.5). Firstly, the 'portfolio role' is most frequently evoked, and, secondly, commissioners more often take on the 'country role'. This behavioural pattern probably reflects that commissioners strived to enhance, in qualitative as well as quantitative terms, the human resources available within their respective remits, while they simultaneously have a close view to the geographical balance as regards senior officials' background (interviews).

Finally, the informants were asked to assess commissioners' role behaviour when items that could clearly have distributional consequences along national lines are on the agenda ('geographical policy'). This policy category could contain elements from all the other policy areas previously discussed as well as the obvious cases, such as location issues. Table 4.6 shows a relatively even distribution among the different behaviours, although the 'country role', as expected, seems to be evoked somewhat more frequently than the others. However, even within this policy category, the 'country role' doesn't take a clear lead. Informants emphasized that on their arrival at the Commission they had been surprised by the

Table 4.6   Geographical policy: how frequently the four
roles are evoked in College

	Frequently				Seldom
Commission role	1	2	3	4	5
Portfolio role	1	2	3	4	5
Country role	1	2	3	4	5
Party role	1	2	3	4	5

limited role played by nationality at College meetings (interviews),
although they also acknowledged that problems related to geography
might have been solved at the cabinet level (interview). The 'commission role' often 'takes the lead at the end of the day', and the *tour de table*
often registers a consensus (interview). Although the organizational structure as well as the informal norms are highly restrictive as regards the role
that nationality might play, it was emphasized that there are, nevertheless, particular situations in which a country orientation is deemed more
legitimate. This would, for example, be the case if a commissioner were
seriously to argue that a certain College decision could mean 'a disaster
in the country I know best' (interview). Also, there might be some relationship between commissioners' future career plans and their liability to
assume the 'country role' (interviews).

Conclusion: understanding commissioners'
multiple role behaviour

The exploratory empirical analysis presented here indicates that the
College can probably not be portrayed as being permeated by national
interests, as claimed by several scholars. Nor do commissioners seem to
act solely in the general European or Commission interest as could be
expected by relying on the relevant Treaty provisions. Instead, this study
suggests that the role most frequently evoked in the College is the 'portfolio role'; that is commissioners tend to champion the interests that are
directly linked to their respective briefs. Since the organizational structure
is specialized according to sector or function, these interests will be sectoral
or functional. They could have been something else, had the arrangement
been otherwise. Another key observation is that commissioners assume
multiple roles: while the 'portfolio role' seems to be most frequently
evoked, both the 'commission role' and the 'country role' are important
ingredients of the College's political life. Less visible is the political 'party

role', although it is there. Moreover, it has been demonstrated that commissioners' role behaviour may be contingent upon the type of policy dealt with. For example, by focusing exclusively on 'geographical policy', it could be shown how a 'representational linkage' might push the 'country role' to the fore.

The assumptions about commissioners' decision behaviour based on organizational theory seem to correspond well with data: the organizational setting leads us to expect multiple and probably often competing role enactments. By combining relevant (given) features of the organizational structure, demography and locus, as well as of the informal norms and culture, we seem to be able to predict fairly well the relative weight that commissioners actually assign to various roles in College. By introducing 'policy type or area' as a conditioning factor, we got some additional cues for specifying the conditions under which various roles are in fact activated. Thus, even if this study builds on rather limited data sources and clearly raises delicate methodological issues, the fact that the results are highly comprehensible in theoretical terms nevertheless strengthens their validity.

Although this study empirically focuses on the Prodi Commission, it is not intended as a study of a particular College. Rather, it aims to describe something of how executive politicians behave under certain organizational conditions. Thus, the theoretical model deliberately ignores the impact of other variables, for example personal factors. This does not in any sense mean that one holds such factors to be irrelevant; only that they are not accommodated in the model, in this case because of an inability to see how they could be incorporated in a meaningful way. Concerning the Commission, most observers seem to agree that the personality of, for example, Jacques Delors did matter (Drake 2000). So, the personal strength of the president could be thought to affect, for instance, the frequency with which the 'commission role' is evoked among the other commissioners.

Within the model applied here, changes in role behaviour are likely to occur subsequent to significant shifts in the organizational and policy area variables. Thus, the arrival of a new team of commissioners does not in itself entail new patterns of decision-making. However, if, for example, they recongregate in the Berlaymont building, one might expect, other things being equal, a slight strengthening of the 'commission role' to the detriment of the 'portfolio role'. A considerable increase in the number of commissioners would, on the other hand, tend to pull in the opposite direction. If a number of commissioners are not assigned (sectoral) portfolios of a certain size (for example if the number of commissioners does not match the number of available Directorates General), they will be pulled between the remaining roles. It can be predicted then that the 'country role' will grow, not only because there are fewer roles left to choose between, but also because the sectoral 'portfolio role' provides displacement of the 'country role'. If the number of commissioners were to become less than the number of member states, as was Jean Monnet's original idea (Duchêne 1994: 240), the 'country role' might be reduced because it would become less appropriate to pursue national interests. In other words, the normative constraints on the 'representational linkage' might be strengthened further.

To conclude, commissioners' role behaviour seems to have much in common with that of national cabinet ministers; they assume multiple and competing roles whose relative weight may vary according to organizational and policy area variables. Both are highly 'portfolio driven', and both are also embedded in a collegial setting that demands a certain collective responsibility. Moreover, commissioners as well as cabinet ministers have their 'local' community back home which imposes certain expectations on them while in office. The modest role that party political affiliation seems to play in the College may represent the biggest difference between the two. If the Commission's relationship to the European Parliament continues to grow, both as regards the appointment of commissioners and their daily policy-making, there is reason to believe that more emphasis will be put on this role in future colleges. Indications of a stronger role for the European-level political parties in the process of selecting the Commission president point in the same direction (Ludlow 2004; Johansson 2005). It should be emphasized, however, that the main purpose of this chapter has been to theorize College behaviour and to outline a method for observing it. The empirical underpinning is, so far, at only a preliminary stage.

What further 'normalizes' executive politics at the EU level is the fact that portfolios are sectoral or functional rather than territorial. Arguably, national executives have been structured according to sectoral or functional principles in order to displace regional tensions within a country. The emergence of ministries specialized by territory, such as the Scottish and Welsh offices within the UK central government, on the other hand, may indicate devolution (Egeberg 2003a). Thus, by having achieved considerable institutional autonomy, and by being organized mainly along non-territorial lines, the Commission adds (inter-)institutional and sectoral conflicts to the European-level pattern of territorial and ideological cleavages (Moravcsik 1998; Marks and Steenbergen 2004). The extent to which cleavages cross-cutting national lines exist at the European level can be seen as a key indicator of system transformation in Europe (Egeberg 2004).

Acknowledgements

I am grateful to two anonymous referees and to participants at an ARENA seminar for their valuable comments on an earlier version of this chapter. A version was also presented at the ECPR conference in Budapest, 8–10 September 2005 at a CONNEX-sponsored panel. Special thanks to discussant and chair Michelle Cini on this occasion.

Notes

1. Sources: (1) Espen Barth Eide, member of the presidency of the Party of European Socialists; (2) one of the interviewees (see section on method).
2. Also mentioned by one of the interviewees (see section on method).
3. Minutes of Commission meetings 2003 (available on the Commission website).
4. Although the organization of the European Parliament and the Union Council clearly embodies sectoral and functional components, this doesn't mean that such components are prevalent within these bodies. The Council, for example, is primarily territorially arranged which, arguably, explains its mainly intergovernmental conflict pattern (Egeberg 2004).

5

EU Committee Governance between Intergovernmental and Union Administration

Morten Egeberg, Guenther F. Schaefer and Jarle Trondal

Introduction[1]

Committees are an essential part of the functioning of modern governance. Some committees are official, whilst others are unofficial or even ad hoc. They play a crucial role in the daily operation of the European Union (EU) system of governance by providing expertise in policy development and decision-making, by linking member states' governments and administrations with the EU level and by increasing the acceptance of European laws and programmes in the member states. EU committees are important arenas for EU governance as well as melting pots of national and supranational government systems. In various guises, committees are active at every stage of the political process within the EU machinery – assisting the Commission in drafting legislation, preparing the dossiers on which the Council takes decisions and supervising the implementation of EC law by the Commission. The latter are generally referred to as comitology committees, although the term is sometimes extended to include all committees (Christiansen and Kirchner 2000).

This chapter is the result of an extensive research project comparing domestic government officials attending Commission expert committees (ECs), Council working parties (CWPs) and comitology committees (CCs). For the first time, survey data that make it possible to compare in a systematic way how the three main types of EU committees really function are presented. One of our main observations is that sweeping generalizations on how the system works should be avoided. Rather than dealing with committees as a coherent mass that basically displays the same characteristics (as in Wessels's (1998) 'fusion thesis'), our portrayal discloses a system of governance with several faces. First, Council groups appear very much as intergovernmental arenas in the sense that participants primarily seem to behave as representatives of their home governments. Officials advocate policy positions that routinely have been subject to coordination processes in their respective national administrations, and they often bring with them instructions on how to act. We think that the general availability of interpreting facilities from all languages into other languages clearly symbolizes the presence of highly intergovernmental components in this particular context. Second, we show that comitology committees exhibit many of the same essentially intergovernmental features as the Council working parties. This is surprising since previous research has tended to portray comitology as an arena in which participants proceed from being representatives of national interests to becoming representatives of a Europeanized inter-administrative discourse (Joerges and Neyer 1997).

Third, our findings suggest that Commission expert committees represent a setting that is significantly different from the two former ones. Here participants usually practice a broader repertoire of roles; thus, the behavioural pattern that follows is more multifaceted than that which characterizes intergovernmental interaction. Moreover, expert committee attendants obviously have more leeway than those on other committees; they are less involved in coordination processes at the national level, and they seldom bring with them a clear mandate on how to act. In addition, the decision situation seems considerably more relaxed as far as language use is concerned: expert committees have in common with comitology committees the fact that interpretation is usually available for only a few languages.

However, the picture of committee governance is more complicated than that. This chapter shows that EU committees also *share* some important properties. First, the role of expertise is pivotal across all types of committee. Participants assign more weight to arguments advocated by members who have demonstrated considerable expertise on the subject matter at hand than to views advanced by colleagues from large member states. Given the huge amount of attention devoted to the formal voting power of the various countries in the Council, this is an interesting result (Golub 1999; Mattila and Lane 2001). Second, a considerable proportion of committee members express allegiance to the committee in which they participate – although this proportion is clearly smaller than the proportion who express loyalty to national institutions. This observation on multiple allegiances is important since it may contribute to diminishing the controversy over whether loyalty transfer from the national to the supranational level takes place or not. While Wessels (1998) asserts that, contrary to certain neo-functional assumptions, no such transfer has occurred, Laffan (1998) seems to take the opposite position. Third, an overwhelming majority of national officials, across committee types, express trust in the Commission in the sense that they perceive Commission officials in committees to act mainly independently from particular national interests. In fact, a clear majority hold Commission officials as among their main interlocutors during meetings. And, finally, 70 per cent say that English is the language most frequently used in informal discussions.

Although the main purpose of this chapter is to report what we see as important findings from an empirical project, the observations noted above raise some crucial theoretical questions. How are the many faces of EU committee governance to be accounted for? The institutionalist turn in European integration studies focuses (or refocuses) on the role that institutions play in shaping actors' role conceptions, interests and identities (Aspinwall and Schneider 2001). However, one could argue that in order to specify the conditions under which this may actually happen one has to 'unpack' institutions (if we are dealing with concrete institutions) to see how they are organized (Egeberg 2004). Thus, the marked difference between Council and comitology committees on the one hand, and Commission groups on the other, may be explained by the different organizational structures that we find in the two settings. The basically territorially arranged Council and comitology setting (in the sense that it builds on the representation of national governments) imposes different role expectations on participants than the sectorally and functionally organized Commission.

Although the Council is essentially structured according to territory, it is sectorally and functionally arranged at the ministerial and working party levels. We find a similar dual structure in comitology committees. The organizational embodiment of functionality across committee types may help to explain the crucial role that expertise seems to play in all committee decision-making. The sectoral or functional affiliation that participants have in common, across nationality, provides a shared frame of reference and a fertile ground for policy-making based on expert arguments. Finally, since EU committees represent secondary organizational affiliations for most national officials (who use more of their time and energy in national institutions), it is no wonder that supranational, or EU-level, allegiances are only partly expressed. However, and understandably from an organizational perspective, these allegiances complement national loyalties.

The chapter proceeds in five main steps. The first section below describes and discusses the data and the methodology underpinning the study. The second section reports on the time requirements and the availability of documentation for domestic officials who attend EU committees. The third section reports the interpretation facilities available for the committee participants and the languages actually used by them. The fourth section reveals the loyalties and identities adopted by domestic EU committee participants, and the fifth section shows how these officials are coordinated domestically.

Data and method

Since 1995 the European Institute of Public Administration (EIPA) in Maastricht has organized seminars for member state officials on the role of committees in the EU political process. In the spring of 1997 we started to distribute a questionnaire[2] to those participants in the seminars who had been involved in one or several committees at the EU level. The questionnaire was designed to get an overview of the experience of member state officials in EU committees: in what type and in how many committees were they involved? How frequently were meetings taking place? How long did they last? What languages were used? How were committee meetings coordinated? And so on. The major part of the questionnaire focused on the question of how member state officials viewed the roles they performed in these committees, how they perceived the roles performed by other participants and how well they were coordinated and prepared before meetings.

Participants at the seminar who had been involved in EU committees were asked to complete the questionnaire on the first day. By distributing the questionnaires on the first day we minimized potential influence or 'noise' from the seminar. Participation in the seminars in Maastricht was very unevenly distributed between different member states. There were very few participants from the southern member states, but regular participation from central European member states, the UK and Ireland. In addition to the seminars in Maastricht, EIPA organized a number of comitology seminars in the member states, particularly those that had joined the EU during the last wave of enlargement in 1995. Unquestionably, this led to a very unbalanced sample, favouring the new member states. In order to correct this, an effort was made in early 1999 to contact the permanent representation of all the member states from which we had a very small number of respondents (N), asking them to help us to get more completed questionnaires from these member states. This effort was successful in the case of Belgium and Spain, but did not result in many additional completed questionnaires from the other member states. The composition of the sample, by member state, is summarized in Table 5.1. The table also shows the type of ministry the respondents came from, differentiating between the foreign ministry, other ministries, agencies and the member state's permanent representation in Brussels.

This sample cannot claim to be representative either with respect to the member states included, or with respect to the type of committees member state officials participated in. From the total sample, 132 respondents participated in expert committees, 134 participated in Council working parties and 76 in comitology committees. Not unexpectedly, 61 respondents participated in at least two types of committees and 31 in all three types. Moreover, the officials studied here are mostly employed within ministries other than the foreign ministry and in medium or lower rank positions. Moreover, our data (not presented in Table 5.1) show that expert committee participants are mostly recruited from sectoral ministries and agencies and less from permanent representations. Council working party participants, in contrast, are recruited to a larger extent from permanent representations and sectoral ministries.

Table 5.1 Composition of the sample, by member state and institutional affiliation

Member state	Ministry or Institution				
	Foreign ministry	Other ministries	Agencies etc.	Permanent representation	Total
Austria		14	3		17
Belgium	2	20	7		29
Denmark	1	5	1		7
Finland	2	17	2		21
France		3	1		4
Germany		7	3	1	11
Greece		1		1	2
Ireland		1		2	4[a]
Luxembourg	1				1
Netherlands	2	10	1		13
Portugal	5	3	1		9
Spain		55	5		60
Sweden	2	23	9		34
United Kingdom	1	4	1		6
Total (N)	16	163	34	4	218[a]

Note: a. One respondent did not answer the question about institutional affiliation.

As in all written questionnaires, there were a considerable number of missing items because of respondents who did not complete all of the questions, even though for most of the questions multiple choice answers were provided. For this reason the N will vary between tables in the following sections.

Time requirements and the availability of documentation

For member state officials, participation in EU committees means consumption of scarce resources, such as time, time that will not be available for national concerns. Table 5.2 shows that time spent on EU matters varies with the place in the hierarchy of a respondent.

As could be expected, the major burden of committee work is carried by head of sections, senior advisers and advisers, the middle and lower middle level of member states' administrations. Nearly two-thirds of the respondents belong to this group. These observations are empirically supported by the studies of Egeberg (1999), Trondal (2001) and Trondal and Veggeland (2003). What is surprising is the relatively large proportion (20 per cent) who come from the director general or deputy director general level.[3] This can possibly be explained by the fact that it is common practice that, on important issues, the top level of member states' administrations will attend committee meetings in Brussels, often accompanied by lower level officials. It may also be taken as an indicator of the importance assigned by member states' administrations to EU matters. The fact that more than 60 per cent of this top-level group spends almost a day or more of their weekly working time on EU matters supports this conclusion. Moreover, Council working party participants report that they seldom attend committee meetings alone. Most of the

Table 5.2 Time consumed in committee work, by position (%)

Working time spent on EU matters	Position			
	Director general, deputy dir. general	Head/deputy of unit/division	Head of section, senior adviser, adviser	Total
15% or less	37	26	24	27
15–50%	43	44	44	44
50% or more	20	30	32	29
Total (%)	100	100	100	100
N	40	27	131	198

time officials go together with colleagues from their own ministry or from the permanent representations.

Involvement in EU affairs may affect one's attitude to European integration. The majority of the sampled officials had positive attitudes towards European integration when they first got involved in EU committee work. Table 5.3 shows that the majority of respondents did not change their attitude towards European integration later. Only 8 per cent indicated that participation led to a negative view on European integration; 57 per cent did not change their attitude; and 35 per cent indicated that their participation led them to view European integration from a more positive perspective. Hooghe (1999) makes a parallel observation within the ranks of Commission officials. She demonstrates that senior Commission officials are generally more supranationally oriented than newly hired Commission officials.

There are significant differences with respect to the frequency and duration of meetings between expert committees, Council working parties and comitology committees (see Table 5.4). The vast majority of the sampled officials attended one or two committees. Only a very small percentage of the officials actually attended more than two committees. These observations might partly reflect the fact that officials at the permanent representations in Brussels are poorly represented in our sample. Lewis (2000) and Trondal (2001) show that permanent representatives attend considerably more Council working parties than officials coming from the capitals. Moreover, almost half the expert committee participants say that they meet no more than one to three times a year while 54 per cent on Council working parties meet eight or more times a year, suggesting that involvement in Council working parties is much more time consuming. Hence, Council working party participants seem to participate more intensively on EU committees than expert committee participants. About 60 per cent say that all types of committee meetings last for one day; half-day meetings

Table 5.3 Working time consumed in committees and change of attitudes (%)

	Working time consumed		
Change of attitudes	15% or less	15–50%	50% or more
More in favour	24	44	34
Unchanged	67	51	54
Less in favour	9	5	12
Total (%)	100	100	100
N	58	83	59

are rare, although one-third on expert committees report that they last more than a day. 'The trend seems to move to one day meetings where member state representatives arrive in Brussels in the morning and leave again in the evening' (Schaefer et al. 2002: 154).

We also found interesting differences with respect to the involvement of member state officials in EU committees between small, medium and large member states. We classified Austria, Denmark, Finland, Ireland, Luxembourg and Sweden as small member states, Belgium, Greece, the Netherlands and Portugal as medium sized member states, and France, Germany, Spain and the UK as large ones. The number of meetings attended per year was by far the highest for officials from small member states. This is particularly the case for expert and comitology committees. In contrast, Council working parties are presumably attended by senior policy officials of large member states who do not participate in expert and comitology committees but delegate these tasks to more 'junior' experts. In small member states, as a result of the smaller size of their administrations, senior policy officials are at the same time the member states' experts.

Finally, a reasonable assumption would be that documentation is a necessary condition for policy preparation. It has been frequently reported that documentation for committee meetings arrives only shortly before the meetings take place (Statskonsult 1999; SOU 1996; Trondal 2002). Table 5.5 shows that in expert committees and comitology committees

Table 5.4 Frequency and duration of meetings in the three types of committees (%)

Number of meetings per year	EC	CWP	CC
1–3	49	15	36
4–8	30	31	34
8+	21	54	30
Total (%)	100	100	100
N	132	131	76
Duration of meetings			
Half day	6	11	10
1 day	58	60	65
1 day+	36	29	25
Total (%)	100	100	100
N	131	126	68

Note: EC = Commission expert committees; CWP = Council working parties; CC = Comitology committees.

Table 5.5　Availability of documentation for the committee meetings (%)

Documentation arrival	EC	CWP	CC
A week before	64	20	55
A day or two before	32	70	31
At time of arrival	4	10	14
Total (%)	100	100	100
N	110	132	71

Note: Abbreviations (see Table 5.4).

in well over 50 per cent of the cases, documentation is in the hands of the participant a week or more before the meeting takes place. The situation in Council working parties is quite different. Two-thirds of the respondents reported that documentation arrives only a day or two before the meeting. This suggests that the pace of work in Council is the most intense and that member state officials are often confronted with documentation at the very last minute. In the case of comitology committees, 14 per cent reported that documentation is only available at the time of the meeting. These are probably committees in the agricultural sector, which meet weekly or bi-weekly. These committees are dealing largely with routine matters where such preparation is not required. The results suggest that the situation may not be as bad as is often pictured: more than 85 per cent of the participants have the relevant documentation in their hands before they arrive in the meeting room. And those attending meetings chaired by the frequently criticized Commission (expert and comitology committees), are in fact better equipped in this respect than those in Council groups.

Availability of interpretation facilities and language use in committees

Participating in EU committees means communication. At the time of data collection (1997–99) there were 11 official languages. From 1 May 2004 the number of languages increased dramatically in the EU, significantly enlarging the need for translation facilities. Hence, the communication and language problems will also increase. Communication, both formally in meetings and informally during coffee breaks, lunches and in the hallways is an essential requirement for effective participation in these committees.

　　Even before the latest enlargement (2004) it was practically impossible to provide simultaneous translation facilities from all official languages into all others in all committee meetings. Common practice was often

Table 5.6 Availability of interpreting facilities in committee meetings (%)

Interpreting facilities	EC	CWP	CC
Translation from all into all languages	17	59	17
From 7 to 9 languages into 3 or 4 languages	56	37	68
Only 2 or 3 languages	20	3	15
Work only in one language	5	1	0
Total (%)	100	100	100
N	118	132	71

Note: Abbreviations (see Table 5.4).

to translate from seven, eight or nine languages into three or four as shown in Table 5.6. Participants may, with few exceptions, speak their own language, but they have to understand French, English or German, or perhaps Spanish or Italian in order to follow the discussions. In some cases the committee may work in only two or three languages with simultaneous translation only between these languages. Our respondents reported a few cases where committees worked in only one language. Table 5.6 also shows significant differences between the different types of committees. In Council working parties, where communication is obviously most important as final decisions are prepared here, almost 60 per cent say that full interpreting facilities were available in the meetings. In Commission expert committees and comitology committees 56 per cent and 68 per cent reported interpreting facilities from seven or nine into three or four languages. Working in only two or three languages is found most frequently in expert and comitology committees. Expert groups sometimes work in only one language, but only in one of twenty cases. Interpretation facilities are clearly most important in Council working parties, although 40 per cent on Council working parties say that full interpretation facilities are not available. Still, Table 5.6 indicates the intergovernmental nature of the Council working parties compared to the expert and comitology committees.

Successful negotiations and discussions in committees do not depend solely on what happens in the committee room, but also on what happens during coffee breaks and in discussions in the corridors and lunchrooms – which is closely related to the capability of participants to communicate in languages other than their own. Not surprisingly we found a relatively high competence in foreign languages among those participating in committees (self-assessment of respondents), particularly in English, as

Table 5.7   English, French and German capabilities, by native language groups (%)

| Language capabilities | Native language groups | | | Total | |
	Germanic	Latin	Other	N	%
English					
Very good and good	98	78	100	167	88
Can manage	2	22	0	22	12
Total (%)	100	100	100		100
N	86	81	22	189	
French					
Very good and good	51	60	69	84	56
Can manage	49	40	31	65	44
Total (%)	100	100	100		100
N	71	65	13	149	
German					
Very good and good	41	25	14	19	35
Can manage	59	75	86	35	65
Total (%)	100	100	100		100
N	39	8	7	54	

Table 5.7 shows. Ninety per cent of non-native English speakers are able to communicate somehow in English, and more than 80 per cent can speak English well or very well. French capabilities are not as widespread, yet there are still 150 out of about 190 non-native French speakers in the sample who can manage to get along in French if necessary. The numbers are much lower for German. We differentiated between Germanic, Latin and other native language groups whereby Germanic languages include German, English, Dutch and the Scandinavian languages, except Finnish. Latin languages include French, Portuguese, Spanish and Italian. Greek and Finnish were categorized as 'other languages' together with a few respondents whose native language is not one of the community official languages. More unexpected is the fact that the English competence ('good' and 'very good') of native speakers of Latin languages is much higher than the French competence of native Germanic language speakers. English is clearly the most frequently used language in Brussels and it can be expected that this will further increase with enlargement. At least for our sample English has clearly become the first foreign language of member state officials participating in committee meetings, indicating a creeping linguistic convergence in the EU.

It can be expected that this development has been reinforced with enlargement since English has become the first foreign language in all

Table 5.8 Language use in and around meetings (%)

	Language most frequently used in committee meetings	Language most frequently used in informal discussions
French	15	19
Spanish	23	7
English	45	70
Other	17	4
Total (%)	100	100
N	210	202

the accession countries. Table 5.8 underscores this impression that English has become the major language in Brussels in informal communications between member state officials. French is still important, but German is almost of no relevance. In meetings, however, member state officials prefer to speak their native language, but if they do not, they are more likely to speak English than French.[4]

Member state officials' loyalties and identities

Civil servants often evoke multiple preferences, interests, roles and identities arising from their multiple institutional embeddedness; they are multiple selves with several non-hierarchical interests and allegiances (Elster 1986; Risse 2002a; Fouilleux et al. 2002). The evocation of one particular interest or identity does not necessarily trump another. By attending different institutions at different levels of governance, officials learn to wear Janus-faces and to live with diversity and partially conflicting interests and loyalties (Lewis 1998). Hayes-Renshaw and Wallace (1997: 279) picture a 'continuous tension between the home affiliation and the pull of the collective forum'. However, particular roles, identities and modes of decision-making behaviour tend to come to the fore in some situations more than in others (March and Olsen 1995).

National officials attending EU committees spend most of their time and energy in national administrations.[5] Accordingly, we expect their dominant institutional allegiances and identifications to be national. However, membership of EU committees imposes additional obligations on officials, although for most these are of a secondary character. They are exposed to new agendas and actors, and are expected to look for common solutions (Egeberg 1999). According to Christiansen and Kirchner (2000: 9), 'committees permit national officials to familiarize themselves with the nature of the EU's administrative system'. However, officials

Table 5.9   Percentage who to a 'great extent' feel allegiance to (identify with or feel responsible to) the following when participating in committees

	EC	CWP	CC
My own government	65	76	69
My own ministry, department or agency	74	81	60
The requirements of the policy arena in which I am working	58	65	58
My own professional background and expertise	60	65	60
The committee or group in which I participate	39	57	44
Total (N)	106	109	58

Note: 'Great extent' is adduced by combining values 1 and 2 on the following five-point scale: to a very great extent (1), to a fairly great extent (2), both/and (3), to a fairly small extent (4), to a very small extent (5). Abbreviations (see Table 5.4).

participating in Council working parties and in comitology committees may be expected to behave more like government representatives than officials attending Commission expert committees. The main reason for this is the territorial principle of organization underlying both Council and comitology groups. In the Commission expert committees, on the other hand, participants are expected to behave more like independent experts. Thus, professional allegiances and sectoral role conceptions are likely to be enacted fairly strongly among the latter.

Table 5.9 shows that national officials who attend different EU committees express more allegiance towards their own national government institutions than towards the EU committees on which they participate. Thus, as expected, EU-level loyalties seem to be secondary to national allegiances. However, some officials feel considerable responsibility towards EU-level entities, particularly the Council working party participants (Lewis 1998; Trondal 2002). Hence, a certain kind of 'system allegiance' seems to be stronger among Council working party officials than among expert committee and comitology committee participants. Inter-governmentalism and EU-level loyalty thus do not seem to conflict but to complement each other (Risse 2002a). Moreover, the vast majority of the committee participants have positive attitudes towards European integration in general and within their own policy/issue area in particular. However, relatively few officials change attitudes in this regard due to committee participation (see Table 5.3 above).

Also as expected, those in Council working parties tend to assign more weight to their relationship with their own government than those attending the Commission expert committees, although the difference is not very big. A remarkably large proportion of Council working party

Table 5.10 Officials' perception of the role of colleagues from other countries when participating in committees (%)

	EC	CWP	CC
Mainly independent experts	33	11	6
Mixed roles	22	12	20
Mainly government representative	45	77	74
Total (%)	100	100	100
N	113	122	66

Note: Abbreviations (see Table 5.4).

participants identify themselves with their own sector administration, policy arena or professional background. This pattern is probably due to the high degree of functional specialization that accompanies participation in the primarily intergovernmentally arranged Council structure. Hence, national officials attending EU committees evoke a highly complex role repertoire.

The respondents were also asked to indicate how they perceived the roles of their colleagues within EU committees. Table 5.10 reveals that civil servants who attend Council working parties and comitology committees tend to consider other colleagues mainly as government representatives (Schaefer et al. 2002: 158; Fouilleux et al. 2002). Commission expert committee participants, on the other hand, tend to perceive other colleagues as having more mixed roles. Here, only a minority (that is 45 per cent) find that their counterparts behave mainly as government representatives. Thus, although role conceptions are highly multifaceted across types of committee (compare Table 5.9), actual behaviour seems to mirror more clearly the prevalent organizational features of the various arenas.

Next, the respondents were asked to assess how much consideration they gave to proposals, statements and arguments from different actors and institutions when attending EU committees (Table 5.11).

First, almost no major differences can be observed between officials attending different EU committees as far as the above considerations are concerned. Second, as to the relative priority given to the proposals, statements and arguments of other actors, one consideration seems to be more important than others: officials attending EU committees pay most attention to what colleagues and experts from their own country have to say. This observation underscores the tendency already indicated in tables 5.9 and 5.10 on the primacy of national allegiances among EU committee participants. Participants, however, also emphasize the points

Table 5.11   Percentage who give 'much consideration' to proposals, statements and arguments from the following when participating in committees

	EC	CWP	CC
Colleagues and experts from my own member state	87	84	81
Colleagues from other member states who have demonstrated considerable expertise on the subject matter at hand	73	70	69
Colleagues from large member states	38	38	30
Colleagues from member states from my own region	42	46	48
Colleagues from member states who share a similar position	61	71	68
Representatives from the Commission	57	60	57
Interest groups and firms I know from my member state	26	32	44
Interest groups and firms I know or have contact with at the European level	17	11	13
Total (N)	113	121	66

Note: 'Much consideration' is adduced by combining values 1 and 2 on the following five-point scale: very much consideration (1), fairly much consideration (2), both/and (3), fairly little consideration (4), very little consideration (5). Abbreviations (see Table 5.4).

of view of colleagues from other member states who have demonstrated considerable expertise on the subject matter at hand. Officials pay much less attention to arguments from colleagues from large member states or to colleagues from member states within their own region. In support of the deliberative supranationalist account (Eriksen and Fossum 2000), the quality of the argument presented by other committee participants is considered more important than the mere size or geopolitical location of the member states they represent. Moreover, the EU Commission is also considered more important than large member states or member states within respondents' own regions. Finally, interest groups and firms are deemed considerably less important than colleagues from other member states. By comparison, however, interest groups and firms from their own country are considered much more important than EU-level interest groups and firms. This observation underscores the general tendency apparent in Table 5.11, namely that national officials attending EU committees pay more heed to national institutions than to supranational ones.

In sum, what we see is that *arguing*, not only *bargaining*, is a salient feature of the system (Lewis 1998; Neyer 1999). Hence, the intergovernmental perspective, picturing national actors entering EU arenas with predetermined and fixed preferences has to be slightly modified. Obviously, deliberation is taking place among actors in which interests may be moved and reshaped on the basis of expert knowledge.

Table 5.12 National officials' perceptions of Commission officials' independence of particular national interests when participating in committees (%)

	EC	CWP	CC
Mainly independent	81	70	79
Mixed roles	13	18	16
Mainly dependent	6	12	5
Total (%)	100	100	100
N	109	112	63

Note: Abbreviations (see Table 5.4).

There is also obviously a good deal of trust in the Commission, as demonstrated by Table 5.12. National officials attending different EU committees seem to agree on the relative independence of Commission officials from particular national interests. Only a very small minority, mostly among the Council working party participants, reports that Commission officials act more in the interest of their country of origin. This shows a good deal of trust in the Commission as an independent supranational executive.

Thus, participation in EU committees tends to affect the institutional allegiances and role perceptions of the participants. Nonetheless civil servants largely retain their national and sectoral identities when attending EU committees. An element of EU-level loyalty does, however, supplement such pre-existing allegiances to some extent.

The coordination behaviour of member state officials attending EU committees

In the last section we demonstrated that national officials attending Commission expert committees probably behave more like independent experts than they do when attending Council working parties and comitology committees where they perceive of themselves and their colleagues from other member states more as government representatives. The different role and identity perceptions of national government officials attending different EU committees may partly reflect different coordination processes at the national level (Trondal 2002). A difference may be expected between officials attending Commission expert committees and officials participating in Council working parties and comitology committees. Officials attending expert committees are expected to be less subject to national coordination, whereas officials attending Council working parties and comitology committees are more likely to participate in committee meetings with clearly coordinated positions derived from their respective national governments (Trondal 2000).

There are two reasons for this difference: the formal organization of the committees and the voting practices within them. First, the Commission expert committees are mainly organized according to sectoral and functional principles. The Council working parties and the comitology committees, although sectorally and functionally specialized, have a stronger territorial component in their organizational structures. Arguably, committees organized by territory are characterized by stronger coordination pressure on the participants than are committees organized by sector and function (Egeberg and Trondal 1999). Second, voting focuses the attention of decision-makers. It also signals expectations from the principals towards the agents with respect to representing agreed-on and often written positions. In contrast to comitology committees, expert committees and Council working parties do not vote in any formal sense (Mattila and Lane 2001; Tuerk and Schaefer 2002). Council working parties are, however, located more clearly in the 'shadow of the vote' than Commission expert committees (Golub 1999; Tuerk and Schaefer 2002). Whereas expert committee participants are not expected to reach any agreements or formal decisions during most committee meetings, officials attending the Council working groups and the comitology committees are expected to reach compromises, majority decisions and often consensus at the end of meetings (Lewis 1998).

Table 5.13 reveals different modes of policy coordination behaviour among EU committee participants. As expected, participants in Commission expert committees seem less coordinated nationally than officials participating in Council working parties and comitology committees. Officials attending comitology committees seem to be even better coordinated nationally than officials attending Council working parties, though the difference is not very large. By comparison, officials in Commission expert committees tend to take positions that are less strongly coordinated back home. Still, when asked whether national interests or professional considerations are deemed vital when deciding what positions to pursue, no major differences are observed between officials participating in different EU committees. Council working party participants seem, however, to pay more attention to national interests than do expert committees and comitology committee participants (Fouilleux et al. 2002). These differences are marginal, however. The most significant observation is that in Commission expert committees, participants have much more leeway to follow their own position than in the Council working parties and the comitology committees.

Table 5.13   Percentage of officials who coordinate their position 'most of the time' before participating in committee meetings

	EC	CWP	CC
I have to coordinate with the foreign office or another central coordinating body	20	47	43
My position has in fact been coordinated with all relevant ministries	28	47	53
My position has been coordinated with all relevant departments in my own ministry	38	55	59
I have clear instructions about the position I should take	28	35	46
I take the position I think is in the best interest of my country	63	72	66
I take the position I think is best on the basis of my professional expertise	43	43	34
If I have no instructions, or if the question is not important for my country, I take the position I think is the best for the member states as a group	52	46	46
Total (N)	110	119	62

Note: 'Most of the time' is value 1 on the following three-point scale: always or most of the time (1), about half of the time (2), rarely or never (3). Abbreviations (see Table 5.4).

Conclusions

The study of European integration has increasingly shifted focus from the horizontal spillover processes at the EU level and the 'grand bargains' struck between the strong EU member states towards the vertical blurring of governance levels across the EU–nation-state interface. This chapter has focused on one such site where government levels interact and affect each other – the EU committees. In the first two sections we observed that many national officials spend a considerable amount of time and energy on EU committee work. In fact almost one-third of our respondents spend at least half of their working hours on preparation, coordination and participation in EU committees. Council working parties are more demanding in this respect than other EU committees. Officials from small member states seem to attend meetings more frequently than their counterparts from larger countries. This is due to the smaller size of their administrations.

Documentation is available earlier in Commission expert committees and comitology committees than in Council working parties, where it commonly arrives only a day or two before meetings. Only a small minority receives documentation at the time of arrival. Interpreting facilities are more widely available in Council working parties than in other committees. For example, in the Council 59 per cent report that all languages are translated into all languages while this holds for only 17 per cent in other committees. English is by far the most frequently used language in formal as well as in informal meetings.

Moreover, as could be expected given the primary institutional affiliation of national officials, national allegiances are more clearly expressed than EU-level identities. However, a considerable proportion also feels loyalty to the committee or committees in which they participate. A clear majority expresses considerable trust in the Commission in the sense that they acknowledge its independence from particular national interests. Commission officials are among their most important interlocutors. Sheer intergovernmentalism is also transcended in the sense that the quality of the arguments seems more important than the country the speaker originates from. The multiple roles and identities evoked by our respondents also point beyond a pure intergovernmental logic. In all kinds of committees they identify themselves heavily with sectoral and functional administrations and policy arenas. The government representative role is most clearly expressed in the Council and comitology settings. It is also in these settings that officials' positions and mandates are most clearly coordinated and instructed back home. As already said, our sample cannot claim to be a representative one. However, our main findings are clearly substantiated by studies based on other sources (Egeberg 1999; Trondal 2001; Trondal and Veggeland 2003).

Recent literature argues that EU committees are sites of vertical and horizontal fusion of administrative systems and policy instruments (Egeberg 1999; Maurer and Larsson 2002; Trondal 2001; Schaefer 2002). We have demonstrated in this study that EU committees are indeed sites of Europeanization of individual civil servants. We demonstrate that the attention, energy, contacts, linguistic practices, attitudes, coordination behaviour and loyalties of European national civil servants are to a considerable degree directed towards Brussels. However, we have also indicated that the re-socializing and transformative powers of the EU committees are heavily filtered and biased by the national institutions embedding the EU committee participants. Last, but not least, we have shown that there are indeed many faces of EU committee governance.

Notes

1. This research has been financially supported by ARENA, the European Institute of Public Administration (EIPA), Agder University College and Sørlandets kompetansefond (http://www.kompetansefond.com/).

2. The questionnaire was jointly developed by Morten Egeberg, Jarle Trondal and Guenther F. Schaefer, together with the 'Comitology team' at EIPA. By the end of 1999, 232 questionnaires had been completed. Eight of these respondents were Norwegian, and in six cases it was impossible to identify clearly the member state affiliation of the respondents. Both these categories of respondents are excluded from this analysis. This chapter is thus based on 218 completed questionnaires as indicated in Table 5.1.

3. It could be argued that this may be the result of sampling. The top level of the member state administrations cannot usually be expected to attend three-day seminars. In fact, this top level may well be over-represented in our sample since it hardly constitutes 20 per cent of a member state's administration. See also Institut für Europäische Politik, *Comitology – Characteristics, Performance and Options*, Preliminary Final Report (Bonn 1987).

4. It is interesting that 20 per cent of the Spanish respondents use a language other than their mother tongue in meetings. At the same time 45 per cent use English in meetings while only 10 per cent of the sample are English native speakers.

5. Almost 30 per cent of the respondents reported, however, that they spent 50 per cent or more of their working time on EU matters (see Table 5.2).

6
Towards a Multilevel Union Administration? The Decentralization of EU Competition Policy

Øivind Støle

Introduction

The very notion of a Union administration may be perceived as a contradiction in terms, given the strong linkage of public administration to the concept of the nation-state. Inspired by, for example, the American and the French revolutions, principles of government reflecting the sovereignty of the people were firmly established in nation-states all over the Western world during the nineteenth century. The foundation for such national administrations was a hierarchically-based political community, gaining its formal and social legitimacy through a majority in the populace. Subordination to decisions made by bureaucrats was thereby deemed acceptable. The impartial bureaucrat, administering state authority in the interest of the community, became a symbol of the nation-state (Nedergaard 2001: 30, quoting Weber 1971). Ulf Sverdrup (2003: 2) recognizes this heritage when stating that: 'Administrative policies have been targeted at resolving tasks and problems within the borders of the nation state and it has been steered and governed by national political and administrative leaders.'

The divisions of tasks and responsibilities in the European Union (EU) have broadly reflected this strong linkage between the nation-state and administration of policy. Although there are variations between different policy areas, the main principle of governance in the EU has been that the European-level institutions shape and decide on policies and programmes while implementation is regarded as the domain of national administrations (Kadelbach 2002; Olsen 1997, 2002b; Sverdrup 2003).

Developments at both the European and the national levels, especially since the 1980s, have changed both the character and the functions of public administrations. They have become less hierarchical, more fragmented and more decentralized (Christensen and Lægreid 2001). A distinctive feature at national level is the decentralization of tasks to independent, regulatory agencies, placed outside the central administrative hierarchy. We also witness the establishment of agencies at the European level, although with more restricted tasks and less autonomy from the central institutions. Additionally, a trend towards developing networked administrative structures, in which national and European-level institutions create closer cooperative arrangements, is an important one. These changes at the European level are attempts at finding workable solutions to a challenge of increasing importance in European governance: how to provide the EU with an administrative infrastructure without delegating direct administrative responsibilities to Community institutions, which is politically inconceivable because of member state resistance (Dehousse 1997b, 2002; Kreher 1997; Egeberg, Chapter 3; Sverdrup 2003).

The ideal model of national administrations as coherent and unitary bodies does not reflect the empirical realities in national politics, where studies have revealed that fragmentation may be a more accurate description (Tranøy and Østerud 2001). In the context of international politics, however, a more unilateral conflict structure organized by territorial criteria has suppressed other lines of conflict (Egeberg, Chapter 2). In most policy fields, disagreements at national levels tend to be less visible in international politics. As such, the ideal model of unitary national administrations may be applicable in the context of European politics.

In this chapter, I will present developments in EU competition policy, leading to the comprehensive reform process initiated by the Commission in 1999,[1] involving a substantial decentralization of the enforcement of EU competition policy to national competition authorities and courts. The purpose is twofold: first, to describe a case that illustrates new administrative arrangements in managing EU policy; second, to explain and seek to understand the rationale behind these arrangements. If this reform signals a development in how the EU is administered, it is truly an interesting change. Close cooperation in policy formulation and implementation between the EU executive and national agencies would indicate patterns of cooperation and conflict that are quite unique in the field of international cooperation. Sensitive to the particularities of the policy field in question, this chapter will give an interpretation of the development of a Union administration based on fundamental features of organizational theory.

EU competition policy

The strong treaty basis of competition policy is an indication of the importance which the architects of the treaty attached to it. Article 3 (f) of the Treaty of Rome sets the objective of ensuring that competition in a common market is not distorted, an objective that is pursued by the rules on competition contained in Articles 85 to 94 of the original Treaty (now 81 to 89 EC Treaty). Further, there are few areas of EU policy-making where the Commission is more central or more autonomous than in competition policy. The responsibility for administering the competition rules was granted to the Commission by the Council in a series of regulations, most importantly the implementing Regulation 17/1962 (McGowan 1999).[2] This regulation concerned Articles 81 and 82, regulating those activities that are usually regarded as the core of anti-trust policy; the range of private business practices which can be construed as anti-competitive. The prohibition of restrictive practices (cartels) through Article 81, and abuses of dominant positions (monopolies) through Article 82 will be the focus of this chapter, as the major reforms mentioned above concern these particular aspects of EU competition policy.

It is necessary to describe Article 81 of the EC Treaty[3] in some detail in order to understand the development towards the recent reform initiatives. Article 81, paragraph 1 [81(1)], prohibits agreements which affect trade between member states where they have as their objective or effect the prevention, restriction or distortion of competition within the common market. Further, paragraph 2 [81(2)] declares that all agreements listed in the previous paragraph are prohibited and thus automatically void. However, this prohibition principle is not absolute, as paragraph 3 [81(3)] declares that paragraph 1 may be inapplicable if the agreement in question benefits the EU as a whole and its advantages outweigh the disadvantages. Companies therefore notify the Commission of their planned agreements – referred to as the notification procedure – applying for exemptions from the general prohibition principle (Cini and McGowan 1998: 66). A very important feature of the system is that the right to grant exemptions under Article 81(3) is an exclusive prerogative of the Commission.

Why the Commission was given such a central role in the enforcement of EU competition policy is a matter of some debate. It may have been the outcome of collusion among an 'epistemic community' of competition officials, a willing delegation of sovereignty by some member states to ensure effective regulation, or a lapse by others, failing to predict how effectively the provisions would be employed (ibid.). Concerning the latter point, the rulings of the European Court of Justice have in general strengthened the role of the Commission (ibid.: 55). Another aspect that was certainly important was the lack of national provisions for regulating competition policy in the late 1950s. Only Germany could be described as having an effective authority with both a full substantive law and the resources to enforce it. Thus, the limited role envisaged for national authorities in this field was seen as a necessity if an effective competition regime was to develop at the European level (Goyder 2003: 447).[4]

The highly centralized mode of enforcement, however, proved to be a double-edged sword, as the Regulation (17/1962) soon became associated with administrative gridlock (Cini and McGowan 1998: 19). The notification system has grown to such an unmanageable extent that the need for reforms has become increasingly evident. Indeed, efforts to improve the situation have not been absent, but they have developed incrementally, as the Commission has introduced remedies to ease its workload, for example through block exemptions, notices on agreements of minor importance, and by settling cases informally using administrative letters or 'comfort letters' (ibid.: 111–13). All of these measures are ways of accepting agreements that are not seen as distorting competition seriously, or that have advantages outweighing the disadvantages involved. They did not, however, satisfy either business, member state governments or the Commission itself, and the need for more fundamental reforms was apparent by the 1990s.

It was never the case that the responsibility for enforcing Articles 81 and 82 lay with the institutions of the Community alone. Some degree of assistance from member state authorities and courts in ensuring that Community law was effectively and uniformly enforced was necessary from the outset. During the first decades, however, the absence of a common competition culture made it too risky to share major responsibility with national authorities (Ehlermann 2000). Today, the situation is quite different:

at present a large number of member states have professional, competent, competition-oriented national authorities, structured to perform their functions with limited political interference – at least with respect to non-merger cases – and with a mandate to enforce the laws based on competition policy, relying on economic analysis, rather than protecting national champions.

(Laudati 1996: 248)

Certainly, this development is not merely a function of EU influence; rather, it is a more general trend in most OECD countries, often labelled

'New Public Management' reforms (Christensen and Lægreid 2001). Although this label can be seen to be ambiguous, including highly heterogeneous means and aims, one central feature has been the effort to make a clearer distinction between politics and administration, and to 'let the managers manage' (ibid.: 96).

In recent years, the resources and abilities of national competition authorities have increased, and with the expansion and refinement of national competition laws substantially based on the principles and language of Articles 81 and 82 has come a greater willingness and ability of these authorities to work more closely with the Commission. During the 1990s, many national authorities took the necessary powers to apply both Articles 81(1) and 82 of the EC Treaty within their national boundaries, a development encouraged by the Commission.[5] The degree to which they now cooperate with the Commission is reflected in the White Paper of 1999, where it is stated that they 'form part of a coherent whole with the Community system'.[6]

The modernization reform

Claus Ehlermann[7] (2000: 3) states that the White Paper on Modernization of the Rules Implementing Articles 81 and 82 of the EC Treaty of May 1999 is the most important policy paper the Commission has ever published in the more than 40 years of EU competition policy. Since its inception, this Commission programme has been succeeded by a proposal for a Council Regulation, as well as the Regulation itself.[8] In the following, these key documents, in addition to information obtained through interviews with officials from both the Norwegian and Swedish competition authorities, form the background material for a short presentation of important features of the reform process and result.

The most important changes in EU competition policy, following the Council Regulation 1/2003, may be summarized in four points:[9]

1. *Harmonization and decentralization.* At present, national competition authorities may choose whether to use national law or to apply Articles 81(1) and 82 of the EC Treaty when treating cases that might impinge upon trade between member states. Further, some competition authorities, as mentioned above, do not have the jurisdiction to enforce EU competition laws at all. According to Article 3 in Regulation 1/2003, however, all national competition authorities are obliged to apply Articles 81 and 82 when the so-called trade criterion is met. It is interesting to note that this particular phrasing was subject to intense

negotiations when drafting the regulation. The wording used in the Commission proposal was:

> Where an agreement, a decision by an association of undertakings or a concerted practice within the meaning of Article 81 of the Treaty or the abuse of a dominant position within the meaning of Article 82 may affect trade between member states, Community competition law shall apply *to the exclusion* of national competition laws.[10]

The final text in the Council Regulation, however, reads quite differently. When national competition laws are applied to agreements within the meaning of Article 81 or 82 of the EC Treaty, '. . .*they shall also* apply Article 81/[82] of the Treaty'.[11] When talking to informants in the Swedish Competition Authority, it was emphasized that member states were pushing hard for these changes in the Council, as the original phrasing was deemed to give the Commission too much leeway compared to the national authorities (interview 30 January 2004; see also Goyder 2003: 446). National competition authorities that did not possess the jurisdiction to apply EC law in these matters had to make the necessary changes before the regulation came into force on 1 May 2004 (Goyder 2003: 438). All 25 competition authorities (following enlargement) should work according to the same rules when trade between member states is affected, notwithstanding the differing contents of their national competition legislation. An informant in the Swedish Competition Authority claimed that 1 May would see 26 competition authorities in the EU (member state authorities and the Commission), as opposed to one under the current system (interview 30 January 2004).

2. *Termination of the notification system.* The most dramatic change following the harmonization and decentralization of enforcing Articles 81 and 82 of the EC Treaty, is that the Commission prerogative of granting exemptions to the prohibition principle in 81(1) and 81(2) is abandoned, giving national authorities the right to enforce all of Article 81, including 81(3). A main motivation for this is surely to come to terms with the ever-increasing load of notifications or applications for exemptions directed at the Commission (Nicolaides 2002). This is done by abolishing the notification system, creating a 'directly applicable exception system' (ibid.), where no prior authorization by the Commission is necessary. It will be up to the companies themselves to evaluate whether agreements fall under the prohibition rules in 81(1) or whether they satisfy the requirements of 81(3). Thus, the system is changed from ex ante evaluation, performed by the Commission, to ex post control,

performed by both the Commission and national competition authorities. If national authorities find that an agreement falls under 81(1),
but at the same time satisfies the demands of 81(3), they will simply
abstain from taking action.

3. *Establishing a network of competition authorities.* Considering the far-
reaching changes inherent in the reform of enforcing Articles 81 and
82 of the EC Treaty, there is obviously a need for closer cooperation
between the different competition authorities. Therefore, a European
Competition Network (ECN) has been established in order to secure a
uniform and coherent application of the new rules. This network will
be an arena for exchanging information between the national authorities, as well as for allocating cases to the best placed authority. If an
agreement between two or more companies charged with evoking
Article 81(1) involves two jurisdictions, for instance those of Denmark
and Sweden, the competition authorities of one of the countries may
be given the responsibility for conducting the investigation.[12] The
Commission itself, represented by DG Competition, is conceived to
be the node in this network, with a main responsibility for coordinating the work.

4. *Strengthening the control mechanisms of the Commission.* In order to avoid
uneven enforcement of EU competition policy, the position of the
Commission as the central regulator is retained in the new regulation.
If, for instance, an agreement is believed to affect three or more member states, the Commission will be the authority in charge. In addition, the Commission may at any time initiate its own proceedings
in all cases, thereby relieving the designated national authority of its
duties. This is perceived to be an important mechanism to avoid a
re-nationalization of Community policy (interview 30 January 2004).
The Commission is also granted more extensive control mechanisms
than envisaged under Regulation 17/1962. This includes extended
opportunities for controlling private homes and business facilities, as
well as conducting interviews with individuals.

Thus, the administration of EU competition policy after 1 May 2004
matches the term 'networked administrative system' (Egeberg, Chapter 3)
quite neatly, in that autonomous national agencies interact directly
with the Commission in preparing and enforcing EU policy, at the same
time as they perform traditional tasks as agents of national ministries.
This development in many ways challenges notions of the coherence of
national administrative systems, and illustrates potential centrifugal forces
in processes of Europeanization.

Framing the development in a theoretical context

Having described some important features of the developments in EU competition policy and the background for recent reform initiatives by the Commission, a theoretical interpretation of the presentation is due.

Intergovernmentalism. There is not one intergovernmentalist perspective; rather there are several, and conceptual heterogeneity prevails, making it difficult to present all the consequences that these somewhat differing views imply when it comes to expectations for European integration. However, the aim of this chapter is to identify a few basic assumptions that characterize a majority of intergovernmentalist perspectives. As such, they will be treated as one approach for matters of simplification.

In general, this perspective is a conceptual approach that emphasizes the centrality of nation-states in the integration process. To cite Nugent (2003: 482), the theory 'is centred on the view that nation states are the key actors in international affairs and the key political relations between states are channeled primarily via national governments'. Renaud Dehousse (1997a) also criticizes the intergovernmentalist tendency of personalizing the state, treating it as an individual endowed with capacity for understanding, a will of its own and a concern to act consistently. According to Dehousse, such a view ignores the fact that behind the notion of 'the state' lies a range of institutions whose objectives and interests vary (ibid.). The work of Andrew Moravcsik (for example 1993, 1998), perhaps the academic most commonly referred to when discussing intergovernmental approaches, has taken this criticism into account in his outline of 'liberal intergovernmentalism'. Nevertheless, this approach still corresponds closely to Nugent, as quoted above, who views the EU member states through the prisms of national governments alone (Bulmer and Lequesne 2002). Although Nugent acknowledges the variety of interests present in national political arenas, his claim is that these are coordinated within national political systems, presenting one national position at the international (EU) level, where negotiations between member states are conducted on the basis of these exogenously determined national interests. Thus, intergovernmentalism basically argues that domestic governance institutions and EU institutions are separate levels of governance.

Neo-functionalism. Whereas intergovernmentalism stresses the autonomy of national leaders, neo-functionalism stresses the autonomy of supranational officials. States are not the only important actors in determining the integration process; in fact, initial delegation of authority to supranational institutions leads to a progressive strengthening of integrationist forces, by ways of spillover and unintended consequences (Strøby Jensen 2003). A famous quote by Ernst Haas (1958/2004: 16) is illustrative of the implicit pro-integrationist assumptions in neo-functional theories:

> Political integration is the process whereby political actors in several distinct national settings are persuaded to shift their loyalties, expectations and political activities toward a new centre, whose institutions possess or demand jurisdiction over the pre-existing national states. The end result of a process of political integration is a new political community, superimposed over the pre-existing ones.

Similar is the claim by Wolfgang Wessels (1998) that constant interaction between national officials at the European level has brought about a 'fusion' of national administrations, where national civil servants no longer consider EU policy-making as foreign affairs in which they act as the guard dogs of national interests, but regard Brussels as an arena in which routine decisions are taken and the officials of other member states as partners. Referring to Wessels's work, Kassim (2003) terms this 'post-national socialization'.

Quite obviously, it is not possible to do justice to the complexities of two of the most widespread theoretical approaches in EU studies within these few lines. Nevertheless, based merely on these few features of intergovernmentalism and neo-functionalism, I will suggest that they are not particularly well-suited to explaining the new administrative arrangements in the EU.

One line of reasoning that is compatible with an intergovernmentalist approach is to view the integration process as a 'turf battle' between member states and the supranational institutions, above all the 'guardian of the Treaties' – the Commission (see, for example, Kassim and Menon 2004). Seen in this light, developments in EU competition policy would seem to strengthen the member states to the detriment of the Commission. As competition policy is decentralized, enforcement is increasingly provided by national authorities, 'bringing the member states back in' into EU policy. On the other hand, however, it is important to keep in mind that it was the nation-states themselves that created the Commission, as they acknowledged the need for strong supranational institutions in order to make the cooperation effective and efficient, enabling the member states to achieve goals that would not otherwise be possible. Moravcsik (1993: 507), for instance, claims that strong supranational institutions are perfectly compatible with an intergovernmental logic, as they are the result of conscious calculations by member states to strike a balance between greater efficiency and domestic influence, on the one hand, and acceptable levels of political risk, on the other. Opportunities for cooperation are enhanced when neutral procedures exist to monitor, interpret and enforce compliance. Neutral enforcement permits governments to extend credible commitments, thus helping to overcome the almost inevitable interstate prisoner's dilemma of enforcement, whereby individual governments seek to evade inconvenient responsibilities, thereby undermining the integrity of the system (ibid.: 512).

When examining the attitudes of national governments to the decentralization reform, it is interesting to see that they have been, at best, diverse. Big and powerful member states, such as Germany and Britain, have been particularly critical, due to fears of uneven practice of competition authorities in different member states (Goldsmith and Lanz 2001; Majone 2002; Boje and Kallestrup 2004). Majone (2002) holds that the opposition of member states shows that the Commission is still perceived as the most appropriate institution for enforcing EU competition policy.

Francis McGowan (2000: 117) states that it is tempting to see competition policy as a prime example of neo-functionalism, as an instance of a supranational bureaucracy expanding its responsibilities as well as playing a key role in creating spillover in economic integration as a whole. However, as mentioned above, the idea of decentralizing enforcement may be seen as a weakening of the Commission and the supranational character of the policy area, and officials within DG Competition have also been highly sceptical of the idea:

> In DG IV, the 'natural' monopoly [over the enforcement of Article 81(3)] theory was an almost religious belief. It constituted for four decades DG IV's main credo. Not to adhere to it was considered to be heresy and could lead to excommunication. A departure from this dogmatic position is the 'cultural' side of the revolution initiated by the White Paper. It is, by the way, a convincing illustration that the widely held view according to which 'Eurocrats' have only one main aim, that is to increase their own influence and power, is wrong.
>
> (Ehlermann 2000: 4)

Majone (2002) explicitly argues that the development is contrary to neo-functionalist expectations, as the Commission becomes increasingly dependent on national administrative systems.

Thus, developments in EU competition policy, involving a substantial increase in administrative cooperation between national competition authorities and the Commission, seem to need other explanatory tools, at least to complement insights provided by intergovernmentalism and neo-functionalism. This is also noted by Alexander Kreher (1997); when studying the increasing administrative interaction between national agencies and EU-level agencies, he questions the relevance of measuring the development in terms of the supranational–intergovernmental dichotomy. A possible explanation for this is provided by Markus Jachtenfuchs (2001), as he states that classical integration theory, like intergovernmentalism and neo-functionalism, predominantly treats the EU polity as the dependent variable, trying to explain the causes for its development. Therefore, in the next section, I will seek to add some value to the understanding of the decentralization of EU competition policy by applying an organizational perspective, treating the institutional configuration of the EU as independent variables.

Suggesting an alternative explanation.   The complexity of the institutional configuration of the EU makes it quite distinct from all other forms of cooperation in the international arena (Laffan 1998). Classic international organizations, for example the United Nations or the WTO, are broadly arranged according to territory, in the sense that key decision-makers formally represent the constituent governments. In the EU, however, the division of tasks between the Council, the Commission, the Parliament and the Court of Justice means that there are more channels for political representation and thereby a potential for inter-institutional conflict (Egeberg, Chapter 2). Here, the focus will be on the Council and the Commission; as the administration of EU policy is the subject matter, it is important to scrutinize the two institutions that interact with national administrations on a routine basis. Two aspects will be paid particular attention to.

A feature of special interest is the division of tasks and responsibilities between the Council and the Commission. The Council is perceived as the most important EU institution, primarily due to its role in decision-making processes. The Commission, on the other hand, plays an important role in preparing, proposing and monitoring policy and legislation.

The Council is primarily organized according to territory, similar to the classic intergovernmental organization (Egeberg, Chapter 3; Hayes-Renshaw and Wallace 1997). Each member state is represented in the different Council formations, acting primarily as guardians of national interests (Kassim and Menon 2004). The Commission, on the other hand, is primarily organized according to non-territorial criteria. The structure of the directorate generals (DGs) is basically sectoral and functional, and Egeberg (chapters 3 and 4) shows how the Commission has continuously sought autonomy from member state influence.

A pertinent question arises in regard to these basic organizational features: How do they matter? Several studies have demonstrated that national officials do not respond uniformly when interacting with different institutions at EU level; whether they are involved in the Council or the Commission structure has an impact on their behaviour (Egeberg et al., Chapter 5; Trondal 2001; Trondal and Veggeland 2003). These studies are predominantly occupied with the behavioural patterns of national officials attending different EU committees, and they evidence interesting differences between participation in comitology committees and Council working groups on the one hand, and Commission expert groups on the other. Participation in comitology committees and Council working parties most clearly evokes role conceptions related to nationality, while the picture is more mixed when it comes to participation in Commission committees. Here, functional and sectoral roles are more pronounced, although the national representative role is still seen to be important. These national officials also display a high degree of trust in the independence of Commission officials from particular national interests. Further, these studies show that the behaviour of national officials participating in the Commission structure are less coordinated nationally than their counterparts in the Council structure and in the comitology structure (Egeberg et al., Chapter 5). These findings illustrate that patterns of cooperation and conflict are, at least to some extent, a function of the organizational structure of the EU institutions. As such, institutions discriminate among conflicts; they systematically activate some latent cleavages while others are routinely ignored (Egeberg, Chapter 3; Trondal 2001). Unlike the findings of for example Wolfgang Wessels (1998), the committee studies do not find that participation by national officials in EU committees leads to any 'fusion' of national administrations, nor that supranational allegiances replace national identities, which was, as mentioned above, expected by functionalist theories.

As EU competition policy has evolved, national competition authorities have gradually become more professionalized and gained more autonomy from political interference (Goyder 2003). This development has been driven by the increasingly tight relationship between the Commission and the national authorities, and has indeed been a prerequisite for the decentralization project. Boje and Kallestrup (2004) refer to the reform of Danish competition law as driven by national bureaucrats and not by politicians. It was clear when speaking to both Norwegian and Swedish informants that this was a trend that was expected to continue with the reform process (interviews 9 December 2003; 30 January 2004). DG Competition was held to be a partner in the enforcement of EU competition policy, and the Swedish political authorities had no role to play in the handling of individual cases.

It is interesting to note, however, that when legislative issues in EU competition policy are at stake, the competition authorities play a double role; when preparing legislation in Commission expert groups and when assisting the ministry in the Council structure. As the committee studies revealed, the work by national officials in Commission expert committees is less coordinated nationally than is the case in the Council structure. Thus, a closer allegiance to the aims and means of the Commission and other national authorities is plausible in this setting. On the other hand, when deciding on legislative initiatives in the Council, the national authorities work closely with their national principals in the ministry, trying to diminish the strength of the Commission. This double role is reflected in Swedish participation in the EU structure; whereas it is the competition authority that attends Commission expert committees and the established European Competition Network, it merely accompanies the ministry in the Council structure when deciding on new legislation (interview 30 January 2004). A corresponding division of tasks is visible in the participation on the Advisory Committee on Restrictive Practices and Monopolies, a Committee where representatives of member states are entitled to comment both on proposed individual decisions and on proposed Community legislation on competition issues. Here, the competition authority attends along with the ministry when legislation is discussed, while the ministry is absent when discussing individual decisions.

Observing actual behaviour in the decision-making process more closely, the division of tasks presented above seems to have quite significant practical consequences. The above-mentioned issue of the phrasing of Article 3 in Regulation 1/2003 is a nice illustration; as one informant stated, the Swedish authorities, represented by both the competition authority and the ministry, worked hard to change the Commission's initial proposal, which gave a much clearer primacy to EU competition law over national law than was finally decided by the Council. Turning to the treatment of individual cases, the attempted merger of Volvo and Scania[13] demonstrates the other role played by the competition authority:

> Even though the Swedish government was supporting the merger and even lobbied for its acceptance in Brussels the Swedish competition authority advised against the merger in the advisory committee. I must therefore stress the importance of the national competition authorities applying EU competition law in close co-operation with

the Commission and with each other. If the national competition authorities would continue to apply national competition law on agreements affecting trade between member states the reform would be a failure, and set us a step back.[14]

Informants in both the Norwegian and the Swedish administrations further comment that there have been instances where a member state has been represented in the Advisory Committee both by the ministry and the competition authority, presenting divergent views of the national position on a particular issue.

Taken together, these observations indicate that the institutional configuration at EU level, with a division of tasks between the Council and the Commission, as well as the different organizational logics in these institutions, have had an impact on the decentralization process of EU competition policy. This has also been facilitated by organizational reforms at national levels, where executive tasks have increasingly been decentralized to autonomous agencies. As such, interactions between the EU and the member states in the field of competition policy seem to follow the institutional configuration at EU level, where officials situated in the national ministries are primarily engaged in the territorially organized Council structure, while officials in the competition authority interact with the functionally organized Commission structure. Thus, both an intergovernmental and a functionalist explanation have difficulties in explaining the dynamics in the reform process because of a lack of differentiation between different actors at the national level. In this way, the findings of this small study are similar to the findings of Trondal (2001: 15–16):

This study argues basically that we have to unpack the organizational structures of the EU system in order to determine which identity, role and mode of action is being evoked by domestic officials attending EU committees. Additionally, we have to carve up the bureaucratic machinery of the nation-state in order to unravel the dual institutional affiliations embedding these domestic government officials, ultimately determining the relative primacy of different institutional dynamics penetrating them.

A networked administrative structure, however, of which EU competition policy from 2004 may be a prime example, differs from a system where national officials sometimes attend committee meetings in Brussels. National competition authorities will participate in a much closer cooperation guided by the Commission, where they are key players in preparing and executing Community policy.

Endnote: pointing at potential transformative consequences

Institutional 'turf battles' between the Council and the Commission are quite common (Egeberg, chapters 1 and 2). However, the above quote by the Swedish MEP shows how these constellations persist, resulting in similar conflicts at the national levels. At any rate, it seems quite clear from the Swedish case that the government is very much aware of the need for stronger coordinating mechanisms to ensure that national agencies in general adhere to the interests of the government (interview 30 January 2004).[15] When it comes to competition policy, where the Commission has an extraordinarily strong position, and national agencies have gained a high degree of autonomy from national political institutions, the chances are that national officials working in competition authorities will see their position as one where they owe allegiance to two principals; their national superiors in the ministry and the Commission. Their position will be what Egeberg (chapters 1 and 3) refers to as 'double-hatted', where they serve as part of the 'Union administration' while remaining an integral part of the national bureaucracy. Stefan Kadelbach (2002: 176–7) perceives the situation in a similar way, albeit from a lawyer's point of view:

> National authorities are thus subject to two claims to obedience, stemming from two legal orders which are different in origin. They find themselves in a situation where they owe dual loyalty. On one hand, they are integrated in their respective institutional hierarchies. On the other hand, national agencies are responsible for the implementation of EU law and thus function as the substructure of the European institutions. That *dédoublement fonctionnel* may lead to conflicts if state officials receive diverging commands from the two orders.

The reform of EU competition policy may increase this challenge, as the setting up of a European Competition Network strengthens both the intensity and the amount of cooperation between national competition authorities and the Commission. This 'double-hatted' position of national agencies may of course be problematic, as it challenges the traditional hierarchical notions of national bureaucracies. It illustrates an observation made by Sverdrup (2003b: 5), of 'the reduced symmetry or overlap between the jurisdictions of the public administration and its territorially based authority . . . where there is often ambiguity, and sometimes conflict, about whom the administration is accountable to and whom it works for'. At least when it comes to competition policy, the statement by the Swedish MEP shows that the reform itself depends on national competition authorities wearing the 'Community hat' when preparing and applying EU competition law. It is not an ambition of this chapter to evaluate potential consequences for the nation-state, but it is clear that the ideal picture of hierarchical and internally coherent national administrations may be increasingly problematic to sustain on the European scene. At least, it does not provide an accurate description when it comes to the administration of EU competition policy as of 2004.

Although it is important to emphasise the particularities of the policy area in question, the more general picture is also interesting. Due to the unique institutional structure of the EU, as well as the fragmentation and decentralization of national administrations, conflicts and patterns of cooperation between different institutions at EU level may penetrate the nation-state and thereby increase the challenges for member state governments in coordinating policy.

Notes

1. White Paper on Modernization of the Rules Implementing Articles 85 and 86 of the EC Treaty, O.J. No C 132/1, May 12, 1999.
2. EEC Council: Regulation No. 17: First Regulation implementing Articles 85 and 86 of the Treaty. O.J. P 013, 21.02.1962.
3. Consolidated version of the Treaty establishing the European Community, O.J. C 325/33, 24.12. 2002.
4. In fact, prior to the drafting of Regulation 17/62, national competition authorities were allowed to apply European competition rules. However, as few member states had competition authorities, not to mention a substantive body of competition law, nothing was achieved in those early years (see also Cini and McGowan 1998).
5. Today, the competition authorities of ten member states have the competence to apply Articles 81(1) and 82 of the EC Treaty: Belgium, Germany, Denmark, Greece, Spain, France, Italy, the Netherlands, Sweden and Portugal (Konkurrencestyrelsen 2003).
6. White Paper on Modernization of the Rules Implementing Articles 85 and 86 of the EC Treaty, O.J. No C 132/1, May 12, 1999, paragraph 4.
7. Former Director General of DG Competition.
8. Respectively, COM (2000) 582 and Council Regulation (EC) 1/2003.
9. Danish Competition Authority, 'Competition report 2003', see http://www.ks.dk/publikationer/konkurrenceredegoerelsen/.
10. COM (2000) 582, Article 3, my italics.
11. Council Regulation 1/2003, Article 3, my italics.

12. See Draft Commission Notice on cooperation within Network of Competition Authorities. See http://europa.eu.int/comm/competition/antitrust/legislation/procedural_rules/cooperation_network_en.pdf.
13. Admittedly, this is a case that does not fall under Articles 81 or 82 as it is a merger case. However, the division of roles by national authorities is the same, and it is therefore used as an illustration.
14. Speech by Charlotte Cederschiöld, Swedish MEP, at a conference of the EP and the Commission on the reform on European competition law, 9 and 10 November 2000 in Freiburg. See http://europa.eu.int/comm/competition/conferences/2000/freiburg/.
15. See also the report by Statskontoret/the Swedish Agency for Public Management – www.statskontoret.se – report no. 2003: 29.

7
Administering Information: Eurostat and Statistical Integration

Ulf Sverdrup

Building European information systems[1]

This chapter analyses the processes and dynamics of institution-building in the European Union (EU). While most studies of EU institution-building have dealt with the birth and evolution of key institutions, such as the legislative institutions, the executives or the courts, the focus is here on a different aspect of democratic governance: the informational foundation of the EU. The chapter examines developments and changes in the organization of numerical information in the EU, in particular the role of Eurostat, the statistical office of the European Commission. How and to what extent can we observe the emergence of a pan-European informational system? How and to what extent has the European information system interacted and worked together with national statistical institutes?

Information is a vital component in any political system (March 1987). Obviously, information is critical for making informed decisions. Without information, decision-making can take place only randomly, or is best understood as the art of guess-work. Information is instrumental for democracy, since it is crucial for enabling citizens to hold decision-makers accountable for their decisions (Alonso and Starr 1983; March and Olsen 1989; Hopwood and Miller 1994). It follows from this that trust in the quality of information, and the institutions generating information, is important for securing trust in government and democracy. The development of a numerical information system at the European level is therefore a central component in the creation of an efficient and legitimate European polity. If the emerging information system in the EU is organized in ways that challenge existing information systems, this can also be seen as one indicator of a transformation under way in European governance.

The argument is as follows. First, national statistics have been supplemented by European statistics, hence statistics are being Europeanized.

Numerical information has become increasingly important in EU decision-making. Over the past fifty years there has been a rapid growth in European statistics. European statistics are distributed more widely, are more frequently used, and are generating increased attention. The more extensive use of numerical information is important for the functioning of the EU, and it also plays an important part in increasing the democratic quality of European governance. Second, over time, there has been a process of gradual institutionalization of the European information system. A separate body, Eurostat, has emerged as a key actor. Rules and procedures have been established, and resources have been linked to upholding these rules and practices. Networks of training and cooperation between European and national bodies have been established. Although the role of Eurostat has been disputed and questioned, it has gradually developed some degree of autonomy and found a place within the larger European institutional configuration. Third, the processes of institution-building have followed some of the well-known dynamics of European integration, such as the functional logic of task expansion, technical problem-solving, and bargaining between parties with different national traditions and standardized routines. However, a striking feature of Eurostat is the importance of pre-existing forms of organized cooperation, and in particular, the importance of the close interrelationship and organized cooperation with national statistical institutes and international statistical bodies such as the OECD and the UN.

The discussion is organized as follows. First, some of the properties of informational systems and some theoretical approaches to statistical systems will be discussed. I then provide a more detailed empirical analysis of the development of the statistical system in Europe, and the relationship between national statistical institutes and Eurostat. Needless to say, the issue of statistics in Europe is large – ranging from the low-attention, refined and highly specialized discussions on methods and modes of measurement, to the high-attention decisions, for instance, determining which states may qualify for membership in the Economic and Monetary Union. In this chapter, the focus is restricted to issues related to the institutional developments of Eurostat and the question of administering information systems.

Statistics and political systems

Most political scientists are consumers of statistics. Few have been interested in seeing information and statistics as a component part of the emerging political system of Europe. Why should we be concerned about statistics?

There are two kinds of response to this. The first relates to key properties of numerical information systems, which should be of particular interest to students of European governance, while the second relates to theories of institutions.

Numerical information systems, such as statistics and accounting, have some properties that make them particularly interesting to the study of Europe. As the EU has become larger and more complex, the need for information enabling comparisons has increased. Compared with textual information, figures are particularly effective in reducing complexities and enabling comparisons. Numerical information also seems to affect the value and trust attached to the information. In general, numerical information tends to signal objectivity to a greater extent than textual information, so it often generates more trust (Porter 1995). In the EU, the lack of a common language makes textual information even more difficult and costly. Finding solutions to overcome the technical, cultural, economic and democratic difficulties related to the many European languages has proven difficult, but numerical information creates a form of communicating across fairly heterogeneous member states. In the EU there is a 'culture of no culture', and in the creation of a unified political and administrative system the 'neutral' language of quantification may therefore prove to be particularly important. Finally, numerical information is a key component of the norm of rationality. Modern societies are characterized by the ubiquity of numerical information, as reflected in the saying, 'what you can't count, doesn't count'. For instance, in modern public administration we observe an 'audit society' characterized by the spread of scoreboards, benchmarking, auditing and the like (Power 1994). These general developments in public administration are also frequently found in the European Union, where we can note the spread of softer governance techniques related to the open method of coordination, as well as the increased use of scoreboards to measure performance, convergence and goal achievements. This ubiquity of numerical information, as well as its particular significance in the EU, makes it interesting to examine the organization of statistics.

The second reason for examining statistics follows from lessons learned from an institutional and organizational perspective on politics. In the literature we can identify different perspectives from which to perceive and view statistical systems. Some see statistics as a neutral, a-political and technical activity that simply mirrors society. From this point of view, changes in statistical systems are likely to derive from technical advances, or changes in society that lead statisticians to measure new areas and policy fields. Others see statistics as a political tool for realizing political aims and ambitions. The famous aphorism that Mark Twain attributed to Disraeli that 'there are three kinds of lies: lies, damned lies and statistics' reflects the view that statistical categories and measures are designed to organize support for distinct alternatives. Numerous studies have shown how the ideal of letting neutral information determine politics can be reversed or perverted, making policies determine data, and there is a huge literature on different versions of 'creative accounting' among both private and public actors (Hopwood and Miller 1994). From such an instrumental perspective, changes in statistical systems are seen as stemming from the changing preferences of the political leaders or changing coalitions of leaders.

However, statistics can also be seen primarily as an institutional practice (March and Olsen 1989, 1995). Figures and statistical systems can be seen as institutions, which, like other political institutions, mobilize bias (Schattschneider 1960; Sangolt 1997). The basic assumption is that the way an institution is organized has implications for how it works. Information serves different purposes, and different information systems can be designed for securing different goals and purposes. Such goals may include maximizing effective decision-making in the European institutions, maximizing the democratic ideal of informing the public and the citizens, and maximizing trust among actors in competitive markets. Sometimes goals and purposes are in conflict with each other. For instance, while secrecy and privileged access to information may sometimes be important for effective decision-making, they can be in conflict with informing the ordinary citizens. Issues such as what to measure, when to measure, who to measure, are not only pure technical decisions, they are also political decisions that can have distributional consequences.

From an institutional perspective it is assumed that different organizational principles skew decision-making in distinct directions. Moreover, it is argued that statistical systems, like institutions in general, often evolve in a path-dependent way. Decisions at time zero create opportunities and constraints for decision-making at a later stage. Perhaps even more than other institutions, statistical systems are conservative: they create and represent the present in the categories of the past. Partly they do so because the effectiveness of statistics is often based upon comparability in space and time, and change in statistical categories reduces the possibilities for comparisons.[2] However, occasionally dramatic crises and external shocks may lead to a situation where the existing rules and categories are not suited for interpreting the world.[3] Under such conditions, when systems fail to provide for meaningful accounts of the world, statistical systems may change rapidly.

In reorganizing the boundaries of the statistical universe in Europe, the European integration process has been interacting with key components of the nation-state. Historically, statistics has been closely linked to the nation-state. In fact, the term statistics itself signals these ties. It was first used in the 1770s to label the science of dealing with data about the condition of a state or community. Initially, the term 'statistics' did not refer to numerical information as such, but was applied to any information on the conditions of the state. The term originated from the German *Statistik*, related to the Latin word *status*, or state, in the sense of circumstances or conditions. *Statistik* originally meant systematized and tabulated textual information. The use of the term 'statistics' as numerical collection and classification of data was first noted in 1829.[4]

Not only is the term linked to the state, but more importantly the emergence of statistical organizations and data has been very closely linked to the construction of the state, its unification and its administration (Desrosières 1998: 8). In the era of the consolidation and growth of European nation-states, the establishment and the growth of national statistical institutes were central components in establishing effective and legitimate government. The emergence of the statistical systems and the budgetary systems of the state also contributed to a shift in citizens' perception of government. From seeing government as a more or less random agglomeration of administrative initiatives, the emergence of advanced budgetary and statistical systems contributed to the vision of a coherent, interrelated and unitary state (Kahn 1997).

Statistics were important not only as a key institution of the state, but also in building a notion of the nation. Many of the conceptions and understandings of self within the nation are closely linked to statistics; for example, ideas about shared and average values, standard deviation and normality, important in 'imagining a community',[5] are all statistical concepts. Stories told about the nation, the 'us' and the 'them', its identities and properties, are often stories told by accountants and statisticians, and they have played a crucial role in generating a national image of the state. For instance, statistical institutions were important in creating Italian nationhood and a national image of Italy, but statistics also contributed to accentuating the internal territorial visions of Italy (Patriarca 1996).

One important consequence of this tight interlinkage between statistics and the development of states and nations is that statistics have become 'firmly entrenched in national administrative structures and practices' (De Michelis 1997: 48). Statistical institutions have developed into national institutions with established rules that infuse the interpretation of the world. Over the years, categories and standards have become taken for granted. The boundaries of inquiry, presuppositions about social reality, classification systems, methods of measurement, as well as rules, routines, organization, resources and capacities for interpreting and presenting data – these have overwhelmingly been structured along the boundaries of the territorial nation-state. Statistical integration in Europe is therefore a case of institution-building in an environment of heavily institutionalized and professional domestic systems.

Goals and resources of European statistics

Statistics have several important functions in the European Union. First, the creation of new statistics for a new Europe has been important for supporting decision-makers on policy choices in Europe. The introduction of new policy fields in the EU increased the functional pressure for reliable and relevant information for decision-making and governance. As the boundaries of what had started as the European Coal and Steel Community changed, there was also a need to change the boundaries of the statistical universe. For instance, the internal market changed the borders of trade, making concepts such as imports and exports within Europe less meaningful. In order to enable comparisons between member states' decision-makers it was necessary to develop harmonized standards of measurement on a huge number of issues, as well as to develop shared modes of classification and methods. Moreover, as border controls in Europe were removed, there emerged a need for new modes of collecting data, since in many instances border controls had provided essential data-collection points.

Second, having new and harmonized statistics was critical for financing the activities of the EU. Since the financial contributions to the budget by the various member states are calculated on the basis of aggregated measures of GNI, it was important to ensure that these economic parameters were measured in the same way in the various member states. Similarly, the basic element of redistribution is also heavily dependent upon methods and modes of determining which states, regions, groups and persons are entitled to receive support from the EU through its various policies and programmes.[6]

Finally, the emergence of European statistics is also linked to the development of some notions of European identity, or at least enabling citizens to learn more about their fellow Europeans and how they live. The policy of dissemination of statistics has made manifest the linkage between statistics and democracy in the EU. For instance, the preface to the first version of the European statistical yearbook, published in 1995, explained that this was a book 'for and about the Europeans', stressing its importance in developing knowledge and trust by enabling its citizens to get to know their 'European neighbours just a little better' (Eurostat 1995: i). The year-book was also intended to link democracy and statistics more closely, see-ing the role of European statistics as serving the people so that 'democracy may flourish'.

European integration has challenged the borders of the nation-state in general, and the statistical boundaries and the organization of the stat-istical information in particular. In order to develop the EU into a full-blown polity, it has become evident that creating a political space both involves and enables the creation of a space of common measurement, within which things may be compared, on the basis of identical categories and encoding procedures (Desrosières 1998: 8–9). This need for statistical cooperation in the EU has been an integral part of European integration since the very start of the European Coal and Steel Community in 1951.

In Article 46 of the ECSC Treaty the objectives which presuppose the availability of statistics were expressed, and in Article 47 it was stated that the High Authority may obtain the information it required to carry out its task. When the High Authority was set up in 1952, it was decided to create 12 divisions and services. Statistics were one of the divisions (De Michelis and Chantrine 2003). From 1959, this unit, which was later named Eurostat, has been at the centre of attempts at integrating statistics in the European Union. Formally, the mission of Eurostat is to provide the European institutions and member states with reliable, comparable and relevant statistical information covering the whole of the EU. That means supplying simple, reliable and timely statistics to the European institutions, the member states, the market and the public. Eurostat aims at creating common classifications and methods, developing organizational structures for comparable statistics by facilitating greater cooperation between the EU and its member states and by developing a uniform European Statistical System (ESS) together with the member states.

The European Statistical System has developed gradually, with the object-ive of providing comparable statistics at EU level. The ESS is made up of Eurostat and the statistical offices, ministries, agencies and central banks that collect official statistics in EU member states, in addition to the mem-ber states of the European Free Trade Association (EFTA) in the European Economic Area (EEA) (Iceland, Norway and Liechtenstein). The ESS functions as a network of statistical bodies. The role of Eurostat is to encourage the harmonization of statistics in close cooperation with the national statistical authorities. As EU policies have been extended, harmonization has been extended to nearly all fields of statistics. The ESS also coordinates its work with international organizations such as the OECD, the UN, the International Monetary Fund and the World Bank, making European statistics a multilevel system of governance, coordinating and producing relevant data and statistics.

In parallel with increased European integration, Eurostat has experienced a noteworthy expansion of its tasks. From primarily being concerned with data in the field of coal and steel, Eurostat is now engaged in most kinds of statistics, including long-term indicators, economy, ecology, structural indicators, employment, innovation, social cohesion, consumer prices, external trade, and more. This expansion has been mirrored in Eurostat's administrative capacity only to a limited degree, but there has been a considerable growth in the size of the organization. From a staff of 58 people in 1959, Eurostat expanded to approximately 730 in 2003. When temporary staff are included, the figure is slightly higher.

As we see from Figure 7.1, the growth has taken place stepwise, rather than incrementally. The stages of growth correspond roughly to the addition of new statistical tasks. For instance, the increase in the early 1960s was primarily related to the merging of treaties and the expansion of statistical fields. Since the mid-1990s it has been related to the introduction of the internal market and, later, especially to the introduction of the Economic and Monetary Union (EMU), which increased the demand for statistics and gave Eurostat the role of monitoring some of the convergence criteria. Although there has been a significant growth in the staff

Figure 7.1   Capabilities of Eurostat, staff 1952–2003
Sources: De Michelis and Chantrine (2003) and Eurostat web page.

of Eurostat, it is still remarkably small compared to its counterparts at the national level.[7] The total staff of the statistical institutes of the EU-15 were calculated at approximately 70,000 in 1998.[8]

Eurostat and its role in the institutional configuration of the EU

There has been a shared understanding of the need for a solid informational foundation of European integration, but the organizational structure of Eurostat and its role in the larger institutional configuration have been contested and disputed over the years.

Eurostat has never been an independent agency: it is organized as a Directorate General (DG) within the European Commission. The limited autonomy of Eurostat sometimes comes into conflict with the views of professional statisticians at the national level, at least in some member states. The autonomous national statistical institutes are often accustomed to making their own plans and being able to act on the basis of statistical arguments and a statistical logic of appropriateness. For Eurostat, by contrast, the first draft of its statistical programme is initiated by the European Commission, which naturally means that it reflects political needs and desires.

Over the past 30 years there have been several discussions as to diverse models for organizing Eurostat. Suggestions have ranged from abolishing the central unit or making it an autonomous body (agency) to proposals for integrating Eurostat more closely into the European Commission. In the early 1980s Eurostat received scant attention from the European Commission, and was generally regarded as an institution of limited importance. It was experiencing internal administrative difficulties, and the national statistical bodies were not particularly concerned about developing European statistics. At the international level Eurostat did not play an important role, being overshadowed by institutions such as the statistical bodies of the IMF, the OECD and the UN. The Eurosclerosis present in Europe during this period was also evident in the field of statistics.

This was the point at which the idea of dividing the statistical unit in the EU was launched. The European Commission proposed that the statistical office should concentrate more on providing the Directorate Generals with the statistical data they need for their work, and it argued that the analysis and interpretation of statistics could be readily done by the various DGs (De Michelis and Chantrine 2003: 77). During the same period, the European Commission also blocked attempts at filling the vacant leading position in the Eurostat – partly due to lack of attention to statistics, but also due to internal personnel disputes in Eurostat. The deep tensions were illustrated by the fact that the responsible leaders of the European Commission did not meet the Director General of the statistical unit. In the early 1980s Eurostat was considered a 'foreign body' inside the Commission; there was talk of breaking up the statistical unit, and instead integrating statistics into the various DGs of the European Commission.

Despite these proposals, Eurostat remained a separate body, for at least three reasons. First, the government in Luxembourg resisted reorganization, not so much because of statistical arguments, but simply because they wanted to keep one of the European institutions within their own borders. Second, the European Parliament, which had gained in importance in the EU after the first direct election in 1979, argued that Eurostat should not be dis-integrated, because they perceived it as a potentially important source of more independent information. The European Parliament even insisted on having a role in shaping the future of Eurostat. Finally, and perhaps equally important, the expansion of tasks in the EU, and in particular the growing interest in creating an internal market, increased the demand for statistical information. The statisticians themselves argued that the quality of statistics would be better with an integrated statistical unit, and that general trust in their figures would be increased if they could maintain some degree of unity.

During the mid-1990s the organizational issue of Eurostat again came to the fore. This time the discussion was reversed. Rather than decreasing the autonomy of statisticians, as advocated during the 1980s, the argument was now that there was a need for greater statistical autonomy. Henning Christophersen, Vice-President of the European Commission, and the Commissioner responsible for Eurostat for six years, argued that 'the best and most coherent solution is to see how we can establish an independent statistical service for the EU – with its own resources and its independence guaranteed by Community legislation and by working with independent national statistical offices' (*Sigma* 1995: 38). This autonomous institutional model for Eurostat would be parallel to the European Central Bank, as well as the model already in use in many member states. The motivation for this proposal was that independence and autonomy as such were held to be good for improving the credibility of the EU and the Commission's proposals, as well as for monitoring and implementing policy within the Union. If member states and markets were well aware that statistical information came from an autonomous body, one that took its own decisions in accordance with professional standards and based upon an independent economic foundation, rather than being influenced by political considerations, this could generate more trust and support.

However, Christophersen also foresaw some difficulties in making Eurostat a more autonomous and independent unit. Since the European Commission controlled the budget, he was uncertain whether the Commission would be willing to pay as much as they had done for the production of statistics in Eurostat. He also feared that it was likely that the Commission would establish competing entities, producing their own statistics within the various DGs or perhaps even out-sourcing the work to other agencies.

Full autonomy has never been granted to Eurostat. But the Amsterdam Treaty, which was signed in October 1997 and came into force in May 1999, represented a significant move in this direction. Article 285 provided Community statistics with a treaty-based foundation for the first time: 'the Council . . . shall adopt measures for the production of statistics where necessary for the performance of the activities of the Community' and '[t]he production of Community Statistics shall conform to impartiality, reliability, objectivity, scientific independence, cost-effectiveness and statistical confidentiality; it shall not entail excessive burdens on economic operators'. This article represented an important step in securing and institutionalizing European statistics. The gradually increasing scope and extent of cooperation within the EU had made it increasingly difficult to ensure the availability of EU statistics purely on the basis of voluntary agreements between member states. The treaty text codified the existing working arrangements and was important in recognizing the role of statistics and Eurostat. The same year a Commission decision[9] clarified further the role of Eurostat as the sole 'Community authority' entrusted with the production of statistics. It also reaffirmed the need for those involved in Community statistics to follow fundamental principles in order to ensure that the results were scientifically independent, transparent, impartial, reliable, pertinent and cost-effective.

The most recent discussions on the role and organization of Eurostat came at the turn of the century, when a management scandal emerged in Eurostat. In 2000, internal auditors discovered that some external contractors had overcharged Eurostat for its services, and showed that some of these firms had been established and owned by major figures in Eurostat. Prior to these accusations, the unions of those employed in the EU had for some time expressed concern about the growing number of temporary staff employed by Eurostat. The huge number of external contractors to Eurostat was partly a result of the limited resources made available for producing statistics within the tight deadlines of the political reforms. The investigation into the financial irregularities developed into a deep crisis in 2002–03, challenging the European Commission.

It was accused of evading responsibility for its activities and by misleading and misinforming the European Parliament. However, rather than seeing this dispute as primarily a matter of statistics, it is more reasonable to consider the context of the institutional struggle for power between the European Parliament and the European Commission, and the larger institutional reforms aimed at securing better and more accountable management systems in the EU. Regardless of the reasons and dynamics of this scandal, it was to have some important implications for the role of Eurostat, since it led the European Commission to initiate reforms to increase cooperation and reporting between Eurostat and the European Commission (Sangolt 2004).

As we have seen, the role of Eurostat and its place in the larger institutional configuration of the EU has been contested. Various reform proposals have been suggested, ranging from having a separate statistical unit to integrating into the DGs of the European Commission; from increasing its autonomy and securing professional standards and self-determination to enabling political instructions and careful political monitoring. Some of these proposals have reflected general trends in public administration. For instance, the idea of having an autonomous statistical body was in line with ideas related to giving more autonomy to expert agencies. Similarly, the increased focus on managerial issues and closer cooperation between the European Commission and Eurostat can be seen as part of a larger public administration reform in the EU, emphasizing the need to ensure accountability and sound management. Alternatively, some of the reforms can be seen simply as by-products of other institutional struggles in the EU – as illustrated by the localization politics in Luxembourg and the struggles between the European Commission and the European Parliament. The development of the role of Eurostat in the larger institutional configuration of the EU is therefore best understood as a series of mutual adaptations and the outgrowth of slowly evolving cooperation between experts, rather than the result of grandiose institutional designs. In fact, the radical proposals have failed.

Eurostat and the national statistical institutes

A gradual transformation of the statistical community in Europe has taken place over a relatively short period of time: an activity formerly conducted primarily within national statistical institutions and the boundaries of member states has seen the emergence of a pan-European statistical administration. The patterns of cooperation with the national statistical institutes have been important in facilitating these changes. In the European statistical system the national statistical institutes are 'double-hatted', in the sense that they serve both as national bodies and as integral parts of the European administration. Several factors constitute this interrelationship. The most important element is the division of labour. Eurostat rarely collects data itself; instead it is dependent upon the transmission of data from member states. Eurostat focuses primarily on the development of harmonized standards of measurement and on comparisons. This division of labour is cost-effective for Eurostat, since data collection is expensive. As noted, there is an asymmetry in resources between the European and the national level. In the field of economic statistics, in which Eurostat also cooperates with the European Central Bank, it has been estimated that there are roughly 100 statisticians at the national or regional level for every one at Eurostat and the ECB combined. The decentralized system for data collection has some advantages but some obvious problems, since the quality and the speed of publication of statistics from Eurostat depend on effective co-working with member states. A study by the Deutsche Bank in 2002 argued that the decentralized model made European statistics of poorer quality than statistics in other countries. The study showed that Europe had fewer indicators than the United States, Japan or Germany. In addition, data in Europe were published significantly later than in the United States. For instance, the United States published weekly data on money supply, whereas in Europe such information was published on a monthly basis. The United States was 29 days ahead of Europe in publishing data on unemployment, 44 days speedier on industrial production, and 103 days faster in producing data on industrial production (*The Economist*, 2002).

Another factor linking European and national statistical bodies is systematic cooperation on methods and standards. As early as 1960, shortly after its establishment, Eurostat decided to strengthen its contacts with national bodies and the statistical departments of the various ministries of the member states. Member states differed considerably in terms of administrative and statistical quality, and there was a need for harmonizing methods and procedures. Eurostat took a gradual approach to harmonizing statistics for the six member states, involving decisions by national experts and the Directors General. Twice-yearly meetings of the 'Working Party of the Directors General of the National Statistical Institutes (NSI)s' were established. Initially, this Conference, as it was later called, had no official status, since it was only a working party, but it still played a crucial role in laying the foundations of the European statistical system. The guiding principle in relations between the EU body and the member states was that data could be collected better by national bodies, and that Eurostat involvement was to be limited to achieving the Community's objectives. The Conference approved a programme containing some key principles for statistical cooperation in Europe. For instance, it defined the role of the Statistical Office (later Eurostat) as 'a central co-ordinating body to unify, supplement and improve the official statistics in the member states which are important for the progress of European integration'. It also decided that 'within the European executive bodies the Statistical Office is the centre where the statistical requirements of the executive bodies are expressed' and that 'it has sole responsibility for conducting statistical surveys'. The Conference made it clear that the tasks of the Statistical Office were not to include economic and social analyses, opinion polls or forecasts. Later in the 1970s this relationship developed further. The Conference suggested 'a reflective approach . . . that would allow the NSIs to think about the functions they fulfilled, such as analysis, processing and dissemination of information, as well as training and co-ordination *from two points of view, national and Community*' (emphasis added). This formulation stated explicitly the dual administrative system that was emerging. On the one hand, the national bodies were seen as the statistical institutions of the member states; on the other hand, they were also encouraged to see themselves as an integral part of the emerging European administrative sphere fulfilling community tasks.

As a result, representatives of the national statistical institutions were present during most phases of the policy process. For example, in relation to the harmonization of statistics, there were approximately 200 meetings of working parties every year, attended by between 10 and 60 representatives from the NSI and European institutions (De Michelis 1997: 49).[10] In addition, the staff of the national statistical institutions stay in regular contact with Eurostat, and national leaders often encourage such contacts. However, although national statistical bodies have recognized the need for harmonized statistics, daily activities at the national level have sometimes overshadowed the European integration processes. In the absence of a legal framework establishing clear priorities, as well as few resources for European statistics, cooperation has at times been problematic. In addition to frustrations at national level caused by the extra workload involved in producing European statistics, one recurrent controversial issue has been secrecy. Member states have been reluctant to give data to Eurostat, fearing that the data could be used by the European Commission or that confidential information could be broadcast. Over time and with increased interaction among member states, such concerns about secrecy have been reduced.

Cooperation between European and national statistical bodies has also been important in training statisticians. Eurostat systematically encouraged the transfer of staff from the national statistical institutes to the European level, and stimulated the development of various exchange programmes between Eurostat and national statistical bodies. In the mid-1980s, an initiative was launched for securing seconded national officials. An increased flow of statisticians from the national statistical institutes to Eurostat brought knowledge, expertise and ideas to Eurostat, while also giving the national institutes a better knowledge of European statistics. Additionally, Eurostat and the NSI set up a large-scale training programme. In 1991 the programme 'Training of European Statisticians' (TES) was initiated. Eurostat, the member states, and the EFTA states sponsored this annual training programme, which was open to other countries as well, for their own official statisticians. Between 1991 and 2002, 377 courses, seminars and workshops were held, attracting 7800 participants – of whom more than 4100 came from statistical offices in the EU and EFTA, about 2100 from Central European countries, 600 from the Mediterranean area, and 600 from republics of the former Soviet Union. In 2004 this programme was reorganized and is now known as the European Training and Research Institute for Official Statistics (Etrios). Compared with other European institutions, Eurostat was a pioneer in developing such organized forms for facilitating interaction between European and national bodies at the level of practitioners and experts. The methods and techniques for promoting cooperation across levels of governance were later used by other European institutions, as well as in relation to the twinning programmes aimed at the new member states in East and Central Europe.

There has in fact been a long history of international cooperation in the field of statistics. International organizations such as the OECD and the UN have historically been important in organizing international statistical cooperation. Eurostat has developed close links with other kinds of international statistical cooperation. For instance, before Eurostat submits a proposal to the Statistical Programme Committee, consultations are made with expert reports and working groups within the EU system, and recommendations are collected from international organizations such as the UN and the OECD. In many instances, the harmonization of European statistics can build upon frameworks for harmonization established in other international statistical units.

As indicated, Eurostat has conflicting roles regarding national statistical institutes. On the one hand, it acts as networker and cooperator; on the other hand, it also serves as judge, making judgements on whether or not to accept the figures published by the various member states. This role came to the forefront in the period when the EMU was launched. Indicators such as public debt, interest rates, exchange rate fluctuations and the balance of payments were to be monitored, and states that failed to meet the initial targets would not qualify for membership in the EMU. The criteria on public deficit and inflation were the subject of monitoring by the European statistical system. Eurostat was suddenly given the role of providing the information necessary for determining which states could qualify for EMU membership and which could not – a daunting task for a small institution.

In order to handle this work, Eurostat introduced two instruments. First, it proposed the creation of a harmonized index of consumer prices (until then, member states had measured inflation differently); and second, it introduced a new accounting scheme called European Standardized Accounts (ESA), an elaborated version of a UN standard for accounting. Although the introduction of these instruments was of a technical character, they also had significant political consequences, since these statistical methods eventually affect economic performance and market evaluations. Some national decision-makers were slow in implementing the new and improved standards. Dieter Glatzel, head of the Eurostat unit responsible for the excessive deficit procedure, argued that the delay was a result of the economic situation in the member states, and feared that the introduction of a new standard could tilt the creation of the EMU. He argued that the '[b]ackground to the delay in applying ESA 95 to the excessive deficit procedure was the economic situation in 1994–95. At that time very few countries were able to achieve or improve on the reference values laid down in the Protocol: 60 per cent for ratio of government debt to GDP and 3 per cent for ratio of government deficit to GDP' (Glatzel 1999).

Eurostat was put under serious strain, caught between professional standards on the one hand and political decisions and aspirations on the other. Since member states wanted to meet the convergence criteria, they sometimes found it easier to manipulate figures than to alter fundamental elements in their economies. Eurostat experienced strong political pressure to accept the data supplied by the member states. The dual role of Eurostat – as an organ for 'neutral' statistics and as a branch of the European Commission, a staunch supporter of the creation of the EMU – made it vulnerable to pressure. Eurostat had to balance the relationship between creative accounting and accurate measurement. For instance, in relation to the French attempt to make one-offs, it argued that 'we do not want all our attempts to build the credibility of data to be undermined' and noted with alarm that 'the credibility of statistics is at stake'.[11] Eurostat expressed a wish not 'to be pushed around by politicians'.[12] Alberto de Michelis, a senior Eurostat official, suggested a relaxing of the interpretation of the statistical figures. He argued that the task of Eurostat was to create a level playing field in the application of statistical rules.[13] The EMU case illustrated that large-scale political reforms focused attention on the European statistical system. The political pressure and the dynamics of the EMU overshadowed other concerns. In part, this momentum led to increased speed in implementing and securing harmonized accounting systems and harmonized consumer indexes; however, it also led to more creative accounting, which in turn brought increased criticism that tended to undermine the general trust in European statistics. This balancing act seemed to have been partly successful for Eurostat, since the professional community of economists and political decision-makers as well as the market in general tended to trust in the data used for supporting the decision as to which states qualified for EMU membership. The EMU example also highlighted some of the built-in tensions created by the double-hatted administrative character of the national statistical system, with Eurostat as both a cooperative body and a European judge.

New technology

The integration of statistics has been the result of political and professional decisions, and organizational principles and rules have gradually emerged in order to secure this integration and harmonization. However, the introduction of new technologies has been important in facilitating integrated statistics. New technology has made possible new ways of producing statistics and has radically eased calculations and comparisons. The introduction of new technology has been important since the late 1970s, when the European Commission computer centre acquired computer equipment that could process data provided by the member states. Even though Eurostat made significant efforts throughout the 1970s in developing software and securing informatics systems, the European Commission resisted the idea of creating an independent computer centre at Eurostat. It was not until the mid-1980s that the real benefits of the new technology came, with the introduction of the personal computer. Ironically, this new technology was not introduced as a result of a large-scale technology investment programme. Quite the opposite, the impetus came from individual Eurostat officials, who for their own personal use and interest had started to buy PCs. Later, and after various shifts in systems and technologies, as well as problems related to different standards, information technology became better organized from the mid-1990s onwards.

New technology was also important in developing the role of Eurostat as a body for providing information for the media and the public, since it radically reduced the costs of producing and disseminating statistics. During the 1970s there was no policy in Eurostat on dissemination of statistics. Statistics were published only in limited series aimed at professional users. As the EU broadened and deepened in the late 1990s, Eurostat increasingly focused on dissemination, changing its publication strategy from the technical reporting of statistics to more attractive publications like the Eurostat yearbook. Eurostat also established numerous so-called 'data shops' in member states in order to disseminate and sell data. CD-ROMs were produced, gradually replacing the 'large' publication series. Later, the Internet became a prime source for disseminating data. The Eurostat website now makes available several series of data, free of charge for various user-groups. In addition to the increased distribution of statistics, the statistical calendar was becoming more fixed, with an established timetable for the publication of statistics which could ensure that information was made available to everyone simultaneously. Organizing such a dissemination timetable is critical in promoting predictability and trust among actors in the markets.

As a result of these developments, comparative data are now disseminated more widely than before. Statistics on everything from social indicators to economic indicators influence the day-to-day activities of EU decision-making – for example, in calculating budgets, forecasting, planning and redistribution. Information produced by Eurostat is also frequently used by other consumers of statistical information, such as governments, businesses, NGOs and researchers. A study of the dissemination practice and the end-users of data (Blakemore and McKeever 2001), however, showed that Eurostat, like most disseminators of official statistics, had various problems: it had little control over the data supply chain, and user-groups were mixed, with differing expectations and needs. In order to meet these occasionally conflicting demands, Eurostat has to balance access rights against data protection and harmonization against specificity, as well as managing to secure the resources for producing statistics while providing free access for the ordinary citizen.

Integrated figures

As we have seen, numerical information is becoming increasingly important in European governance. The expanding EU agenda has triggered an increased use of numerical information in order to reduce complexity and ease comparisons. The growing use of numerical information in the

EU is also an important element in enhancing the democratic quality of European governance, since it enable citizens to evaluate information and hold politicians accountable. European statistics can also be seen as one of several instruments for developing European self-awareness and even for the creation of a shared (numerical) language. As indicated in this chapter, the processes of building statistics and statistical institutions in the European Union share a number of characteristics with the development of statistical institutions in the era of state- and nation-building. Over the past few decades, Eurostat has become institutionalized. It has gradually developed rules, principles and capacities, as well as some degree of autonomy, and has found its place in the larger European institutional configuration. There is a clear path-dependency in the incremental development, but at different times Eurostat has been exposed to more radical reform attempts, some of them only partly related directly to the field of statistics. The 'living' institution has evolved through processes of mutual adjustment and a variety of patterns of cooperation – not so much by grand design and treaty revisions, as through the long-term involvement and commitment of professional statisticians and the gradual utilization and cultivation of pre-existing national and international institutions. As a result of these developments, a multilevel system of governance in European statistics has emerged. National statistical institutes are central to this system of double-hatted administration. They operate within the boundaries of the nation-state serving national-level tasks and purposes, but in addition, they are key elements in the European administration. The extensive cooperation is the result of the division of labour between the two levels, in much the same way as with the implementation of ordinary legislation. In the field of statistics, cooperation has also been stimulated by the establishment of organized systems for the training and exchange of staff. So far, we know little about the potential tensions built into this kind of multilevel system, or how the different roles, responsibilities and tasks are balanced and fulfilled in instances of conflict or political pressure.

The growth in European statistics has only partly been met by a corresponding increase in the staffing and budgets of the statistical authority. There has been an imbalance between ambitious tasks and limited capacity. Attempts have been made to bridge this gap by the division of labour, extensive exchange of personnel with national-level institutions, the introduction of new technologies and close cooperation, and the utilization of pre-existing forms of international cooperation. All the same, Eurostat officials have argued that 'politicians tend to think that statistics can be produced for no money out of thin air'.[14] This was particularly so in relation to the EMU, where there was a pressing need for additional resources to produce reliable statistics within extremely tight deadlines. One consequence of the limited resources, European statisticians some-times argued, was that 'there may not be high-quality data available'.[15]

So far, the European Union has produced data that have been trusted. An increasing number of actors and decision-makers use EU data as infor-mation sources, and the data contribute to shaping perceptions of Europe and Europeans. However, we should recall that figures do not always generate trust: sometimes they also generate distrust. So far, Europe and Eurostat have avoided generating mistrust in information regarding key indicators in European governance, although there have been instances where data have been lacking, problematic or subject to creative account-ing. It remains to be seen whether this trust in European statistics will continue. There have been instances where statistics produced by Eurostat have been accused of being systematically biased in favour of specific policies and outcomes.[16] Such accusations are very serious for an institution that seeks to be seen as a legitimate and trustworthy source of information for all. Elsewhere in the world we have recently seen serious distrust in national accounts (as in the Asian crisis), and there have been serious flaws in private accounting practices in the USA and in Europe, generating deep distrust in accounting and statistics (Stiglitz 2003). Lack of trust in Eurostat's figures could prevent decisions from being made, reduce the opportunity for citizens to hold decision-makers accountable, and potentially undermine the broader trust in and support for European integration and European institutions. For a proper understanding of the informational foundation of EU decision-making, we must move beyond the organizational issues addressed here and critically examine the figures that are being produced and used.

Notes

1. I would like to thank Morten Egeberg, Ken Endo, Susan Høivik and colleagues at ARENA for comments and help. Parts of this chapter were written when I was a Jean Monnet Fellow at European University Institute, Florence.
2. To illustrate, in Germany, a large EU-inspired reclassification exercise in early 1995 involved 6000 specific types of goods. Only one-fifth of the figures gathered and reported in 1996 were comparable with those reported 16 months earlier (*Financial Times*, 9 April 1996).
3. On statistical absurdities see for instance the *Daily Telegraph*, 1 December 1996. The figures presented by Eurostat to ECOFIN showed that the EU had a $102 bn trade surplus with itself! The article also refers to an analysis finding that 'even with the restricted group comprising six countries, discrepancies in the data are so massive as to forbid any serious knowledge of trade position

of this zone and the way it has been developing in recent years. The monetary policy committee of the European central bank is simply going to operate in the dark from this point of view.'

4. See online etymological dictionary: http://www.etymonline.com/index. php?search=statistics&searchmode=none.

5. See for instance Anderson (1983).

6. For instance, Ireland lodged an application with Eurostat in 1998 to divide the country into two regions; one of them would then qualify for Objective 1 structural funds from the EU, the other for the 'transitional funds' (Boyle 2000).

7. For instance, the French statistical office, INSEE, has a staff of 6500.

8. *Financial Times*, 15 June 1998.

9. Official Journal (97/281/EC) 21 April 1997.

10. The average was 30.

11. *Financial Times*, 31 October 1996.

12. *Financial Times*, 31 October 1996.

13. *Financial Times*, 22 February 1997.

14. *Financial Times*, 24 June 1996.

15. *Financial Times*, 24 June 1996.

16. An article in the newspaper *European Voice* called on the public to focus not only on the management of Eurostat but also its statistics. The authors showed that in relation to enlargement there were significant changes in the data reported. 'In the case of eight central European countries set to join EU next year, extrapolated PPPs from a 1993 benchmark study (by Eurostat and the OECD), show their average GDP per head in 2002 at 35% of the EU-15 level: still poor but less so than at market rates. For the next (1996) benchmark study and all subsequent ones (1999 and 2000) Eurostat brought in various revisions to the methodology . . . this greatly improves the picture for most central European countries: to an average of 46% of the EU-15 level in 2002 . . . Extrapolated back to 1990, the numbers show the central Europeans to be much richer than in previous studies . . . Against all common sense, the Prague region is far above the EU average.' They concluded that '(the) more you look into Eurostat's numbers, the harder it is to escape the conclusion that they are upwardly biased', and argued that 'it is time to look at . . . the numbers the agency produces' (Franklin 2003).

8
National Regulators between Union and Governments: a Study of the EU's Environmental Policy Network IMPEL

Maria Martens

Introduction

Recent studies of implementation in the EU literature have to a large extent focused on differences between member states in relation to their individual ability or capacity (or lack thereof) to implement Community law (see, for example, Mendrinou 1996; Tallberg 1999; Peters 2000; Knill 2001; Mbaye 2001; Bursens 2002; Sverdrup 2003a). The focus in this chapter is rather on the interplay between different actors at various levels of governance, including a description and analysis of a specific implementation arrangement, namely networks between the European Commission and national regulatory agencies. This is an arrangement to be put into action *after* the laws are incorporated into the domestic legal systems and before the practitioners on the ground are to implement the legal acts. The specific case to be analysed is the IMPEL network, an informal network composed of representatives from the national environmental inspectorates in 29 countries – including all member states of the European Union, the three candidate countries Bulgaria, Romania and Turkey, and Norway – and the European Commission.

My approach is in line with the so-called multilevel governance literature in the study of European integration, in which the EU is considered 'a system characterized by co-decision-making across several nested tiers of Government' (Marks 1993: 407). My aim is to study how a multilevel networked governance structure can be applied to the implementation of the EU environmental policy, with particular focus on the 'contents' and 'directions' of the relationship between the European Commission and the national agencies. How can we describe and understand the relationship between these actors? More specifically, I will address whether and in what ways the national regulatory agencies are serving as agents of the European Commission.

Implementing Community law: the last stronghold of national control?

It is almost considered conventional wisdom that while European legislation is made by the European institutions, it is implemented at the national level (Cini 2003a: 350). This division of responsibilities between the EU and its member states was intentional; those drafting the original treaties in the 1950s felt that it would be both inappropriate and, indeed, unworkable for the Community to involve itself in all aspects of the policy process (ibid.: 351). Thus, although the European Commission oversees the enforcement of EU law, its implementation functions are, in all but exceptional cases, restricted to monitoring and carrying out investigations (Peters 2000). Implementation of Community law has been considered the 'last stronghold of national control' (From and Stava 1993).

From an integrationist point of view, reliance on national governments for implementation of EU policies reflects the 'old inter-governmental order'. Implementing through national governments exposes common policies to considerable influence from national politics and administrative traditions (Dehousse 1997b; Knill 2001; Olsen 2003; Sverdrup 2003a) and may hamper a uniform and effective enforcement of Community law.

A clear-cut Community solution would be to give EU institutions direct administrative responsibilities. This would be enhanced for instance if the Commission ran its own agencies at the national level. Such a system would ensure both Community control and harmonization of the legal systems across national borders. This model is, however, neither politically realistic for the time being nor even desired by the Commission due to lack of capacity (Dehousse 1997b: 246).

We do however see in the EU a trend towards developing networked administrative structures in which national and European-level institutions create closer cooperative arrangements (Graver 2002). The European Commission has also intensified its work on alternative and non-legal instruments for improving implementation by developing a wider repertoire of organizational instruments involving national administrations (Sverdrup 2003b). These changes at the European level can be considered attempts at finding a workable solution to the above-mentioned problem: how to secure coherent and uniform implementation without transferring more direct power from the national to the supranational level (Dehousse 1997b; Egeberg, Chapter 3; Sverdrup 2003b). These networked administrative structures are our point of departure.

National regulatory agencies within a new context

I believe we have to stop thinking in terms of hierarchical layers of competence separated by the subsidiarity principle and start thinking, instead, of a networking arrangement, with all levels of governance shaping, proposing, implementing and monitoring policy together.[1]

Changes at both European and national levels serve as important background for this chapter. As mentioned above, we see a trend towards developing networked structures in the EU, and the idea of a 'networked administrative system' – in which the Commission could partly 'dispose' of national agencies – has been launched.[2] At the same time, we have witnessed an important development with regard to national administrative systems; in most Western states these have changed during the last few decades, especially since the 1980s, and have become less hierarchical, more fragmented and more decentralized (Christensen and Lægreid 2001). Explanations and possible motivations for these changes are certainly plentiful, and so-called New Public Management (NPM) ideas, with their market-inspired character, come easily to mind. One central feature in this approach has been to make a clearer distinction between politics and administration, with administration perceived as a *craft*, best performed at an arm's length from political considerations (ibid.: 96). A possible way of gaining political leeway is through the decentralization of tasks to independent regulatory agencies placed outside the central administrative hierarchy. Although these ideas have had a major impact on national administrations in Europe, concerns related to possible consequences for accountability of administrative actions and for political control over the executive apparatus have persistently been at the centre of attention.

The reason for studying the role of national regulatory agencies in a European context is threefold. First, regulatory agencies constitute an important part of the national political system in the member states, both in policy formulation and implementation. They 'matter' in political terms. Second, there is a lack of knowledge regarding the role of national agencies in European cooperation, with the focus having rather been on the founding of agencies at the European level (see for example Dehousse 1997b; Majone 1997, 2000; Kreher 1997; Yataganas 2001).[3] Finally, as observed above, the European Commission has shown increased interest in these organizations when Community law is to be implemented; and due to their relative independence from national ministries, these agencies may be well placed to collaborate with actors at the Community level and to take part in network structures across levels of governance (Egeberg 2003a).

Our knowledge of national agencies in a European context is limited. Profound cooperation between the European Commission and these entities could create new and interesting patterns of cooperation and conflict on the European scene. In that respect, this chapter may contribute to our understanding of the dynamics of European cooperation and the change in dynamics between institutions at different levels of governance. The next section outlines the EU's environmental policy and the case of the IMPEL network; the theoretical framework of the chapter follows.

The EU's environmental policy and the IMPEL network

As the 1957 Treaty of Rome did not contain any reference to environmental protection, environmental policy was, in the 1970s and 1980s, a domain of innovation in the European Union (Sbragia 1999). Under the Single European Act (SEA), environmental policy was finally formally recognized as a proper competence to be exercised at the European level, and under the 1992 Treaty on European Union (the Maastricht Treaty), it became possible to pass most environmental measures through the Council of Ministers by qualified majority (Weale 1999). To quote Weale (1999: 40), 'Completely unanticipated in 1957, environmental policy had moved from silence to salience within thirty years.'

Environmental policy is now one of the major policy areas in which the EU plays a role, and covers a very wide-ranging set of regulations that contain the critical environmental media (water, air and soil) and a range of industrial products (Zito 2002). However, the political salience of environmental policy has gradually declined over the past fifteen years, and the political commitment to impose regulations has consequently diminished. Governments seem at times willing to approve comparatively stringent rules, while subsequent compliance is often patchy and slow, or at worst nonexistent. In practice, therefore, legislation does not always have as far-reaching an impact as might be expected. A growing concern, both in member states and at the European level, about this issue of disparity serves as the backdrop for the foundation of the IMPEL network (Sbragia 1999).

The origins of IMPEL can be traced back to the Dutch EU Presidency in 1991, which placed environmental issues high on its agenda. On the basis of a report on insufficient implementation of environmental law, the Council proposed that an informal network be formed between national environmental authorities, initially known as the Chester Group (after the first meeting in Chester in 1992). A plenary meeting was then installed on a bi-annual basis, alongside four working groups assigned to core areas of legislation (Schout and Claessens 1999).

At that time, a proposal was already circulating in the Commission to address the issue of disparity in the field of environmental law. The Commissioner for Environment at that time, Ripa di Meana, favoured a European Environmental Inspectorate. This proposal was however never realized due to concerns about the Commission having such an enforcement or supervisory role within member states (Sbragia 1999).

The Chester Group was reborn in 1993 as IMPEL, in response to the Fifth Environmental Action Programme's proposal for a more structured network through which to canalize information, advice and implementation consensus. Work was organized within projects chaired by the member states with a particular interest and competence in the relevant topic. It was further decided that the work of IMPEL was to be pursued in partnership with the Commission which would co-chair six-monthly plenary meetings with the presidency. In 1997, the Commission further agreed to share the work programme costs and host an IMPEL Secretariat in Brussels where a seconded national expert would be employed (ibid.).

The Commission has recently proposed extending the scope of the network to include policy-making or, more specifically, to involve the network when relevant legal acts are in the pre-pipeline phase. The Commission wants in particular to know whether the relevant legal acts seem reasonable from the practitioners' points of view. Due to uncertainty among the members as to how to manage this in practice – as well as scepticism, especially among many at the British Environmental Ministry, about including 'inspectors' in law-making – this proposal is still on hold, to be revisited at a later stage (interview 7 October 2004).

Theoretical framework

There are several angles from which this subject might be approached. This chapter is in line with the so-called multilevel governance literature, an approach that for some time has pointed to the fact that international institutions may provide opportunity structures that encourage transnational coalitions (Hooghe and Marks 2001). The literature heavily criticizes the 'state fixation' in the studies addressing intergovernmentalism (see for example Moravscik 1993, 1998; Hoffman 1995), claiming that it offers only a partial representation of both integration and EU governance (for example Kohler-Koch 1999; Hooghe and Marks 2001).

According to Bauer (2002: 771), 'it was hoped that it would be possible to offer an empirically informed explanation of day-to-day integration in the tradition of neo-functionalism that would be able to compete with – or rather "co-exist" with liberal–intergovernmentalist research agendas'. Arguably, the multilevel governance literature gives a vast empirical description of an important development in the EU; the question we have to ask in this respect is whether and how we can use this perspective for analytic purposes. Is it possible to apply it as an analytic tool, as a basis for crafting hypotheses about the subject we are interested in for the purposes of this chapter? To use Jachtenfuchs' words (2001: 259); 'The governance perspective offers a *problematique*, but does not constitute a coherent theory.' From my point of view, it seems difficult to craft fruitful hypotheses about the relationship between the Commission and the national agencies purely on the basis of a multilevel governance perspective. We may state that these networks 'matter', and that they represent a challenge to the authority of the member states. This could be a useful starting point, a theoretical assumption that we might try to test out. At the same time, it seems difficult to move forward, especially if we want to reveal underlying mechanisms for behaviour and single out relevant variables for explaining different outcomes. An institutional perspective might help us a step further in that respect, a theoretical approach I will outline in the next section with special emphasis on the organizational dimension.

Institutionalism and an organizational approach

Institutionalists of all kinds seem to agree that actors' behaviour is influenced by their institutional context. Institutions tend to impose particular world views, ways of thinking that guide behaviour and stabilize expectations (March and Olsen 1989).[4] An important assumption in one branch of this literature is that players are viewed as boundedly rational; it is not possible for them to attend to everything simultaneously or to calculate carefully the costs/benefits of alternative courses of action, as attention is a scarce resource (Simon 1957/1965). Institutions provide simplifying shortcuts, cues and buffers that can lead to the enactment of particular role conceptions among individuals. Human rationality may thus be described as institutionalized, embedded or contextualized (March and Olsen 1989).

Based on these general remarks on institutionalism, we now adopt a specific approach within this literature,[5] namely, an organizational perspective. The study of European integration through institutional prisms has to an increasing extent been influenced by organization theory perspectives. From this point of view, the extent to which institutions (might) impinge profoundly on people's pre-established mind-sets depends on how these institutions are organized (see for example Bulmer 1994; Egeberg 2001, 2003a; Trondal 2001). Thus, to study processes in the EU, we need first to reveal the institutional architecture at the European level and to take a closer look at the organizational principles upon which they are based. The notion is not, however, that the institutional architecture of the EU *determines* political behaviour, only that it makes some patterns more likely than others.

A feature of special interest is the division of tasks and responsibilities between the Council and the European Commission. One may argue that these institutions are organized according to two different basic and general principles in administrative life. Parallel to the sectorial and spatial institutional build-up of the domestic political–administrative apparatus (sector ministries and agencies versus foreign ministries), the Commission may be seen as exhibiting functional principles; conversely, the Council may be viewed as demonstrating spatial and territorial principles of organization since the key decision-makers formally represent the constituent governments (Egeberg et al., Chapter 5).[6]

Existing studies show that national officials do in fact play different roles in these respective organizational contexts in the EU. National officials operating within the Commission's working groups and committees seldom perceive themselves primarily as government representatives (Egeberg et al., Chapter 5; Trondal and Veggeland 2003). Participation in comitology committees and Council working parties, on the other hand, more clearly evokes role conceptions related to nationality. Further, these studies show that the behaviour of national officials participating in the Commission structure is less coordinated nationally than that of their counterparts in the Council structure (Egeberg et al., Chapter 5). These findings demonstrate that patterns of cooperation and conflict are, at least to some extent, a function of the organizational structure of the EU institutions; and that institutions as organized entities discriminate between conflicts, systematically activating some latent cleavages while others are routinely ignored (Egeberg, Chapter 2; Trondal 2001).

To be able to answer our questions on the basis of an organizational approach, we also need to trace the ways in which administrative life is formally organized at the national level of governance (Knill 1998). As stated earlier, we see a trend towards administrative decentralization at the national level in the member states, where more tasks and functions are hived off from ministerial departments and put into quasi-autonomous agencies. Studies show that government officials employed at the agency level in the national administration are more likely to evoke intra-sectorial modes of coordination than officials employed at the ministry level (Trondal 2000; Trondal and Veggeland 2003; Egeberg 2003a). This 'agencification process' may have provided a window of opportunity for running 'double-hatted' regulatory agencies at the national level; the national agencies constitute an integral part of the national bureaucracy as originally intended, however, due to their relative independence and the compatible organizational structures in the European Commission, they may also be well placed, in organizational terms, to act as local agents at the Community level (Egeberg, Chapter 2). By connecting up national agencies in issue-specific administrative networks, the European Commission would, in a sense, create the opportunity to extend its organization down across the levels without formally erecting its own offices. Hence, on the basis of an institutionalist perspective we address organizational components at both the national and European level and anticipate that certain developments have cleared the ground for a new 'double-hatted' position for the national regulatory agencies on the European scene.

In search of empirical dimensions

As stated, the aim of this chapter is to explore the character of the IMPEL network and whether the agencies are playing a 'double-hatted' role in the EU. The pertinent question is, then, where to look when studying the IMPEL network or, in other words, which questions can provide us with relevant answers.

Multiple identities? The first dimension to explore is the degree of identification between the different actors at these two levels. To what extent do the Commission and national experts consider themselves part of a community? Institutions tend to impose particular world views, identities and ways of thinking – a particular 'logic of appropriateness' (March and Olsen 1989). The question here is not whether the national experts have changed their identification and institutional affiliations completely, but rather whether their belonging to the national administration has been extended to include an affiliation to the Community network or if so-called multiple identities have been developed (Egeberg, Chapter 3).

The Commission in charge? The European Commission and the national regulatory agencies are formally equal members of the IMPEL network.[7] However, we are interested in the actual functioning of the network; as I have indicated that the agencies may work as agents for the European Commission, the second dimension I will address is the hierarchical relationship between the Commission and national agencies. Is there an asymmetric relationship between them? Does the Commission have a grip on these agencies and the opportunity, consequently, to steer them in their work?

Ministerial control? The third dimension to address is the role of the national ministries. Do they control and steer the work of the national agencies in the IMPEL network, or do they leave matters to the agencies? If the national ministries are in fact heavily involved in the network, it would be difficult to talk about 'double-hatted' agencies, serving two different masters in their work.

Talking or acting? Last, but not least, I will explore whether cooperation between the two levels matters in a broader sense. Does the IMPEL network actually affect the way different member states implement legal acts? Does it make a difference? If it makes no political difference, the idea of new patterns of cooperation and conflict between these two levels of governance could be no more than an illusion.

A note on methodology and data

The study of the IMPEL network is a single case study: one particular network in a specific policy field is presented and analysed (N = 1). 'A major problem in any form of social research is to reason from the parts we know to something about the whole they and parts like them make up' (Andersen 1997: 135, quoting Becker 1992: 213). My aim in this chapter is not to tell the 'whole story' and draw general conclusions about the relationship between national regulatory agencies and the European Commission. I have foremost an exploratory ambition; I want to know more about this phenomenon and the study of IMPEL may help develop a first impression, a hint and a piece of the broader picture. Second, I want to examine whether these theories can explain and shed light on this specific case. Are they able to capture the dynamics of the relationship between the actors involved? Do we have to refine or alter concepts in our theoretical framework to be followed-up in other studies of these actors? This study can be considered primarily a starting point for future research.

Given the small number of IMPEL members it would make little sense to do a statistical analysis of the group. I chose therefore to conduct qualitative interviews with open-ended questions, the advantage of such an approach being the possibility of receiving broad reflections and extensive information from the actors involved. Given the exploratory nature of my project, the opportunity to acquire as much information as possible from the relevant actors seemed most strategic.

I chose to interview twelve national experts and one representative from the Commission in the IMPEL network.[8] My ambition was not to examine differences between the member states in their relation to IMPEL, but rather to capture a general impression of the network arrangement with special emphasis on the relationship between the national experts and the European Commission. While it was concluded that these twelve informants could provide adequate information about the general functioning of the network, we should nevertheless be aware that not all potential voices in the network are necessarily heard.

I began by sending network members an e-mail briefly describing the project and including the questions I intended to ask. After a few days, I made a follow-up phone call and went through the questions. The interviews lasted between 45 minutes and one hour. An important challenge in analysing the data was the selection and weighing of the various observations. However, the level of convergence among responses turned out to be quite high, despite certain differences between new and old member states in how they viewed the network in general and, more specifically, the role of the Commission. These differences are addressed in the following analyses when considered relevant. In addition to the interviews, I consulted written sources such as the IMPEL multi-annual work programme, IMPEL work programme 2004, the Commission's sixth environmental action programme and the European Commission's annual Internal Market Scoreboard, in addition to several documents on the internet homepage of IMPEL. These sources helped provide an overview of the practical work of IMPEL, the organizational structures, meeting frequency and formal procedures. The interviews, however, were the most useful instrument for gathering highly valuable information regarding the character of the relationship between national experts and the European Commission.

Presenting and analysing the data

If we consider the last question first, whether the experts are 'talking or acting', we can conclude that the members of the network are indeed acting, not just talking. The guidelines and standards developed in the network are followed up in the different member states; we are not, then, dealing with an empty partnership that looks good on paper but that doesn't really matter at the end of the day. The IMPEL network has significant practical consequences in relation to how the member states actually implement the legal acts in this specific policy area. According to the informants, the reason for this is the direct involvement of the technicians on the ground: they are the people in charge, the actors on the scene. This finding may be understood within a so-called bottom-up perspective within the implementation literature; the assumption is that lower-level actors – that is, those responsible for implementing policy on the ground – are as important as those who originally drafted the law. Bottom-up studies further show that policies are 'ineffective not because they are poorly implemented but because they are poorly conceived on the ground' (Cini 2003a: 355). Having stated that the IMPEL network matters in practical terms, we now turn to our main focus in this chapter, namely the relationship between the different actors involved in this cooperation.

The relationship between the national experts and the European Commission in the IMPEL network has clearly changed over time. As we have seen, the initiative to create the network surfaced at the national level, and the participation of the European Commission was not part of the original plan; in fact, the national experts actually expressed concerns about admitting the Commission. This scepticism about including the Commission gradually drifted away: 'By the end of 1993, however, familiarity with individuals and the good working relationships developed during the relatively unstructured phase of the Network seemed to have dispelled those concerns' (Duncan 2001: 2). The Commission and the national experts became accustomed to each other, and gradually built a spirit of cooperation, mutual trust and companionship; as such, 'increased familiarity' might accurately describe how the relationship between the national experts and Commission developed over time. This increased familiarity among members goes hand in hand with formal changes in the relationship between national experts and the Commission: namely, the Commission's role as co-chair of the six-monthly plenary meetings (1993), and Commission (DG XI) as host for the IMPEL Secretariat (1997).[9]

However, lack of hostility, a kind of familiarity, and contact on a (partly formalized) regular basis do not seem sufficient to conclude that the Commission and the national regulatory agencies consider themselves as part of the same community, that they have developed a common 'logic of appropriateness', a 'we'. The strongest companionship seems in fact to have developed among the national experts. The members emphasize that they have common tasks and share the same practical experiences back home, while the representatives from the Commission, on the other hand, know the field but are 'not technicians on the floor like us'.[10] It can thus be argued that the national experts' professional affiliation in their home countries is sustained and reassessed through their contact and discussions with colleagues in the transnational group.

It is also worth noting that the national experts have more contact with each other than with the Commission. They exchange e-mails and speak on the phone on a weekly and sometimes daily basis, whereas contact with the Commission is more typically on a monthly basis. Thus, it is possible to argue that the common professional background and high degree of contact between the experts create a sort of common identity that reaches deeper than the companionship with the institutions at the European level. According to one of the experts:

> The Commission has become more active ... The Parliament has actually also paid more attention to the network lately. Their view is that the network should be doing more, function more like a police force, discover and report infringements ... be more confronting and challenging.[11] That is not our style. And the member states wouldn't like it either.

> The Commission looks for procedures and partners [that] will help to improve its performance and bring it closer to the citizen.
>
> (Kohler-Koch 1996a: 361)

Having examined the *identity* dimension of the relationship between the different actors in the network, we now turn to the question of *authority*. To what extent does the Commission steer the work of the national experts? We have seen that the Commission is formally an equal member of the IMPEL network; it is clear, however, that the Commission has certain resources that make it something more than an equal partner, first and foremost money. The network operates to a large extent through different projects with the Commission as its main economic contributor, and through this funding the Commission can influence which projects are realized. The Commission does not dictate what is to be done, but the money ties make it difficult for the national experts to initiate different projects without the Commission's acceptance. According to the Commission representative: 'we have great interest to benefit from IMPEL projects and it is thus important to pay attention that priority areas for IMPEL and the Commission correspond to each other to the extent possible'.

Second, the Commission has knowledge and expertise, resources that are less visible but no less influential. The Commission people know the content of the relevant legal acts, they know the institutional history of IMPEL and they have an overview of the organization. In addition, they are housing the IMPEL Secretariat, the latter functioning as an important connecting link, bringing the experts closer to the Commission and vice versa. According to the representative from the Commission: 'the secretariat provides the network with information stemming from the Commission and liaises with the Commission.'

The European Commission functions, therefore, not only as an actor with certain knowledge and expertise, but also as a facilitator and co-ordinator of the network. The informants point to the fact that the recent expansion has resulted in a larger and less informal organization where the Commission's overview and expertise are needed to an even greater extent.

It is worth noting that it is the experts in the new member states who are the most enthusiastic about the Commission's knowledge and expertise. They focus on the help and encouragement the Commission has provided to get them on board in this collaboration, and stress that the Commission's strong involvement in the network gives the network prestige and more influence in the outside world. Some of the national experts from the old member countries, however, are more sensitive to the active role of the Commission; they are aware that it can become problematic if the relationship gets too close and the Commission gains too much control. Some of the experts referred to a recent incident at a plenary meeting where the Commission proposed two projects that would have taken up almost the entire budget, and where the national experts made the Commission withdraw its proposals. According to one of the experts, 'We drew a line in that case.'[12]

In conclusion, the European Commission has worked itself into the network and become an influential member of the IMPEL family; according to one of the experts, it has taken the role of 'the father of the family'. It steers the direction of the network's projects not only by its funding, but also through its expertise and knowledge and role as coordinator. Hence, if we are to describe the relationship between the Commission and the national agencies, we can point to two important if partly contradictory dimensions that define it: familiarity and partnership on the one hand, and use of authority on the other. The familiarity and partnership dimension appears however the slightly weaker of the two, as the Commission's influence and position in the network are linked to its resources and use of authority rather than to a common identity among the actors across the two levels of governance. In addition, it should be noted that an element of conflict also exists in this relationship, with some of the experts expressing mistrust and a degree of irritation in relation to the active role of the Commission.[13]

What about the national ministries? What role do they play? Are they active or passive players in this cooperation? The role of the national ministries in the IMPEL network varies to some extent between the different countries, and it is therefore difficult to draw any general conclusions. In Finland for instance, the ministry is strongly involved; the ministry of environment is eager to gain all relevant information and participates in the plenary meetings as well as in the concrete projects involving Finland. An example of the opposite is Norway,[14] where the ministry of environment participated in a couple of the initial plenary meetings, only to conclude that the work was of too technical a nature to warrant its involvement. In most countries, however, the ministries are kept informed but are not directly involved in the practical, daily work of the network.[15] One of the national experts further mentioned that the Germans occasionally sent 'politician-types' from the federal government to join the project groups, leaving the impression that 'these people were probably there to control us and did not fit in'. Though the general picture is, then, that the regulatory agencies 'run the business', we should nonetheless be aware of the differences between countries regarding involvement at the ministerial level in the work of IMPEL, and that not all potential voices have been heard in this study. Examining and explaining the differences between the countries is outside the scope of this chapter, and to be followed-up in further studies.

It does not seem feasible to provide any categorical answers to the questions posed in the introduction. There is indeed a strong link between the national regulatory agencies and the European Commission, and it is clear that the intergovernmental ideal, where 'street-level' implementation of Community law is seen as a pure national domain, is not an accurate description. We have seen that the European Commission is heavily involved in the actual functioning of the network, it possesses important resources, and seeks to steer the work of the network in certain directions as a tool to fulfil certain goals. Thus, it may be difficult to portray the national regulatory agencies in IMPEL as solely national agents. They could be said to be 'double-hatted' in the sense that the IMPEL aspect of their work is influenced by the Commission, while the rest is devoted to the ordinary business of the national regulatory agency.[16]

On the other hand, however, we have seen that the involvement of the different ministries in the IMPEL network varies among member states, and we lack extensive information about how they conceive of and react to the situation. We need therefore to explore further the relationship between the different ministries and the national regulatory agencies before drawing any clear conclusions about the degree of leeway the regulatory agencies actually enjoy in a network like IMPEL.

Balancing efficiency and accountability

The issue of balancing efficiency and democracy has received increased attention in recent literature discussing multilevel governance and networks in Europe (see, for example, Dehousse 2002; Kohler-Koch 2002; Sørensen and Torfing 2004). One of the key issues is the balance between securing effective problem-solving capacity and maintaining legitimate administrative structures subject to political control. The first type of concern may be linked to the concept of 'output democracy' where the focus is on the superior performance of the agency, relative to the result that would be likely if elected politicians were to perform the functions themselves (Thatcher and Stone Sweet 2001). In the case of IMPEL, we have seen that the network clearly contributes to securing a more effective implementation of the legal acts on the ground and contributes to enhancing a harmonized internal market in the field of environmental policy. This might be even more salient if policy-making were included in the scope of the network, as the laws might become more 'enforceable' and in consequence easier to implement for the technicians on the ground. The informants are positive about such a development, and consider it a necessary advance. In the words of one of the experts, 'we have so many practical problems with the directives, so it is necessary that we have a word to say when the laws are in process'. Hence, a network such as IMPEL may be a workable solution both for the Commission and the member states to the problem of how to secure uniform implementation without transferring more direct power from the national to the supranational level. Such an arrangement can be viewed through 'intergovernmental lenses'; in other words, as an arrangement securing an important political goal for the member states, that of harmonizing the Internal Market.

However, we have also seen that the national experts in the regulatory agencies have to alternate between different principals, and it can be argued that such a 'double-hatted' role may blur the relationship between different actors, making it difficult to distinguish the real owners of competencies and responsibilities. In Wessels and Rometch's words (1996: 365): ' "Fusion" becomes also "confusion" since we are increasingly less able to make individual institutions and persons accountable for their action.' In this respect, it is possible to argue that the IMPEL network challenges traditional notions of the functioning of national administrations and in so doing also challenges the notion of democratic governance.[17] In relation to agencies at the European level, there is growing awareness in the EU of the need to ensure the autonomy of experts while at the same time securing political and legal control through increased transparency, codes of conduct and principles of good administration (Dehousse 2002; Sverdrup 2003b).[18] In my opinion, this awareness may also be expressed in relation to the role of national regulatory agencies on the European scene.

Conclusion (and a starting point)

Organizations direct and redirect patterns of conflict by adhering to different principles of specialization (Egeberg 2003a). By weakening the principle of territorial organization in a political entity by imposing smaller functional entities as the main building blocks, the focus of conflict may be shifted from territorial lines and towards other lines of conflict. Consequently, it may be argued that a harmonized implementation of EU policy in its member states that is based on organizing administrative policy across territorial lines would be a more far-reaching transformation of the EU as a political system than harmonization due to member state adherence to EU-level legislation. Sverdrup (2003b: 17) puts it this way: 'These developments challenge the traditional principle of sovereignty that has been a fundamental building brick in the European administrative order. The principle of institutional independence is gradually being stretched and it is gradually being replaced by an idea of administrative interdependence.'

As stated earlier, this study is tentative and exploratory, and my remarks have been restricted to one particular area, one network. The purpose of the study has been to pinpoint future research efforts rather than offer any clear answers. We have some indications and a notion of a puzzle to be examined further: it would for instance be interesting to dig deeper into the relationship between the national ministries and the regulatory agencies in a European context. Why do states differ in relation to the national ministries' involvement? How do national ministries react to and perceive the situation?[19]

I would also like to explore further different mechanisms explaining the dynamics between the various actors at their respective levels; it would be interesting for example to examine more thoroughly the concepts of 'partnership' and 'authority' that have been pointed out in this analysis. Are these concepts useful for understanding the cooperation between national regulatory agencies and the European Commission? A relevant question is whether we find the same type of relationship between the European Commission and national regulatory agencies in all types of networks. One possibility would be to compare the first network of pollution authorities with one dealing with matters where national interests are more salient, for instance a network of agencies in the energy sector. Does the European Commission have the same grip on the agencies when there is more at stake for the member states? Is the familiarity dimension equally strong? If we found the same pattern in this latter case, it would serve as indication of the robustness of the mechanisms involved. Hence, the IMPEL network is a stepping-stone, hopefully a useful and fruitful stepping-stone, which will contribute to our understanding of the dynamics between different institutions in the European Community.

Notes

1. Speech by Romano Prodi to the European Parliament, 15 February 2000.
2. See 'Externalization of the Management of Community Programmes – including presentation of a framework regulation for a new type of executive agency' (COM (2000) 788 final).
3. Agencies at the European level (for example the European Environmental Agency) have not been granted the needed authority to enforce Community acts at the national level and function mainly as information-gathering institutions (Majone 2000; Kreher 1997).
4. There is a vast diversity of institutionalist literature. This diversity may, according to Checkel (1998), be divided into three branches: rational choice institutionalism, historical institutionalism, and sociological institutionalism. As one moves from rational choice to sociological institutionalism, the effects of institutions change. For rational choice, the focus is on behaviour, instrumental self-interest and strategies; sociologists, on the other hand, emphasize the prescriptive and legitimizing role of institutions. Underlying these distinctions are two radically different logics of action. Rational choice scholars posit a model of human action based on utility maximization. Interests are given a priori and exogenously. Structures and institutions constrain the choices and behaviour of pre-existing agents who operate under a logic of consequences. Sociological institutionalists favour a different model where utility maximization is replaced by rule-governed action, and where logics of appropriateness, derived from social norms, prevail (ibid.: 4).
5. The literature I draw upon in this respect falls mainly under the category 'new institutionalism'. As an approach to political science it is 'new' in the sense that it is not identical to the old institutional interest in politics in

which attention was almost exclusively paid to the formal aspects of decision-making and this mostly in a descriptive way. The difference between 'old' and 'new' is then, that the new institutionalism not only points at the importance of rules and traditions in decision-making processes, but also the role of routinization and socialization in these (Kerremans 1996: 3).

6. There are several contending organizing principles within the European Commission and the Council of Ministers. Within the Commission a geographical principle runs parallel to the sectorial principle, while a sectorial principle of organization is present within the Council, supplementing the area principle. I will argue, however, that the dominating and uppermost principles are mentioned above.

7. Cf. the IMPEL Annual Work programme at IMPEL's homepage: http://europa.eu.int/comm/environment/impel/workprog.htm#multiannual.

8. I wanted to include the Nordic countries, some of the new member countries and the 'major' EU members: the UK, France and Germany. I also wanted to include a representative from the southern part of Europe and the Benelux countries. My informants represent therefore the following countries: Denmark, Finland, Sweden, Lithuania, Slovenia, the Czech Republic, the United Kingdom, Germany, the Netherlands, Greece, France and Norway.

9. It is interesting to note the 'intergovernmental' elements built into these organizational arrangements, such as (the) *co-chairing* with the current Presidency (in practice the member from the country holding the Presidency) and the seconded *national expert* working in the Secretariat. These intergovernmental elements may serve as an illustration of the aim to balance different concerns (for example 'national' and 'European') in the European institutional architecture.

10. The informants were promised anonymity before answering the questions, consequently all quotations lack direct references.

11. IMPEL is not directly involved with the European Parliament, however IMPEL reports are occasionally sent to the EP for discussion (Schout and Claessens 1999).

12. One of the experts in one of the old member states is concerned that the Commission goes too far in collecting specific information about implementation gaps in the different countries. He pointed to the possibility that the Commission may use this information as a basis for infringement procedures.

13. A member of the network expressed her view on the role of the Commission in this way: 'La Commission a tendance à devenir plus dirigiste, et être moins respectueuse des choix et décisions des membres d'IMPEL, elle essaie de plus en plus souvent d'imposer ses vues et ses objectifs propres.'

14. Norway is not a member of the EU, but participates in the IMPEL network (and several other EU forums) through the EEA (European Economic Area) agreement.

15. In some of the countries, the ministry is formally in charge, but an employee in the relevant agency is the actual coordinator at the national level. In Germany, the national coordinator is actually situated in the ministry.

16. The national experts devote in general approximately one-third of their time to the IMPEL network and the rest to their ordinary work for the agency.

17. The fundamental political concept of 'democracy' is of course multi-faceted and may be understood and interpreted within different theoretical

frameworks. It is not possible within the limits of this chapter to do justice to this political concept; my aim here, however, is primarily to point to the fact that an arrangement such as IMPEL may be understood and considered in different ways, dependent on the student's 'glasses'.

18. This is explicitly outlined in COM (2002) 718 final: Communication from the Commission. The operating framework for the Regulatory Agencies.

19. See the report from the Swedish Agency for Public Management (Statskontoret 2003: 29) regarding an increased need for further coordination of the work of the national regulatory agencies in Europe: www.statskontoret.se.

9

The European Commission and the Integration of Food Safety Policies across Levels

Trygve Ugland and Frode Veggeland

Introduction

Regulation of food safety has a long and troubled history in the European Union (EU). However, a fragmented and restricted framework of actions has, over time, been replaced by a more comprehensive and integrated approach to food safety at the EU level (Ugland and Veggeland 2004, 2006). This reorientation reflects two interrelated developments. First, despite its cross-cutting nature and its obvious links to agriculture, consumer affairs, the internal market, external trade, public health, and other sectors, food safety has increasingly been recognized as an independent subject area.[1] Second, food safety has gone from being the sole responsibility of the member states to being an area of shared responsibility, characterized by cooperative arrangements between national administrations and the EU. These two developments reveal an increased status of food safety at the EU level vis-à-vis both other subject areas and the member states.

According to the General Food Law of 2002, EU food safety policy is based on an integrated policy approach (European Communities 2002). Policy integration can be defined in terms of consistency, interdependence and structural connectedness (Ugland 2003), and food safety policies are integrated to the extent that they are coherent and interlinked with the objective of ensuring safe food, and in as much as this objective penetrates all relevant policy sectors and all levels of government. This chapter takes an in-depth look at the EU project of establishing an integrated approach to food safety across different levels. Towards this aim, we illustrate how new multilevel administrative relationships have emerged and how they have profoundly changed the way food safety is regulated. Particular attention will be paid to the role of the European

Commission, which has gradually been assigned increased competences and more resources in order to ensure safe food for Europeans. The European Commission is involved in each phase of food safety regulation from the proposing, drafting, making and implementation of policy, to international representation. This chapter argues that this development is a product of explicit institutional interests on behalf of the European Commission, as well as of specific organizational and institutional features present at different points in the history of the EU. It will be shown how the European Commission's increasing involvement in the area of food safety has been institutionalized through a number of small steps, as well as through several big leaps related to the emergence of major transnational food crises that have put the health of European consumers at risk during the past decades.

We highlight three main changes that have occurred in the *modus operandi* in the area of food safety in the EU over the last decade. First, cooperative arrangements between the European Commission and national administrations have increasingly been developed in connection with the drafting of policy proposals. This can be identified in the work of the expert committees[2] under the European Commission, in comitology committees such as the standing committees, and through EU-level 'agencification' represented by the establishment of the European Food Safety Authority (EFSA). Second, cooperative arrangements between the European Commission and national administrative agencies have also become more prevalent in connection with the implementation of EU food law. Here, the DG Health and Consumer Protection in general, and the Food and Veterinary Office (FVO) in particular, play important roles. Third, the European Commission plays an increasingly active role as a representative of the whole EU when dealing with food safety matters in international forums such as the World Trade Organization (WTO) or in the United Nations food standards body, Codex Alimentarius Commission.

In addressing these issues, the chapter will proceed as follows. The next section looks at the status of food safety, and the integration of food safety objectives across the EU viewed as a multilevel entity. The mixture of intergovernmental and supranational features is complex when it comes to food safety, and the three types of cooperative arrangements between national administrations and the EU level mentioned above will be presented in greater detail here. The European Commission's participation in the Codex is considered to be an apposite illustration of the multilevel relationships between the European Commission and the national administrations of the member states; this case will be given particular attention. The following section discusses why the networked administrative system of food safety regulations has emerged in the EU. We also discuss how these multilevel administrative relationships have changed the roles of the European Commission and ultimately the European Union itself. It will be argued here that the European Commission has enhanced its autonomy vis-à-vis national governments over time, and thereby increased its potential to act independently as an executive in the area of food safety in the EU. Thus, clear indications of the emergence of a genuine multilevel Union administration, characterized by policy networks operating across different administrative levels, can be identified in this area of public policy (Egeberg, Chapter 1).[3]

Food safety policy integration in the EU

The food sector plays a significant role in the European economy. The agri-food processing industry is the biggest in the world, and it is among the largest industrial employers in the EU. However, due to a series of crises concerning human food and animal feed, food safety has become a major concern for consumers, industries and national governments. The spread of 'mad cow' disease (Bovine Spongiform Encephalopathy – BSE) and its onward transmission to people through consumption of beef, and the contamination of animal feed by dioxin have received much attention. These crises stimulated comprehensive reforms of the established design and application of food legislation in most European countries, as well as at the EU level.

The first EU Food Directive concerned colours in foodstuffs and was adopted by the Council in 1962 (O'Rourke 1998). For many years the EU approach to food legislation was based on the objective of ensuring free movement of foodstuffs throughout the common market. During this period, food policy was dominated by the economic objectives related to the Common Agricultural Policy (CAP). Food safety and health protection were given less attention, as these areas fell under the competence of the member states. The process of developing food safety legislation at the EU level was thus slow and fragmented, and it was characterized by different national traditions of member states (O'Rourke 1998). Furthermore, a coherent and coordinated approach to food legislation was undermined by the fact that different sector units of the European Commission were responsible for managing different food policies.

Ambitions to establish a more integrated food safety policy framework at the EU level were expressed in connection with the single market initiative. However, the responsibility for managing food safety and public health policies remained dispersed across several different administrative units in the European Commission; DG III (Industry), DG V (Social Affairs) and DG VI (Agriculture) were the most important. This fragmented approach to food safety was, however, challenged immediately after the United Kingdom announced a probable link between BSE and human health in March 1996. The announcement was followed by a massive critique of the European Commission's handling of the BSE problem since the mid-1980s (European Parliament 1997).

The EU has undertaken comprehensive reforms in their approach to food safety over the last decade (Vos 2000; Skogstad 2001). As this chapter will illustrate, the European Commission has been a central actor in all stages of this reform process from the proposing, drafting, making and implementation of new food safety regulations at the EU level, to the external representation of this new approach to food safety in international forums. The White Paper that was published by the European Commission in 2000 constitutes an important starting point for the EU project of establishing a consistent, interdependent, and structurally connected approach to food safety within the European Commission itself, and also across different levels of government (Ugland and Veggeland 2004, 2006). The stated objective is to organize the food safety area in a more 'coordinated and integrated manner' (European Commission 2000a). Towards this aim, the Commission proposed the establishment of an independent European Food Safety Authority at the EU level which would be responsible for providing independent scientific advice on all aspects relating to food safety; improved operation of rapid alert systems and communication of risks; an improved legislative framework covering all aspects of food products 'from farm to table'; greater harmonization of national control systems; and an improved dialogue with consumers and other stakeholders.

The proposals from the European Commission were followed up in 2002 through the adoption of the General Food Law (European Communities 2002). The General Food Law formally established the European Food Safety Authority (EFSA). EFSA replaced the eight existing scientific committees and reinforced the rapid alert system for human food and animal feed. Furthermore, the comitology system was reformed; a new Standing Committee on the Food Chain and Animal Health was set up to replace the Standing Committee on Foodstuffs, the Standing Veterinary Committee and the Standing Committee on Animal Nutrition. It also took over the Standing Committee on Plant Health's responsibility for plant protection products and pesticide residues. This particular reform was implemented with the aim of creating a more structurally connected approach to food safety. In addition, the European Commission was granted special powers, allowing it to take emergency action when the member states themselves were considered to be unable to contain a serious risk to human or animal health.

This rapid development may seem puzzling to many observers. The EU competencies in public health are less developed than those in other areas (Holland and Mossialos 1999). Under the principle of subsidiarity and given the limitations of the treaties, the development of public health policies is primarily the responsibility of the member states. Despite this, this short historical background illustrates how food safety, a key domain of public health, has gained increased status over the last decade. This will be further illustrated through a detailed analysis of the central role that the European Commission has been assigned in order to ensure safe food for Europeans.

The European Commission and the drafting of food safety regulations

Cooperative arrangements between the European Commission and national administrations have increasingly been developed in connection with the drafting of food safety policy proposals. This can be identified in comitology committees, such as the former Standing Committee on Foodstuffs and the newly established Standing Committee on the Food Chain and Animal Health; in the work of expert committees under the European Commission, which are often set up on an ad hoc basis to deal with particular aspects of food legislation; through EU-level 'agencification' represented by the establishment of EFSA; and through cooperation between the European Commission's food inspection service and national food inspection bodies.

A Networked Committee System.   The foodstuffs sector is a field in which the committee systems have been a forerunner to other policy fields (Joerges and Neyer 1997: 610). Hence, the Standing Committee on Foodstuffs was established as early as 1969 and the Scientific Committee for Food was established in 1974. The EU's institutional regulatory framework in the foodstuffs sector is thus well established and advanced. At the core of this framework is the establishment of cooperative links between member state administrations, formally independent scientists and European Commission officials.

A closer look at the role of the expert committees under the European Commission and the comitology committees reflects a networked administrative system dealing with food safety regulations (Trondal and Veggeland

2003). Thus, in the food safety area, the committee system highlights the development of an extensive policy network involving actors from a number of different food safety bodies from member states as well as from EU institutions.

Expert committees are chaired by European Commission officials and consist of national officials from EU member states, as well as officials from EFTA countries participating in the EEA Agreement. The work of the expert committees is an important part of the policy preparation phase of the EU's work on food policies, that is the phase when the European Commission prepares proposals for new food legislation and, thus, has a need for technical expertise. Studies have shown that participants in expert food committees take part by virtue both of their role as national representatives and their role as technical experts (Trondal and Veggeland 2003). This is further underlined by the fact that national officials in these committees normally come from specialized ministerial food policy units or food agencies, typically health and veterinary units and food inspection bodies. In this preparatory phase, the European Commission has a tradition of consulting independent experts, including members of the Scientific Committee for Food (now integrated into EFSA's Scientific Committee and Panels). Originally, the members of the Scientific Committee for Food were appointed by national governments, even though they were supposed to represent their disciplines rather than national interests (Joerges and Neyer 1997: 615). However, this was changed by the reforms that followed the BSE crisis.

Today the members of EFSA's Scientific Committee and Panels are appointed on the basis of their scientific expertise following an open call for expressions of interest, and they come from all over Europe, even in some cases from beyond Europe. These scientific experts nevertheless participate in the same network of food safety experts within which national delegates from EU member states are also involved. A practical illustration of this participation will be presented below.

The standing committees of the EU (comitology committees) are also chaired by European Commission officials. The Standing Committee on Foodstuffs has played an active part in the EU's food regulation for a long time, and is an important meeting place for officials from the European Commission and member state administrations. The committee was set up as a regulatory committee, which means that if the European Commission wishes to adopt measures 'which are not in accordance with the committee's opinion, or in the absence of an opinion, it must without delay submit to the Council a proposal of the measures to be adopted'

(Vos 1999: 25). If the Council has not acted on the European Commission proposals within three months, the European Commission can then adopt the proposed measures. The committee has been important for the European Commission in getting support and assistance from member states in drafting proposals, as well as for the member states to be able to control the European Commission. It is also important to note that many of the people who participate in expert committees also participate in the meetings of the standing committee. Sometimes an expert committee can even transform itself to a standing committee by evoking the regulatory committee procedures and can subsequently put a proposal to a vote. However, compared to Council and comitology participation, those attending European Commission expert committees in the food sector are considerably less subject to being coordinated and mandated by foreign ministries or other central authorities (Trondal and Veggeland: 2003).

The comitology procedure of 1987, which was adopted in connection with the internal market programme, ensured that member states could maintain control over the European Commission, especially with regard to implementation (Vos 1999). However, the Single European Act of 1987 also introduced qualified majority voting under which the Standing Committee on Foodstuffs operated. The European Commission can thus push through its proposals by taking them to a vote. Furthermore, the European Commission can place great demands on the technical expertise of the member states' delegations. These demands can be difficult to fulfil, thus enhancing the European Commission's influence. The mandate of the successor to the Standing Committee on Foodstuffs, the Standing Committee on the Food Chain and Animal Health, covers the entire food supply chain. It is supposed to assist the European Commission in the development of food safety measures and operates principally under the same procedures as the Standing Committee on Foodstuffs.

The expert committees and standing committees under the European Commission, as well as the working groups under the Council, have contributed to the establishment of a network between European Commission officials and officials from national administrations involved in the preparation and drafting of food policy proposals. Thus, the officials have frequent contact in the sessions of the committee meetings as well as outside. Moreover, many delegates meet and consult with each other in other international food safety forums, such as the Codex Alimentarius Commission (see below). The committee system illustrates the development of a comprehensive European food policy and food safety network characterized by extensive coordination and consultation between the European Commission and national officials and technical experts.

The establishment of agencies at the EU level has been considered partly as a functional alternative to comitology (Dehousse 1997b), and although comitology still plays a crucial role, increasing 'agencification' can be identified in the food safety area. The European Commission is a key actor behind the establishment and the operation of these agencies. The objective of establishing an independent agency that could provide advice on food safety matters at the EU level was set out in the European Commission's White Paper of 2000. Two years later, EFSA was legally established through the adoption of the General Food Law.

The European Food Safety Authority.   In principle, EFSA operates independently of other Community institutions, but important links have been established with a vast number of EU-level and national institutions. EFSA has explicitly stated that it will seek to build scientific networks involving Community institutions, national food safety authorities and scientific institutions in and outside the EU as well as in international organizations (European Food Safety Authority 2005). EFSA is primarily committed to the task of providing scientific advice through risk assessments and communicating existing and emerging risks. It has no decision-making powers, but the risk assessments provide risk managers (consisting of EU institutions with political accountability, that is the European Commission, European Parliament, and Council) with a sound scientific basis for defining policy-driven legislative or regulatory measures required to ensure a high level of consumer protection with regard to food safety. Risk assessment has traditionally been an area of policy in which national sentiments are strong, and EFSA is also required to establish cooperative networks with similar bodies in the member states. In this way, EFSA contributes to the coordination and integration of food safety policies across different levels.

EFSA's many close relations with the European Commission constitute a key aspect of the new administrative system of food safety regulations that has emerged in the EU. First of all, the European Commission and EFSA work closely together in the area of risk assessment. However, this is not new. The former scientific committees, which were placed in the European Commission, also worked in close contact with European Commission officials in providing risk assessments. What is new, however, is that the risk assessment capacity at the EU level has been considerably strengthened through the establishment of EFSA. Second, although EFSA is funded entirely from the Community budget, the funding is based on a proposal from the European Commission. Third, EFSA is managed by an executive director, who in turn is answerable to a management board. The shortlist for the position of executive director is put together by the European Commission (European Communities 2002). Additionally, there is always one European Commission representative on the EFSA management board, while the remaining members are appointed by the Council in consultation with the European Parliament from a list drawn up by the European Commission. However, the board members are appointed on the basis of their individual expertise and competence and none of them represents any government, organization or sector. The organizational structure of EFSA nevertheless demonstrates that the European Commission is actively involved in managing risk assessment activities in general and in the functioning of EFSA in particular.

The EU member states have also retained some influence on EFSA activities, first and foremost through the Advisory Forum, which is EFSA's consultative body. The Advisory Forum is made up of representatives from each of the member states' national food agencies or other national authorities with similar responsibilities, and is chaired by the executive director. A representative of the European Commission participates with observer status in the meetings of the Forum. The establishment of the Forum illustrates the member states' efforts in seeking to monitor and control activities at the EU level. The tasks of the Forum include advising the executive director in general and advising on scientific matters, priorities and the work programme. The Forum also forges close links between EFSA and the 25 EU member states. The goal is to build strong collaborative networking between EFSA and the national food agencies and authorities working in the fields of risk assessment and communication. This forum also facilitates the sharing of information and collaboration between the national authorities themselves (European Food Safety Authority 2005).

All in all, EFSA can be seen as a response to the need for increased excellence, independence and transparency of scientific advice, and to the necessity of separating scientific advice from regulative activity. This new institution has more or less exclusive responsibility for performing risk assessments for EU institutions, and together with the European Commission, EFSA contributes significantly to food safety policy integration across levels in Europe and to the development of European food safety networks, which operate outside direct hierarchical control of national ministries.

The European Commission and the implementation of food safety regulations

The European Commission has also become increasingly involved in the process of implementing food safety regulations. This implies that the European Commission plays a more active role in monitoring and assisting national governments in the correct implementation of EU law. The DG Health and Consumer Protection in general, and the Food and Veterinary Office (FVO) in particular, play important roles in this respect. Furthermore, cooperative arrangements between the European Commission and national administrative agencies have also become more prevalent in connection with the implementation of EU food law.

As a guardian of the treaties, the European Commission is responsible for ensuring that food safety regulations are followed up in practice. In the area of food safety, the completion of the internal market accentuated the need for greater control with food products (Egan 2001). The two most important directives regarding food and veterinary controls were Council Directive 89/397/EEC of 14 June 1989 on the official control of foodstuffs and Council Directive 89/662/EEC of 11 December 1989 concerning veterinary checks in intra-Community trade with a view to the completion of the internal market. These directives regulated food and veterinary control and inspection in the member states, involved a harmonization of national controls, and arranged for coordinated inspection programmes at the Community level. Furthermore, the completion of the internal market involved both the removal of veterinary border controls between EU members and a strengthening of such controls towards third countries.

The European Commission was assigned a key role with regard to food control and inspection. In 1991 the Office of Veterinary and Phytosanitary Inspection and Control (OVPIC) was created within the Directorate General (DG) for Agriculture in the European Commission. OVPIC gained considerable inspection powers, and it was empowered to conduct inspections of food production and processing facilities in a range of areas. In addition, the EU enacted legislation giving the European Commission the responsibility to evaluate member states' general systems of food safety control (Kelemen 2004: 135). However, a limited number of staff and resources (only about 10–15 inspectors in the period 1990–94) restricted the scope of its activities (Chambers 1999: 104; Kelemen 2004: 136). In fact, it was estimated that 100 inspectors were necessary to carry out the tasks assigned to OVPIC (Chambers 1999: 104). Thus, OVPIC was not able to cover all areas that fell within its mandate and was forced to confine itself to meat safety. In 1993, the European Council decided to move OVPIC to Ireland. The formal responsibility for the office was, however, kept in DG Agriculture. According to Chambers (1999: 103), the decision had little to do with criteria of efficiency, good budgetary management or the operational capability of the inspectorate, but more with the 'pork-barrel' share-out of Community agencies between member states. The decision to transfer OVPIC to Ireland was perceived by the European Commission as posing considerable problems, mainly because the inspectors needed close contact with the member states' missions to the EU, which were, and still are, located in Brussels. The actual moving of the office was delayed when the BSE crisis hit Europe and the European Commission decided to create a new food and veterinary office.

The Commission was not satisfied with the performance of OVPIC, mainly because of the problems inherent in attracting sufficient resources and staffing. Thus, with the aim of strengthening the EU's food inspection service, the European Commission put forward a proposal to the Council on transforming OVPIC into an independent European agency with its own source of funding (Kelemen 2004: 136). However, the Council did not follow up on the proposal, and it seemed difficult to bring food safety regulation and control to the top of the EU agenda. This situation changed dramatically as a direct result of the BSE crisis.

In 1997, OVPIC was reformed into a new unit, the Food and Veterinary Office (FVO). FVO was then transferred from DG Agriculture to DG XXIV and moved to new locations in Ireland. DG XXIV was subsequently renamed DG Consumer Policy and Consumer Health Protection (today: DG SANCO or DG Health and Consumer Protection). Today, DG SANCO is responsible for managing the food inspection service of the EU, as well as for coordinating national food inspection programmes. The inspection service will check on compliance with the stricter EU requirements of food safety and quality and veterinary and plant health legislation that have been developed in recent years. The EU has also decided that food legislation, to a larger extent, should be issued as regulations instead of directives in order to avoid the problems of transposition of EU rules into national law. For instance, both the general food law of the EU, and the European Commission's proposal on official feed and food controls were issued as regulations (European Communities, 2002, 2004). As a result of these developments, national governments have less room for manoeuvre with regard to how EU rules should be implemented and enforced.

In the mid-1990s the European Commission introduced formal audit procedures in order to allow an assessment of the control systems operated by the competent national authorities. Today, it is the FVO that is responsible for evaluating member states' general systems for food inspection and control. The new approach to food safety also implies that closer and more coherent inspections will be performed vertically all along the food chain: 'from farm to fork'. Also, the FVO has grown significantly in size and has steadily expanded the scope of its activities and responsibilities vis-à-vis the member states since 1997. In particular, the number of European Commission food inspectors has increased substantially (Kelemen 2004).

Member states have fewer discretionary powers than before with regard to how their national food inspections are to be carried out. These powers may be even further reduced as a consequence of the adoption by the European Parliament and the Council of the European Commission's proposal from 2003 for a regulation on official feed and food controls (European Communities 2004). The proposal was a follow up to the European Commission White Paper on Food Safety of 2000. It was adopted in April 2004 with an application date of 1 January 2006, with the exception of the provisions on financing which will apply from 1 January 2007. The title of the regulation was amended before adoption to reflect its wide scope: 'Regulation (EC) No 882/2004 of the European Parliament and of the Council on official controls performed to ensure the verification of compliance with feed and food law, animal health and welfare rules'. The new regulation specifically focuses on enforcement measures and particularly on the imposition of sanctions at the national and Community level with regard to serious offences or negligence in following EU rules. It also contains new tools for the European Commission to enforce the implementation of Community feed and food law by the member states.

All in all, the European Commission through DG SANCO in general, and FVO in particular, is playing a central role in ensuring the implementation of EU food safety regulations in the member states. This process must be considered against the background of the completion of the internal market, the increased importance of defending Community interests in the international context, the BSE crisis, and the need for better coordination between different activities relevant to food safety in the European Commission and the different national food inspection systems responsible for enforcing EU rules. The FVO already plays an important role in this respect, which is, inter alia, reflected in the many inspection reports published on the European Commission's homepage (http://europa.eu.int/comm/food/fvo/).

The European Commission and the external representation of the EU's integrated approach to food safety[4]

The EU is a member of the WTO in its own right and is normally represented by the European Commission in WTO meetings. In addition, all EU member states are WTO members. Altogether the EU therefore makes up 26 WTO members. However, while the member states coordinate their positions in Brussels and Geneva, the European Commission *alone* speaks for the EU at almost all WTO meetings. Hence, at these meetings the member state delegates are normally confined to the role of observers. This is also the case for the meetings in which food safety issues are primarily discussed in the WTO, that is within the framework of the SPS Committee's meetings where the European Commission's DG SANCO leads the EU delegation.

The WTO SPS Agreement covers measures related to food safety, animal health and plant health and entered into force in 1995. WTO members can fulfil their obligations under this agreement by basing their national regulations on international standards (Veggeland and Borgen 2005). In this context, the SPS Agreement refers to three international standardization bodies: the OIE (animal health), IPPC (plant health) and Codex Alimentarius Commission (food safety). The agreement gives these standardization bodies a more significant role to play. This is particularly true for the Codex Alimentarius Commission, whose standards have been an issue in several WTO trade disputes (Veggeland and Borgen 2005). Since 1962, the Codex has been responsible for managing the Joint Food Standards Programme of the Food and Agriculture Organization of the United Nations (FAO) and the World Health Organization (WHO) (FAO/WHO 1999). Today, it is the single most important international reference point for developments associated with food safety standards. Thus, the Codex is an essential part of the international work on shaping national food safety policies.

In the EU, the importance of the Codex is illustrated by the references to Codex standards in adopted food directives and regulations. However, the role of the European Commission in the meetings of the Codex Alimentarius Commission was, until recently, quite different from its role in WTO meetings. Until 2003, the EU was not a member of Codex in its own right, even though the member states were all members. The European Commission nevertheless participated in Codex meetings with an observer status. Further, the European Commission and the member states coordinated their positions in Brussels prior to the meetings, and also arranged for ad hoc coordinating meetings to be held on the spot. The member state holding the EU Presidency spoke on behalf of the EU on matters covered by harmonized EU food law.

The European Commission worked for several years in order for the EU to be accepted as a member of Codex. The fact that the EU became a member of the FAO in 1991 (but not of the WHO) provided the legal entitlement to apply for membership of Codex. Further, EU member states were actually committed by treaty obligations to support an application for full membership in Codex. The European Commission used this to push for the EU to become a full member instead of simply maintaining observer status. The Council authorized the European Commission to negotiate conditions for such membership as early as 1993. However, the negotiations were halted for many years by disagreements between the European Commission and the member states on the roles and responsibilities of each and by scepticism towards EU membership among some Codex members, such as the United States. Nevertheless, after a vote in July 2003 of the Codex members, the EU was allowed by the Codex Commission to apply to become a full member (Codex Alimentarius Commission 2003).

In November 2003, the European Council formally decided that the European Commission should send a request for accession to Codex and adopted at the same time an arrangement between the European Commission and the Council regarding preparation for Codex meetings, statements, and exercising of voting rights (European Communities 2003). The EU is normally represented by the European Commission's DG SANCO when food safety issues are on the agenda in Codex. The European Commission speaks on behalf of the member states and exercises the voting rights on those matters covered by harmonized EU law. Furthermore, the Codex work involves an extensive system of coordination between the European Commission and the member states, which takes place in Commission meetings and Council meetings, as well as on the spot in the meetings of the many Codex committees (European Communities 2003; interviews).

Together with the other proposals put forward in the White Paper on Food Safety, full membership in Codex has been considered by the European Commission to be an important step towards strengthening the EU's competence in food safety matters.[5] Thus, in Codex meetings today the European Commission speaks on behalf of the EU. However, according to the Codex procedures, member states of a Regional Economic Integration Organization (such as the EU) are still free to take part in the discussions. When the new Codex procedures were adopted in 2003, this was an essential point both for the delegates of the EU member states and for several other national delegations in order to allow for a continued diversity of Codex debates. Nevertheless, in Codex discussions the delegates from the EU member states must be mindful of their responsibilities under the EU treaties (as was the case before 2003). Thus, the role of the European Commission in representing the EU in food safety matters has been strengthened while at the same time the need for coordination between the European Commission and the delegations from the member states has been upheld.

Even though the attendance of delegates other than food experts and food agency officials (such as diplomats and trade experts) has increased over the years, Codex is still primarily an arena for government officials with backgrounds from science, food safety agencies and primary industries (Veggeland and Borgen 2005). Officials with these backgrounds are well represented in the national delegations of the EU member states. Thus, Codex has become an important arena where officials from the European Commission (in particular DG SANCO) and experts from national food agencies and other governmental food safety units meet and coordinate positions on how to shape the international food safety agenda. However, these activities do not take place without friction. Food safety experts from member states' administrations have stressed the need to maintain their professional independence; hence they are wary of any attempts by the European Commission or even national ministries (for example foreign affairs ministries) to limit their freedom to put forward scientifically based views.[6] Thus, on the one hand, the development of coordinating arrangements between the European Commission and national food safety experts could undermine national governments' control of international activities which actually have a substantial impact on the development of food safety policies; while on the other hand, the strengthened role of the European Commission is also conceived by national food safety experts as a possible threat to their freedom to act as technical experts.

The EU's representation in both the WTO SPS Committee and, in particular, the Codex Alimentarius Commission, illustrates the development of yet another important aspect of what can be called the EU's multilevel Union administration in the food safety area. The EU's external representation in food safety matters is characterized by the European Commission's active role in collaboration with food safety experts from national administrations. Many of the same people who meet in EU committees and working groups also meet in other important international forums where food safety issues are discussed, thus extending the activities of the EU's food safety policy network to the global level.

The growing importance of the EU's food safety policy network does not in itself imply that the influence of national food safety agencies is increased at the expense of national ministries. However, the increased importance of the policy networks involving these agencies nevertheless creates opportunities for food safety experts who are interested in shaping European and global food safety agendas. One example illustrates this. A deputy director general of a national food administration in an EU member state has previously held the position of professor of toxicology (until 1990) and is an acknowledged food safety expert with a large number of publications in international scientific journals. He has long been active and participated in Codex work, the European Commission's Working Group on Scientific Cooperation (SCOOP), and in many FAO/WHO expert meetings on food safety and risk analysis and international programmes related to food contaminants. In 2003 he was elected chairperson of the FAO/WHO Codex Alimentarius Commission, and in 2005 he became the chair of EFSA's management board (European Food Safety Authority 2005). Accordingly, this person has occupied a number of different roles (and sometimes simultaneously) – scientific expert, national representative, representative of international bodies – in some of the most important arenas in which food safety matters are discussed.

Of course extensive international participation has always been an inherent part of being a scientific expert. However, this example illustrates how experts from national food agencies can play an important role in policy networks that have grown in importance in recent years, both at the EU level and at the global level. Furthermore, many food safety experts, like the one presented above, tend to hold different positions under different (formal or informal) 'principals' in these policy networks. Moreover, national ministries are not actively involved in many of these processes. Hence, the development of a multilevel Union administration in the food safety area, including the development of a food safety policy network, leads to a situation where national agencies increasingly play a 'double-hatted' role, which may subsequently undermine the influence of national ministries in this policy area. Thus, the traditional model of national hierarchical governance is challenged.

Towards a genuine multilevel Union administration in the food safety area?

In the EU, an advanced multilevel Union administration has developed in the food safety area. The treaty provisions in relation to food safety have considerably increased since the early 1990s. Thus, the European Commission has gained real competencies in several ways. Following the internal market programme the member states have delegated more authority to the EU level in food safety matters; thus, more responsibility is transferred to the European Commission with regard to initiating food law proposals, to monitoring the implementation of the EU's food law, and to representing the EU externally. These powers were further enhanced by the reforms that were implemented following the BSE crisis. The European Commission's capacity to act in food safety matters was also enhanced by the creation of a special DG for consumer and health protection with the responsibility for food safety policies, and by the strengthening of this DG, including FVO, through a considerable increase in staff and resources. The European Commission has thus increased both its room for manoeuvre and its capacity for acting independently of the member states.

The European Commission is a key player in the development towards a consistent, interdependent, and structurally connected food safety policy network both within and beyond Europe. In addition to the European Commission's officials from DG SANCO, the EU's food safety policy network involves food safety experts working in national food agencies and specialized food safety units, as well as independent scientific experts. The committees under the European Commission, EFSA, and international forums such as the Codex Alimentarius Commission, are all important meeting places for the participants in this network. Furthermore, following the completion of the internal market and the establishment of the WTO, this network is actually involved in important policy-shaping activities that have greater repercussions on formal policy decisions than before. Still, many of the activities normally take place without or with minor ministerial control. The same applies to food inspection activities involving cooperative arrangements between FVO and national food inspection agencies, that is the implementation and enforcement of EU rules.

Hence, an important aspect of the multilevel Union administration of food safety policies that has evolved in the EU is that national ministries are often partly bypassed by the European Commission and national food agencies in the policy preparation phase, the implementation phase and in the EU's external representation. However, member state governments have also retained several control mechanisms, as illustrated by the comitology procedures, member states' representation in EFSA's advisory board, and of course the ability of the Council to amend or reject the European Commission's proposals and to model mandates for the European Commission's external participation. Further, national governments have the option of inducing tighter control on its own representatives, for example, by modelling stricter mandates for national officials who attend meetings in EU committees and in other relevant international food safety bodies.

A mixed picture therefore emerges with regard to the integration of food safety policies in the EU. The European Commission has clearly strengthened its position vis-à-vis the member states and a multilevel administration with increased responsibilities has emerged. One aspect of this multilevel administration is that national food safety agencies, to an increasing extent, perform important food safety tasks on behalf of or in cooperation with the European Commission while at the same time serving national governments (double-hattedness). The member state governments are only partly circumvented in these processes as they have retained a potential for controlling important parts of the policy process. What all this amounts to are indications of the development of a new type of governance system in the food safety area where important tasks in relation to policy preparation, implementation, and external representation are handled by policy networks dominated by the European Commission and national food safety experts. Thus, harmonization of food safety policies at the EU level and a subsequent strengthening of the role of the European Commission have been followed by a more intense integration of food safety policies across several administrative levels in the EU. In particular, governmental food safety agencies in member states have become tightly linked to the EU level through cooperative arrangements and coordination systems with the European Commission.

The development of a Community food safety administration and the role of the European Commission as a key actor in this administration can be illustrated by the discussions on the precautionary principle. The European Commission referred to the precautionary principle in the White Paper on Food Safety in 2000 and subsequently issued a Communication on the principle the same year with the aim, inter alia, to 'establish a common understanding of the factors leading to recourse to the precautionary principle and its place in decision making, and to establish guidelines for its application based on reasoned and coherent principles' (European Commission 2000b: 9). In this Communication, the European Commission stressed that the precautionary principle is a general one that should apply among all member states and EU institutions as well as across different policy sectors.

DG SANCO has actively promoted the precautionary principle both internally in the EU and in meetings in the WTO and the Codex Alimentarius Commission (WTO 2000a, 2000b; Codex Alimentarius Commission 2001). Although the European Commission has not managed to convince all WTO and Codex members of the benefits of developing such a principle with general application, the European Commission has succeeded in convincing the EU member states of such benefits. Hence, as a follow-up to the Commission's Communication, a European Council resolution on the precautionary principle was adopted at the European Council Meeting in Nice on 7–9 December 2000 (European Council 2000). The precautionary principle was subsequently included as Article 7 of the General Food Law (European Communities 2002). A general principle on the understanding and application of precautionary measures, which is binding for all member states and provides guidance for the management of food safety measures across all administrative levels of the Community, has therefore been developed. This process illustrates the central role of the European Commission with regard to the shaping of food safety policies in the EU, as well as with regard to the representation of these policies externally. Moreover, by developing general principles that are applicable to all levels of a multi-level food safety framework, the EU is increasingly moving towards an integrated approach to food safety.

Notes

1. The official website of the European Union, EUROPA (http://europa.eu.int), contains a list of 32 EU activities. Each activity represents a subject area in which the EU manages programmes, organizes events or passes legislation. Food safety is included in this list as an independent subject area.
2. In this chapter we use 'expert committees' as a collective term for the working groups, working parties and expert groups under the European Commission where national officials are represented.
3. This comparative study draws on a wide variety of empirical sources. In addition to the documentary information, the study relies on qualitative interviews with European Commission officials working with food safety issues, as well as with national officials participating in EU veterinary and foodstuffs committees and in Codex meetings. The study further relies on personal observations made as a participant in four Codex meetings (Codex Committee on General Principles (CCGP) Meeting, Paris, April 2001; Codex Committee on Fish and Fishery Products Meeting, Aalesund, June 2002; Codex Commission Meeting, Rome, July 2003; and Codex Committee on Food Import and Export Certification and Inspection (CCFICS) Meeting, Brisbane, December 2003).

4. The section on the EU's involvement in WTO and Codex Alimentarius Commission draws on Veggeland and Borgen (2005), interviews with European Commission and member state officials, our own observations made at Codex meetings, and documents and minutes from WTO and Codex meetings.
5. Reports from the meeting in CCGP in April 2001 and the Commission meeting in July 2003 (see: http://www.codexalimentarius.net), and interviews with DG SANCO officials in 2000 and 2003.
6. Stated by several Codex delegates in interviews.

10
National Limits to Transnational Networking? The Case of the Danish IT and Telecom Agency

Gitte Hyttel Nørgård

Introduction

Administration policy has traditionally been linked to the nation-state as a symbol of its autonomy and sovereignty. However, an interesting development has taken place in line with the expansion and widening of the European project. Even though the legal influence of the EU on national administration policy remains limited, an evolving standardization of administration and implementation processes and practices across the member states can be observed (Olsen 2003; Sverdrup 2003b).

Studies show that EU institutions have developed an increased interest in administration and implementation activities over the last years (Sverdrup 2003b). The expansion of policy areas adopted at the EU level has caused a broadening of the tasks of EU institutions, especially those of the Commission. As a consequence, the need for convergent implementation practice has also grown. However, this development has not been matched by a transfer of administrative resources and competences to the EU level; on the contrary, nation-states have been remarkably unwilling to make such transfers, resulting in an overload of work at the EU level (Majone 2000).

Attempts to enhance the efficiency of Brussels have led to new institutional arrangements regarding the administrative tasks of the EU Commission. 'Agencification' at the EU level is an example of this development, whereby partly independent agencies assist the Commission in administrative matters without formally adding to its competences and manpower. Decentralizing some of the Commission's tasks to the national administrative level is another option supporting the idea of a 'Union administration', where (parts of) national bureaucracies are integrated in the EU administration. An example of this is the development of a networked administrative system, where semi-autonomous national regulatory authorities have a 'double-hatted' function in serving (i) the national government as part of the national bureaucracy and (ii) the EU Commission as part of the Union administration (Egeberg, Chapter 3; Kadelbach 2002: 175). Such systems build upon contemporary decentralization initiatives in many nation-states by which semi-autonomous authorities are delegated regulatory tasks from ministries. Arguably, the changing role distribution indicates a significant change in both EU and national implementation policies (Nørgård 2004). With national regulatory authorities directly linked to the EU level, the establishment of a multilevel Union administration becomes feasible.

In this chapter I will present developments in EU telecommunication policy based on a case study of the Danish IT and Telecom Agency (ITTA). The focus of the case study is the preparation and implementation of a New Regulatory Framework for Telecommunication in the EU. The purpose is twofold: first, to explore the extent to which a transnational networked administrative system might be able to incorporate parts of a state apparatus that has been seen as one of the most coordinated within the Union (Pedersen 2000); second, to explain and seek to understand the establishment of such a transnational system.

How to identify a networked administrative system

A network can be defined as a relatively stable, independent, non-hierarchical relationship between actors with shared interests in a policy field (Börzel 1998: 254). Arguably, the character and state of relations between these actors are of particular relevance; by analysing patterns of cooperation and conflict it is possible to shed light on actor relations at several levels. Crucial to the existence of a networked administrative system in the EU are inter-institutional patterns of conflict and cooperation cutting across traditional territorial lines. Thus, cleavages follow functional or institutional logics in addition to a territorial one.

In order to identify patterns of conflict and cooperation between the Danish ITTA and other actors, I will, first, look at the tasks of the ITTA in the preparation and implementation of the new regulatory package. To indicate the existence of a networked administrative system, the study must show that the regulatory agency has two masters – serving both the Ministry of Science and the Commission. Second, I will focus on the role, identity and interests of the ITTA when participating in different settings. Studies show that officials participating in transnational activities over time start to identify themselves to some extent with the transnational group (Egeberg 1999). Furthermore, studies indicate that officials often play multiple roles depending on institutional characteristics. In this study it will thus be of interest to explore whether actors from the ITTA evoke multiple roles, identities and interests. If the analysis shows a co-existence of national and European identities and interests, it will support the thesis of a networked administrative system linking the EU and national levels. Third, I will look at interaction between the IT and Telecom Agency and other actors, covering both vertical coordination within the national administration and horizontal coordination with sister agencies in other countries. Furthermore, contacts with supra-national institutions such as the Commission and Union Council will be studied. Changing patterns of interaction may reflect an increasing international cooperation in general and are not in themselves evidence of a networked administrative system. Thus, changing patterns of interaction must be seen in concordance with multiple roles, identities and interests in order to indicate the kind of development that we trace.

The following variables are expected to affect the emergence of a networked administrative system:

- *Institutional structure of the EU.*   An advanced division of labour and competences between the Commission, Council, Parliament and Court characterizes the institutional structure of the EU system. This differentiation fosters a complexity of behavioural patterns where each institution itself inspires different patterns of conflict and cooperation. Interaction between the actors is a source of multiple cleavages, either coinciding with or cutting across national boundaries.
- *Organizational structure in the national administration.*   A high degree of vertical specialization in the central administration provides ground for relatively autonomous agencies. Such agencies are characterized by discretion in decision-making, hence there is little subordination to their central ministry. Furthermore, physical distance between the agencies and ministries will emphasize their relative independence.

The study conducted is an exploratory case study. Using a variety of data sources such as semi-structured personal interviews, legal and official EU documents and national policy documents, the analysis draws on both primary and secondary sources.[1]

Theorizing the development of a networked administrative system

Several theoretical perspectives could be of relevance in explaining the emergence of a networked administrative system. The theoretical framework of this chapter draws on three perspectives with differing perceptions of the European-level political order. From an intergovernmental perspective, EU integration reflects the will of national leaders who are considered the dominant actors in the European policy process. Thus, member states act as coherent units led and coordinated by national governments (Moravscik 1998). In the EU arena, national governments act with pre-defined preferences formulated at the national level. Without any direct channel of representation, sub-national actors, as well as a variety of non-governmental actors, are deemed to go through their national governments to have their interests represented at the EU level. Following the intergovernmental approach, EU institutions are regarded as arenas for reducing transaction costs among nation-states. Without any independent role beyond the authority delegated to them by member states, EU institutions act as instruments of the national governments (Moravcsik 1993).

In a multilevel governance perspective, EU integration is characterized by interaction between multiple actors at multiple levels of governance, making integration a complex international as well as national phenomenon. The core argument of multilevel governance is that EU integration has led to a loss of competence for the nation-state, while the tasks and competences at the supra-national EU level and the sub-national, decentralized level have been strengthened (Marks et al. 1996). Integration has opened possibilities for sub-national actors to act directly in the EU arena, bypassing national governments (Jeffery 2000: 3). Without national governments serving as gatekeepers, sub-national actors may become partners in transnational networks. According to Jachtenfuchs (2001), it is the EU's fragmented institutional structure as well as the absence of a strong power centre that have given rise to the variety of actors and multiple channels of access. This environment works as a stimulus to the development of multilevel networks between actors.

The key assumption of the organizational perspective is that organizational structure influences the behaviour of actors. In a European integration context, this means that the organizational structure of EU institutions affects the behaviour of actors interacting within these institutions. As the EU institutions are characterized by various structures and organizational principles, a range of cleavages appear. The institutions may be structured in ways that either underpin or challenge a state-centric order (Egeberg 2004). For example, the Council is primarily organized according to territory, as are classic intergovernmental organizations such as the UN and OECD. In the various Council committees, actors of the member states represent first and foremost national interests. By contrast, the Commission is primarily organized according to non-territorial criteria, with actors representing sectional and functional interests in the different Directorates General (DGs). The division of work between EU institutions such as the Commission and the Council provides for inter-institutional conflicts and multiple contact points for national governments. In this process the Commission may add to the complexity by searching for 'partners' within national administrations.

In addition to the institutional architecture at the EU level, the national administrative structure is of relevance. The development of semi-autonomous regulatory authorities strengthens vertical specialization. Thus, regulatory authorities become more independent of national political leadership (Egeberg 2003a) and may have autonomy to serve both the national political system and the EU Commission in a 'double-hatted' manner. An 'unpacking' of institutions is necessary to expose the conditions for transformation of actors and political processes. A primary organization structure is the setting where actors spend most of their time and energy. National administrations typically constitute the primary structure of national officials. In a secondary structure, actors interact, but without the same amount of energy as in the primary structure. However, such a structure also widens the frame of reference by adding new agendas, obligations and participants (Egeberg 2004). A typical example of such a structure is the EU committee system.

Exploring the development of a networked administrative system

In order to understand the policy context in which the ITTA is operating, it is necessary to describe the recent legislative changes in the telecommunication sector known as the New Regulatory Framework. In 1999, the Commission reviewed the existing telecommunication legislation in the EU and initiated a set of directives to expand competition in the sector. On 7 March 2002, these directives were adopted by the EU Parliament and the Council and set to be implemented throughout the member states by 1 July 2003. The New Regulatory Framework contains four directives: the Framework Directive (2002/21/EF) sets the main principles for regulation of electronic communications in the EU and specifies the tasks of the national regulatory authorities, the Universal Service Directive (2002/22/EF) lays down the rights of consumers and the obligations of the industry, the purpose of the Access Directive (2002/19/EF) is to harmonize the rules of access and traffic between telecommunication suppliers in the EU, while the Authorization Directive (2002/20/EF) simplifies the rules of telecommunication licences. The New Regulatory Framework introduces several new decisions to the policy field, for example by transforming the procedures of regulation. Whereas a market share exceeding 25 per cent was previously considered an indicator of dominance, this is now to be assessed individually by regulatory authorities based on market analysis. If a dominant market position is found, the regulatory authorities are authorized to enforce conditions of competition. However, they are obliged to take into careful account the guidelines specified by the Commission (EU Commission 2002b).

Furthermore, the Framework introduces a notification procedure, whereby national regulatory authorities are obliged to notify other regulatory authorities as well as the Commission before implementing regulation. The feedback from these actors must be taken into account; formally, the Commission can veto an activity if it is thought to counter general Community objectives. Introduction of the notification procedure is obviously inspired by EU competition policy – a field which has been comprehensively reformed by decentralizing enforcement to national authorities and courts (Støle, Chapter 6).

The revision of regulatory procedures has significant consequences for national regulatory authorities. As these authorities are now in charge of market analysis, they are authorized to make decisions concerning market positions, obligations and remedies based on individual discretion. In several interviews it is emphasized that revision has increased the autonomy of the ITTA; at the same time, the framework has decreased opportunities for the Ministry of Science (MS) to lay down specific national rules (MS interview 25 February 2004; ITTA interview 25 February 2004). These observations support Dehousse in his arguments for a strengthening of *administrative* at the expense of *legislative* processes (2002: 220).

The IT and Telecom Agency and the Commission

In general, the New Framework has intensified cooperation between the ITTA and the Commission. Given its special veto right, the Commission acts not just as a central partner in EU telecommunication but also as a principal to national regulatory authorities. The New Framework has increased the national-level discretion of regulatory authorities yet subordinated them more directly to the Commission. Furthermore, the notification procedure gives the Commission a legal opportunity to interact in the implementation of policies.

As indicated by the pre-notification procedure, both formal and informal relations have expanded. The pre-notification procedure is an informal preparatory procedure, whereby national regulatory authorities present their notification drafts to the Commission. Thus, the latter's comments are taken into consideration before the formal notification is produced, reducing the risk of a veto. Following intensified cooperation with the Commission, a change of attitude has appeared in the ITTA; where the agency was previously reluctant to interact with the Commission – maintaining the exclusiveness of national affairs – the attitude is now more relaxed and characterized by interpersonal relations (ITTA interview 25 February 2004).

Interestingly, interaction between the Commission and regulatory agencies has been fairly limited in preparation of the New Framework. This distinguishes the case dealt with here from previous studies which have shown that the Commission is assisted by national expertise in preparation of legislative drafts (Egeberg et al., Chapter 5). When preparing the telecommunication framework, the Commission primarily made use of internal expertise and evaluations of previous legislation (ITTA interview 25 February 2004). However, the Commission has on several occasions consulted national regulatory authorities for feedback on legislative implementation. This has indirectly given regulatory authorities a chance to offer input to the framework preparations. An example of such input is the licence-free system, which was introduced in Denmark as early as 1996, thus giving the ITTA a chance to document its potential of impacting on Commission decision-making.

The IT and Telecom Agency and the Ministry of Science

As the ITTA has legal authority to act without instruction from the Ministry of Science, it can be defined as an independent authority. However, this independence only encompasses regulatory activities. In many areas of general administrative work the IT and Telecom Agency assists the ministry; furthermore, it acts as a central partner in the ministry's EU activities. As prescribed by the formal coordination system in Denmark, legislative drafts from the Commission are discussed in special committees with participants from the ITTA, the Ministry of Science, telecommunication companies and consumer representatives. Furthermore, Danish positions presented in Council negotiations are prepared in cooperation with the ITTA. As regards national transposition of EU directives,[2] the ITTA has played a crucial role. In sum, much preparatory work has been characterized by close interplay between the ITTA and the Ministry of Science.

This style of cooperation is carried to activities at the EU level as well. Admittedly, as national experts are often invited to assist national delegations in Council working groups, the presence of the ITTA in the Danish delegation is not extraordinary. The ministry is rarely expected to possess detailed technical knowledge; such negotiations are therefore often left to national expertise (MS interview 25 February 2004). However, the process of cooperation based on a common working document indicates that the ITTA is present not only when technical matters are negotiated, but throughout the entire negotiation process. According to informants in the ITTA, a closely knit delegation – with a combination of technical and political skills – gives strategic advantages; the Danish delegation is thus considered to have considerable influence in the Council working group (ITTA interview 25 February 2004). The Ministry of Science has also included the ITTA in the Communication Committee (CoCom) of national resort ministries. Thus, informants from both institutions can take for granted that they share the same interests on the international scene. This case study shows that the ITTA is capable of separating its roles as (i) part of its resort ministry in the Council delegation group, and (ii) as an independent authority in regulatory activities (ITTA interview, MS interview 25 February 2004).

ITTA's role as administrator of national legislation raises the question of inconsistency between two principals; with Kadelbach (2002) one may ask how a regulatory authority is to act if the national implementation of EU directives is not approved by the Commission. Informants from the Ministry of Science and the ITTA emphasize governmental responsibility for transposing EU directives into national legislation. The Commission will address the national government in matters of inconsistency. Following these arguments, national regulatory agencies are not in danger of being caught between two principals; as a working rule, they are to follow national legislation. However, examples indicate that these kinds of dilemmas have occurred. In the case of Finland, the Commission considered the implementation of directives unsatisfactory and addressed the regulatory authority directly in this matter (ITTA interviews 12 January 2004, 25 February 2004).

The IT and Telecom Agency and international cooperation and networks

The internationalization of the telecommunication sector is not solely the outcome of the development of the European Union; international cooperation has existed for decades. One example is the International Telecommunication Union, established as early as 1850. In 1997 the national regulatory authorities formed the Independent Regulators Group (IRG), a non-binding forum for exchange and debate on telecom practice.

The forum was established at the initiative of regulators, and the group has no formal role in the policy-making process. However, parallel to negotiations in the Council, the IRG group discussed and made several proposed amendments to the New Framework directives. According to informants in the ITTA, the IRG interaction provided qualified knowledge to the Council debate, clarifying a range of details (ITTA interview 25 February 2004). Interestingly, this indicates a certain influence from regulatory authorities on the decision-making process at the EU level, in spite of their lack of formal access.

Aside from traditional cooperation in the telecommunication sector, the Commission has been eager to create a common European approach to this field. In the revision of telecommunication legislation in 1997–99, the Commission took the initiative in establishing a European Regulatory Agency – receiving only moderate support from the member states. Instead, it was recommended that coordination and communication between national regulatory agencies should be enhanced; inspired by the IRG, the Commission proposed establishing a High Level Communication Group to manage these activities (EU Commission 2000). After some amendments from the EU Parliament (EU Parliament 2000), a decision was made to set up a European Regulators Group (ERG).

Interestingly, the proposal for a regulators' group in the EU has met with scepticism among national regulatory authorities. Certain countries in the IRG have been enthusiastic about such a group, perceiving that closer cooperation with the Commission would enhance the legitimacy of regulatory work. However, a majority has been resistant to the set-up of a new group, emphasizing the capacity of established groups such as the IRG/CEPT/ECTRA[3] to handle emerging tasks. According to informants in the ITTA, some countries fear a loss of independence to the Commission, and are not ready to give up the IRG for the new ERG. With the continued existence of IRG, an option to exit the ERG is still present (ITTA interview 26 February 2004).

Nevertheless, the ERG was set up as part of the New Framework with the purpose of promoting cooperation and coordination between national regulatory agencies in order to secure uniform employment of the directives (2002/21/EF). The ERG network is decidedly different from the working groups established under the Council. With the purpose of guiding and assisting the Commission in consolidating the internal market, the group has a common European focus, its members acting as regulators rather than national representatives.

Procedures of implementation and best practice (PIBs) are one of the ERG initiatives to increase harmonization. However, these procedures are of a non-binding character and function primarily as advice and recommendation. The Commission is not without influence in this work; if regulatory authorities do not succeed in formulating common procedures, it is authorized as principal to make recommendations. Furthermore, the ERG works to increase harmonization by deciding remedies; in cooperation with the Commission, the regulatory authorities specify obligations for a dominant market actor in a given situation. Again, the specifications are of a non-binding nature.

The composition of PIBs and the nature of available remedies illustrate a decreasing separation between legislation and implementation (Dehousse 2002). These activities are divided between the political objective of harmonization and the administrative principle of individual discretion. Harmonization can be strengthened by uniform guidelines for national regulatory activities; such guidelines, however, may wipe out the discretion of national administrations, leaving them with legislative processes instead of implementation. In the ERG this problem has caused some disagreement. While the Danish approach has been to make the procedures as non-binding as possible to avoid conflict with national legislation, the Dutch have attempted, conversely, to give the procedures legislative effect (ITTA Interview 26 February 2004).

Interestingly, the ERG has until now been characterized by a rather high degree of internal conflict. The ITTA has even questioned the concept of voting, as decisions are not binding. Definition of members has also been a matter of debate; the Commission refers to 'relevant national regulatory authorities', which in some countries also include national ministries (EU Commission 2002a). Petitions from ministries to participate in ERG have provoked serious opposition; according to informants in the ITTA, this has been of 'almost religious' significance to some authorities, with threats to boycott the ERG if ministries were admitted (ITTA interview 25 and 26 February 2004). This refusal to accept ministerial participation obviously questions the idea of a uniform national delegation at the EU level. However, the representation conflict has not been present in Denmark. The Ministry of Science has never wished to participate in the ERG – neither would the ITTA oppose its participation.

As indicated, the members of the ERG clearly have different expectations from network cooperation. A few examples serve to illustrate this. When the European Parliament addressed national governments for feedback on New Framework consequences, the Dutch and a few other regulatory authorities wanted to present their own statements as well. The Danish ITTA took strong opposition to this idea, seeing it as a way of bypassing national ministries. Moreover, the Dutch regulatory authority reacted promptly when a legislative issue was handed to the CoCom. As the Dutch ministry had not involved their regulatory authority in the work – as several other ministries, including the Danish, had done – the Dutch regulatory agency was without any influence in this setting. These examples illustrate the widely differing patterns of interaction between regulatory authority and ministry in the Netherlands and Denmark. An informant from the ITTA goes as far as arguing that the Dutch regulatory authority identifies more with other regulatory agencies than with its own ministry (ITTA interview 26 February 2004).

From interviews in the ITTA it is possible to identify both national and common European interests when the agency participates in ERG activities. However, it is obvious that national identity remains most important, confirming organizational studies of primary and secondary identities. An informant from the Ministry of Science emphasizes the legality aspect: as long as the ITTA acts according to the legislative framework, international inspiration is non-problematic (MS interview 25 February 2004). Several observations indicate that the traditional perception of national administrative officials often clashes with the demands they meet in international forums. Even though the ERG explicitly works to promote a common European mode of regulation, a glimpse of bad conscience is still discernible when informants from the ITTA describe their involvement in common problem-solving (ITTA interview 25 February 2004). Despite a change of context, the traditional definition of an official's obligation to serve national interests is still perceived as the relevant frame of reference.

On the whole, the New Framework has had considerable effect on international interaction in the telecommunication sector. The autonomy granted to regulatory agencies within the New Framework is matched by the notification procedure securing closer coordination and harmonization between national regulatory activities. Consequently, growing European engagement has expanded the European focus and orientation in the Danish ITTA and made international cooperation more binding (ITTA interview 25 February 2003).

The empirical evidence of a networked administrative system

The New Framework has strengthened the idea of an evolving Union administration by fostering systematic cooperation between national regulatory agencies and the Commission. Indeed, the ERG's work with remedies and PIBs has supported harmonization and enhanced the opportunity for common administrative practice across national boundaries. The ITTA's will to participate in this work is, however, conditioned by the possibility of implementing the ERG procedures within the existing Danish legislative framework. It is, consequently, more or less up to the other countries to adapt to Danish legislation for a common practice to be obtained. This intransigence on the part of the ITTA may modify the effect of harmonization.

Revision of the telecommunication sector has enhanced the regulatory competences of the Commission and consolidated its role as principal vis-à-vis national agencies. This has created a situation where regulatory authorities are accountable to two principals. However, being functionally independent, these authorities are capable of serving both the national administration and the Commission at the same time. In serving the Commission, the ITTA is not in danger of confronting the Ministry of Science, as cooperation with the Commission is related to an independent sphere of regulatory activities. This leads to the notion of the ITTA as being 'double-hatted'. Nevertheless, the argument of several principals can be questioned. In strictly legal terms the regulatory agencies are only responsible to national legislation emanating from the resort ministry. Where inconsistency occurs between EU directives and their implementation, the regulatory agency must follow national legislation and leave the Commission and national government to clarify the inconsistency.

The case study has shown the ITTA to be characterized by multiple roles and capable of separating these roles in different settings. In contexts where the Ministry of Science is the prominent actor – such as in preparatory work, Council working groups and CoCom – the ITTA acts as an integrated part of the ministry administration with a nation-based interest. In contrast, within the ERG, the agency participates as an independent regulatory agency cooperating with similar agencies and the Commission to solve regulatory matters in a common European context. Multiple identities seem conspicuously present within the ITTA, the study thus confirming previous accounts by Egeberg et al. (Chapter 5). We have also seen how dispositions of roles and interests vary considerably between regulatory agencies. For the Danish ITTA, national attachment is primary and European attachment secondary, whereas the opposite seems to be the case for the Dutch regulatory agency.

Certainly, patterns of interaction have changed for the ITTA. Relations with sister agencies in other member states as well as with the Commission have been strengthened, albeit not at the expense of cooperation at the national level; the Ministry of Science remains the most significant partner for the ITTA. Moreover, changes of interaction have resulted in a widening of the ITTA's relations and tasks. Arguably, neither the ITTA nor the Ministry of Science finds this change problematic. Given that their relationship is based on trust, neither seems to perceive or notice any effect on their internal relations. Testifying to these close relations, the ITTA has not used the new interaction patterns at EU level in any conscious attempt to bypass the ministry.

New patterns of communication may, nevertheless, profoundly disrupt the interaction between national actors. In countries characterized by inter-institutional conflict, Europeanized relations may be applied in order for such institutions to bypass each other. This seems to be the case in the Netherlands, where the regulatory agency is eager to make ERG cooperation as binding as possible while excluding the ministry from participation. Likewise, the ministry has excluded the agency from the Dutch delegation in the Council working group and CoCom. Evidently, changes in patterns of interaction at both the EU, national and sub-national levels accentuate a certain national disintegration. However, as this case study has shown, national disintegration does not necessarily replace national cooperation, as relations at the national and international levels may be complementary.

Explaining the development of a networked administrative system

In general, the intergovernmental perspective builds on a logic of territory, where conflict and cooperation follow a geographical pattern. From an intergovernmental point of view, the European project remains a bargaining arena for autonomous nation-states. Hence, fundamental transformation of the national and European political system is not an option. Furthermore, there is no room for the development of a networked administrative system where sub-national and EU actors interact directly. In this respect, the intergovernmental perspective does not account for the existence of different institutions with diverging interests and objectives within the confines of the state (Dehousse 1997a). From an intergovernmental point of view, EU integration is considered to strengthen national integration through a coordinated process at the national level, thereby disclaiming the possibility of national disintegration.

The empirical finding of 'double-hatted' regulatory authorities confronts this traditional idea of hierarchy as well as the concept of coherent nation-states. Furthermore, the Commission's appearance as a principal challenges the intergovernmental idea of EU institutions as neutral and controlled by the nation-states. From an institutional point of view, on the other hand, institutions are defined as 'living organisms' in constant evolution, progressively acquiring a life of their own by generating interests and preferences (March and Olsen 1989). A neo-functional perspective adds the notion that transfer of sovereignty from the nation-state to EU level promotes a spillover process, in which integration weakens nation-state control (Haas 1958/2004).

These empirical findings seem to lend credence to a multilevel governance approach, by which network replaces hierarchy as the governing frame of reference. Multiple points of access provide the opportunity for more or less institutionalized and structured cooperation between actors at EU and sub-national levels. From a multilevel governance perspective, direct interaction between the EU and sub-national levels does not replace but rather supplements inter-state relations. Thus, it is possible for sub-national actors to serve several principals, reflecting the concept of being 'double-hatted'. Following an organizational perspective, the ITTA's ability to perform in a 'double-hatted' manner and the Commission's role as principal can be explained by 'unpacking' the organizational structure in and between institutions. The vertical specialization between the ministry and the ITTA functions as a pre-condition for serving both the Ministry of Science and the Commission in a 'double-hatted' fashion.

Also, the existence of multiple roles, identities and interests challenges an intergovernmental perspective. In line with the unitary state concept, the intergovernmental perspective claims that preferences are formed at the national level, as national actors appear with predefined preferences and interests in the international arena. Focusing on formative decision-making processes, the intergovernmental perspective neglects the fact that EU integration covers several policy processes and involves multiple actors. Admittedly, the fact that national interests remain relevant to the ITTA in the ERG – the forum for independent regulators – seems to support the intergovernmental argument. However, as the ITTA is motivated by both national and European interests in the ERG, it may seem more relevant to emphasize the dual structure of interests and identities.

From an organizational perspective, structure affects not only tasks but also the development of values, norms and identities. Accordingly, the conception of primary and secondary structures becomes relevant. In line with this argument, the national environment is the primary structure for the ITTA as this is the setting where the agency expends most time and energy. Naturally, the agency will continue to be affected by the primary structure in international activities. The European identity and interest evolve as the ITTA participates in international activities in the ERG or the

IRG, which constitute the secondary structures. From an organizational perspective, these secondary structures supplement the primary structure, thus creating a dual basis for identity and interest.

The identification of multiple interests, identities and roles is, however, not enough to substantiate the existence of a networked administrative system, as the patterns of interaction disclose how and when these identities, interests and roles are put into action. From an organizational point of view, the interaction between national and EU levels follows the institutional structure at the EU level as national ministries are primarily involved in the Council structure, while the regulatory authorities interact with the Commission. The revision of telecom directives has decreased the national ministries' legislative influence and increased the administrative competences and discretion of regulatory authorities. Furthermore, the New Framework has increased the influence of the Commission and given the institution a legal opportunity to intervene in national regulatory activities. This direct interaction between the ITTA and the Commission illustrates the loss of a gatekeeper role for national governments. Thus, the intergovernmental idea of coherent and centralized nation-states is once again challenged by the empirical findings. The ERG can be described as a policy community, as the interaction has both a formal and informal character and is exclusive in its criteria for participation. The work in the group is guided by formal procedures and rules, but an informal practice of consensus-seeking characterizes the interaction as well. This illustrates that the group has to a certain extent become institutionalized (Selznick 1957).

Conclusion and reflections

This chapter has presented an exploratory case study of the Danish IT and Telecom Agency (ITTA). As the purpose of this study has been to identify possible signs of a networked administrative system, patterns of cooperation and conflict have been analysed. A primary observation is that the ITTA is 'double-hatted' in serving both the Commission and the national ministry; furthermore, the ITTA embodies multiple roles, identities and interests, and it has over time experienced a change in patterns of interaction. These observations support the notion of a networked administrative system. While the intergovernmental approach is a highly appreciated integration theory, it is not capable of explaining the existence of a networked administrative system; it is primarily its state-centric and one-dimensional concept of integration that disqualifies this approach as a relevant framework for explanation. The multilevel governance approach, on the other hand, brings to light a highly complex pattern of interaction across different levels of governance.

However, as the multilevel governance perspective may be seen primarily as a descriptive framework, the explanatory potential of the approach is limited. Thus, organizational theory supplements the multilevel governance approach with more comprehensive explanatory tools. Claiming that the structures and settings of organizations affect the behaviour of actors, the organizational perspective has proved to be a relevant explanatory framework. In this context, the development of a networked administrative system is related to the division of tasks and responsibilities between institutions in the EU system. Combined with a decentralized administrative structure in the nation-states, where semi-autonomous authorities are decoupled from ministries as regards regulatory activities, new patterns of cooperation and conflict arise between actors at the national and EU levels.

A short reflection is appropriate before concluding this chapter. Even though the organizational perspective appears as the most relevant explanatory framework for the changes in the telecommunication sector focused on here, this perspective can be criticized for not theorizing the degree to which new patterns of cooperation and conflict have emerged. The empirical study indicates that this development has not been the same in all countries. As the case study suggests, cooperation between the Danish Ministry of Science and the ITTA is based on consensus and trust. The contrary seems to be the case in the Netherlands, where cooperation appears to be characterized more by conflict than consensus. In order to conceive of these variations, an institutional perspective focusing on national administrative traditions might be fruitful (Olsen 1992, 2001). The study presented here indicates that varying traditions of cooperation have influenced the behaviour of national actors. The close cooperation between actors in the Danish administration can be explained by the formal and hierarchical EU coordination system in Denmark, with procedures for hearings in special committees and a high degree of parliamentary control. Furthermore, the tradition of formal coordination in Denmark may have induced the development of an informal norm of cooperation, expressed by the actors' willingness to cooperate with each other (Pedersen 2000).

A transnational networked administrative system can, in other words, be modified by administrative culture and political agency at the national level. Denmark can be seen as a critical case in this respect. Thus, when this study unequivocally indicates that new patterns of cooperation and conflict have emerged, it supports the argument of a general development of a networked administrative system in Europe. Such a development seems even more likely to take place in countries with less formal coordination procedures and parliamentary control.

Acknowledgement

I would like to thank Morten Egeberg at ARENA for inspiration and comments in relation to this chapter.

Notes

1. Literature consulted for this chapter also includes the author's Master's thesis, submitted in 2004 (Nørgård 2004).
2. The main principle of governance in the European Union makes the EU level responsible for policy initiation and decision-making, while the nation-state is in charge of policy implementation. This is known as the principle of shared competences and institutional autonomy (Sverdrup 2003b).
3. IRG: Independent Regulators Group; CEPT: The European Conference of Postal and Telecommunications Administrations; ECTRA: The European Committee for Telecommunications Regulatory Affairs.

11

Transnational Networks Meet National Hierarchies: the Cases of the Italian Competition and Environment Administrations

Dario Barbieri

Introduction

One of the most important outcomes of the Italian administrative reform during the 1990s was the creation of new institutions characterized by a variable degree of independence from the ministries. Some studies have shown that the content and strategy of this reform did not represent a paradigmatic change (Capano 2003), but rather an evolutionary adaptation to external pressures, mainly from the New Public Management (NPM) approach (Peters 1997). The NPM approach was characterized by the aim of finding new solutions to challenges common to most of the western public administrations through promoting, among other things, privatization, decentralization, flexibility and, more generally, suggesting the application of private administrative principles to the public realm (Hood 1991).

Reorganization of the Italian ministries and the development of independent structures with a certain degree of autonomy were explicit results of NPM-inspired reforms occurring in the Italian public administration. In 1999 alone, nineteen agencies were created or completely reorganized. I focus my analysis on the Environment Agency (Agenzia per la Protezione dell'Ambiente e per i Servizi Tecnici – APAT), which was originally formed in 1993 as Agenzia Nazionale per la Protezione dell'Ambiente, with a different structure and mandate. The existence of so-called independent administrative authorities (independent institutions with regulatory and inspection competences) in the Italian public administration goes back to the early 1970s. However, the majority were initiated during the 1990s, including the Antitrust Authority (Autorita' Garante della Concorrenza e del Mercato – AGCM), the other institution considered in this chapter.

Reforms of the Italian public administration responded primarily to the ideological pressures of NPM and to the increasingly pressing problems of administrative inefficiency and public discontent. Adding to this, administrative adaptation to EU requirements as well as the 'central penetration of national systems of governance' (Olsen 2002b) by European institutions played a role in the process.

Before discussing the concept of Europeanization, it is worth noting that EU directives may specify requirements as regards the independence of national agencies from ministries. The question to consider here is whether new patterns of interaction between national agencies and EC executive bodies could partly bypass national ministries (Egeberg, chapters 1 and 3). To give a satisfactory answer one must also investigate whether interorganizational relations between Italian agencies and ministries might have changed.

Theoretical framework

Europeanization processes have been widely debated among political scientists and management scholars, both from a 'top-down' and a 'bottom-up' perspective (Börzel and Risse 2000). Nevertheless, no unambiguous definition of the concept has hitherto been given. Olsen (2002b: 923–4) focuses attention on *what* is changing, listing five areas: (i) changes in external boundaries, (ii) development of European-level institutions, (iii) central penetration of national systems of governance, (iv) exportation of forms of political organization and (v) political unification. As Egeberg (2004, 2005) argues, European integration may both strengthen national coherence and consistency and, under certain conditions, generate a slight disintegration of national political systems. The EU, in order to govern, depends on its member states; governing power must be anchored in consensual and negotiated agreements between its components, rather than in authoritative decisions (Kohler-Koch 2002). Such consensus-building gives relevance to the concept of networked multilevel governance within the EU system (Kohler-Koch 1999). Characteristics of this system include 'co-decision-making across several nested tiers of government, ill-defined and shifting spheres of competence and an ongoing search for principles of decisional distribution that might be applied to this emerging polity' (Marks 1993: 407).

This chapter seeks to address whether a networked governance structure can be applied to EU policy-making in the environmental field by assessing the role of the Italian Environment Agency and its relation with the European Environment Agency and the European Commission. The Italian Antitrust Authority case will be analysed in order to determine whether the same considerations can be applied to the relations this institution has developed at the national and European level. In my research I assess the influence that national administrative traditions may have on these relations (Knill 1998). What I expect to find, however, is a direct link between national agencies and the European Commission (or EU agencies) which might to some extent bypass the ministerial structure (Egeberg, chapters 1 and 3).

To single out the factors behind processes of change at the national level, particularly the effects of EU policy penetration of national bureaucracies, the model developed by Olsen (1992) will be used, evoking macro-, micro- and meso-levels of analysis. Macro-level analysis implies that characteristics of the environment can influence structural changes, as the latter are dependent on contextual factors and driven by efficient competitive selection (Olsen 1992: 248). Thus, structural change may stem from factors such as instrumental performance, economic competition and technological development. In this logic, inefficient institutions disappear due to dwindling support and legitimacy. The micro-level effects study relies on the assumption that structures are chosen by the organizations' decision-makers; thus, change is driven by human intention, design and power. Following Child's assumption (1972), the strategic choice to change institutional structures implies establishing and modifying structural arrangements, and choosing appropriate performance standards and alternative environments. Institutional structures can be created or modified to reduce transaction costs or because of political authority and power struggles (Olsen 1992: 249). The meso-level concentrates on institutional robustness, defined as the impermeability of political and administrative institutions to environmental transformations and purposeful reorganization. Indeed, many scholars (Kaufman 1976; Kimberly, Miles et al. 1980; Romanov 1981) consider, from different point of views, institutions as 'self-organizations'.

Research questions

The macro-level is represented by the EU and its capacity to penetrate national governmental structures. At the micro-level, characteristics of Italian decision-makers and their influence on the Italian governmental structure will be discussed. The meso-level refers to the centripetal forces of the Italian public administration, with regard to both its formal structure and its administrative culture. Thus, the independent (macro) variables considered are (i) EU policies, in the sense of its administrative policies, and (ii) the EU's institutional structure which, due to its peculiar complexity (at this level), is supposed to trigger centrifugal forces at the national level (Egeberg, chapters 1 and 2). Dependent variables are (i) the organization of Italian agencies and authorities and their relative independence from national ministries, and (ii) the type of interaction between agencies, European institutions (primarily the Commission, but also EU agencies) and the Italian ministries.

Cultural influence from what has been called 'the hegemonic paradigm' of Italian administration (meso-level) is expected to mediate changes in the relations between Italian agencies and other actors. Aspects of the national institutional framework, such as hierarchy and legal coherence, may indeed moderate the effects of external factors on inter-institutional relations (Capano 2003: 786–7; Leyland and Donati 2001). A moderating effect may also stem from policy-makers aiming to counteract a particular development (micro-factors). Thus, my research will start from the theoretical assumption that European-level arrangements may have transformed the territorial state structure (Kohler-Koch 1999; Hooghe and Marks 2001); the scale and quality of these changes, however, being influenced by mediating factors.

Empirically, I will focus on relations that might have developed between APAT and AGCM, on the one hand, and corresponding European institutions and other Italian bodies on the other. In the case of APAT, such institutions comprise primarily the European Environment Agency, the European Commission and other national agencies. With regards to AGCM, the European Commission and other national authorities take precedence. On this basis I will investigate whether a direct link has been forged between Italian and European actors, thus partly bypassing national ministries. I will provide some empirical observations concerning APAT and AGCM structures and strategies, and – more specifically – regarding contacts and interactions with ministries as opposed to EU-level institutions.

Method and data

Qualitative data from the relevant institutional archives constitutes the empirical basis for this research. The research follows an exploratory design, in which a set of theoretical concepts and testable evaluation criteria are crucial. What is expected from this type of analysis is a clear representation of the institutions analysed, with particular stress on our a priori expectations stated above.

Adaptation of national institutions to the European decision-making environment can be documented by official documents and secondary literature. At the European level these sources have been website documents, white papers, legislation and other publications. At the domestic level the sources have been website documents, reports, and domestic documents concerning institutional budget, structure and organization in general. As my focus is on structural pressures from the European level, a lot of the relevant information can be found in open sources and official documents. A vast amount of secondary literature about the issues in this chapter has also been taken into consideration. Interviews conducted by means of semi-structured questionnaires with key personnel in the institutions under study supplement these sources.

Debates about the pertinence of case studies in analysing Europeanization have not reached an unequivocal conclusion (Andersen 2003). Nevertheless, applying this method should give the opportunity to develop an 'analytical generalization' (Yin 1989) from the relevant case. Naturally, this approach poses some problems: the difficulty of controlling and testing the effects of unexpected mediating variables, possible biases of the archival data, and attempts to generate *hic et nunc* scientific conclusions about a phenomenon – namely, institutional relations – which is by its nature dynamic. Trying to formulate conclusions to an ongoing process of change is always difficult because of the limited timeframe and danger of defining as permanent what is just transitory. Properly assessing this possibility is usually a problematic issue: further studies in the future, with a wider sample and a longer time horizon, could answer these doubts. In this study, recognizing these shortcomings prevents any false aspiration for definitive conclusions.

Investigating the Italian case: semi-independent agencies bypassing national ministries?

How should one describe the administrative paradigm permeating Italian bureaucracy and its public administration? Always remembering that it is worth being cautious when trying to define an ideology applying to an administrative reality as daily practice can be different from the label we try to put on it. Capano (2003) summarized the Italian administrative paradigm as characterized by (i) the perception of law as an expression of administrative action, (ii) the separation of political decision-making from administrative implementation, (iii) the importance of legality, impartiality and neutrality principles, (iv) formal rules as instruments of administrative action, and (v) attention to organizational structures more than to policies and the control of legitimacy.

The legal paradigm has been considered for decades as a shared framework for the entire Italian administrative community. Changes occurring in the Italian public administration during the last twenty years should be interpreted as paying great attention to this point. Reconsideration of the Italian hegemonic paradigm has involved a shift from the principle of conformity to law to conformity to NPM ideas, as laid out in the introduction. The Italian public administration became committed to reconciling new principles with old ones, thus rendering them compatible. Factors deeply rooted in the Italian administrative culture influenced the reform, allowing the hegemonic paradigm to survive in a new and revised form, but without having changed its core structure (Capano 2003).

The creation of a number of agencies was a direct consequence of this wave of reforms, apparently causing a 'revolutionary' remodelling of the Italian public administration. Although such agencies have sometimes been denoted as 'autonomous administrations', they have, however, been under close ministerial supervision (Hine 1993: 228). The concept of independent institutions refers to legal provisions for autonomy in organizational, financial, accounting and personnel policies. In the Italian public administration this juridical transition occurred with the Antitrust Authority, now recognized as having considerable autonomy from political and economic pressures. In general, we can divide the independent institutions existing in the Italian public administration into two categories: the 'authorities' and the 'administrative agencies'. Authorities are characterized by a considerable degree of autonomy; not subjected to governmental directives, they are organizationally as well as financially autonomous.[1] A distinguishing feature of this autonomy can be found in the election of authority directors who are usually chosen by parliament or by the President of the Italian Republic, rather than the government. Administrative agencies, on the other hand, comprise more than twenty institutions in different sectors ranging from environment to health care. Some of their distinctive features are as follows:

- They operate under ministerial jurisdiction, with policy implementation as their main function;
- Their roles and objectives are stated by law;
- They enjoy managerial as well as financial autonomy, though within the constraints of a fixed budget;
- They have flexible hiring rules;
- They are obliged to give periodic reports on their activities to the government;
- Their budget is subject to control by the Supreme Audit Institution.

As argued by Capano (2003), the creation of agencies did not represent a 'revolution' in the real sense, its consequences being comparatively limited in relation to administrative reform in countries such as the UK and New Zealand. Continuity is related to the fact that the organizational format of Italian agencies draws on models from the past, in particular the 1980s. Moreover, the managerial approach that is manifest in agencies corresponds surprisingly well with traditional bureaucratic ministerial style in Italy.

The Environment Agency: new inter-institutional relations?

The Italian Environment Agency (APAT) can be defined as the operative branch of the Ministry for the Environment. It was created in 1999, its activities in accordance with the traditional rule that 'functionaries manage and ministries control' (Morbidelli 2000). APAT operates on the basis of a three-year programme subject to yearly approval, which necessitates full accordance with the work priorities and budgetary framework given to it by the Environment Ministry. At the organizational level, the APAT directorate has a director general and four other members, all nominated by the state and regional governments.

APAT is structured according to a sectoral principle: the directorate maintains coordinating power over all the divisions, each of them responsible for a particular environmental field. The responsibility of the director general is to manage the relations of APAT with other environmental organizations at the state, sub-state and European levels (source: APAT). The main responsibility of APAT is to operate as the hub of a networked system of linked organizations at the national level and to cooperate with the European Environment Agency (EEA).

It is possible to identify two distinct levels inside this network and, likewise, three different hub organizations, one of them being APAT, the focal point at the Italian level. At the communitarian level the environmental policy development is driven by the Commission's DG Environment. Some studies (for example Everson et al. 1999) have investigated the characteristics of relations between this DG and the EEA. In this chapter, however, no particular attention will be paid to this topic. The EEA can be considered the second European hub for environment policy: its mandate is to provide the European Commission and the member states with accurate information about the environment, in order to facilitate the elaboration and implementation of environmental policies. The EEA operates on behalf of a European network of member state institutions (EIONET). Every member state appoints a National Focal Point (NFP), a hub of the national institutional network, responsible for collecting data and coordinating the activities of sub-national institutions.

The structure of the Italian environment network is based on six national topic centres (Centri Tematici Nazionali – CTN) and 21 regional focal points (Punti Focali Regionali – PFR) (source: SINANET). APAT represents the Italian NFP on the European scene, its representative being nominated and mandated by the Environment Ministry. APAT also represents the National Reference Centre as part of the European Topic Centre network. Within Italy it operates as the hub of a national network of environmental institutions and with close working ties to the Environment Ministry. This double-sided role of APAT gives the initial impression of a clear separation between its technical and political activities. Were this correct, the possibilities of 'bypass' by creation of a direct link between this agency and European institutions would be viable. If the macro-level influence is taken into account, it could be argued that the creation of APAT and the environmental institutions' network in Italy might be a consequence of European adaptation pressure.

However, the creation of APAT has to be contextualized in the framework of Italian administrative reform as it occurred in the 1990s: the distribution of power and authority inside the Italian system between the ministry and APAT is wholly biased in favour of the ministry. The APAT director and deputy directors are appointed by governmental decision; furthermore, all issues concerning strategy and budgetary resources of the agency are resolved through co-decisions with the ministry. Ministerial influence has been further enhanced by the centralization of APAT activities over the last years.

In line with Italian administrative tradition, agencies were created and mandated for technical purposes. The continued prevalence of this attitude suggests that no real bypassing of the ministry has hitherto occurred. Relations between APAT and EEA are limited to purely scientific topics, the government maintaining its role in managing environmental policy development and relations with EU institutions. To assure the coordination of APAT activities at the communitarian level, the Environment Ministry takes precedence. Thus, APAT experts attend meetings at the EU level at the request of the ministry. Furthermore, the Environment Ministry has recently created its own office in Brussels in order to follow the activities of the DG Environment, adding to its presence at the country's permanent representation. As far as relations with the Commission are concerned, it is usually the ministry that takes the lead while APAT is assigned only an auxiliary role. APAT may attend Council working parties as well, but the experts who are sent to the meetings are appointed by the ministry, and the lines they are supposed to pursue are laid down by that same ministry. No concrete attempts at really bypassing the 'controller' – the

Environment Ministry – seem to have occurred. The resistance of the Italian bureaucracy to the European pressure for change remains strong.

APAT and the network created for administering environment issues in Italy represent an interesting case of the Europeanization of a national structure in the sense that the EU model can be compared to that of the Italian administration. It is not possible to determine whether this phenomenon represents a case of isomorphism (Di Maggio and Powell 1983) or, more likely, an answer to the European request to implement a structure mirroring the communitarian one. The reaction of the Italian government to communitarian pressure has been to transform the network of regional and provincial institutions with environmental functions previously reporting to the ministry, into a network of formally independent institutions reporting directly to a centralized technical agency.

In order not to lose political control over environment policy formulation and implementation, the government created a structure without decision-making power, dependent on the ministry from an organizational, managerial and budgetary point of view. Hence the creation of APAT was problematic: its statute was approved only in 2002, and its management was for a short period controlled by an emergency commissioner. To create APAT and to formulate the current structure took some time, because it was necessary to harmonize different statutes and already existing structures and to concentrate them in a unique organization.

The Antitrust Authority: a case of institutional independence?

The Italian Antitrust Authority (AGCM) represents a peculiar case in Italian public administration. AGCM is a concrete example of an independent institution, as demonstrated by its autonomy in selecting a board of directors. The AGCM is collegially organized, with a president and four co-directors on seven-year, non-renewable mandates.[2] This board is autonomous as regards organizational management (within the constraints of 50 permanent staff members), finance (concerning the state budget) and accounting (constrained by external revision of budget).

The Authority has the responsibility to act when mergers and inter-company agreements substantially reduce competition; it also sanctions, more generally, abuses of market dominance. AGCM is organized in six sectoral directorates. The Directorate for International Relations, supervised by the president, is responsible for information and consultation vis-à-vis the European Commission as well as other member states' antitrust authorities.

Its institutional structure and mandate give the AGCM a formal guarantee of non-interference from the government in administrative matters. Studying AGCM's relations with the European Commission could thus improve our understanding of the developing autonomization of institutions in the Italian public administration. However, the resort ministry of AGCM – Ministero per le Attività Produttive – plays a considerable role at the European level. While ministerial influence weighs heavily as regards Council decision-making, the AGCM is in fact the main Italian actor in preparatory work as well as implementation. In the formalization phase of Council deliberations, an ad hoc working group is created in which the ministerial delegation is supported by AGCM expertise. Such technical support gives considerable leverage in policy formulation, although political approval remains pivotal. In politically sensitive issues it is normally the ministry alone that makes the final decision, taking into account the AGCM position.

EU competition authorities went through a 'soft revolution' on 1 May 2004. Hitherto, the system had been largely centralized, meaning that exemptions to EU rules were to be applied or administered by the Commission.[3] The new system gave these powers to all enforcers – namely the Commission, national competition authorities and civil courts (see Støle, Chapter 6). A requirement for effective application of this system is the diffusion of a European competition culture and a common administrative approach. With regards to longer-term consequences, one could reasonably expect more efficient law enforcement as well as a potential re-nationalization of competition policies. Further studies will be needed for a firmer assessment of the actual results. What remains the focus in this chapter is the possible effect on relations between the European Commission and the national antitrust authorities. With all enforcers enabled to apply Articles 81 and 82 of the EU Treaty, the reform envisions a more efficient and coherent application of communitarian law. This requires, however, a strengthened *vertical* cooperation between the European Commission and national antitrust authorities as well as enhanced *horizontal* cooperation between the national authorities themselves. Cooperation includes the possible exchange of confidential information in anti-trust judicial proceedings.

In order to prepare the reform, a study group composed of national representatives of old as well as incoming member states was set up. Established as the European Competition Network (ECN), it was mandated to provide procedures for coordination and information exchange. The establishment of this forum exemplifies the strengthening of independent authorities vis-à-vis ministerial rule, although national ministries typically retain rights to consultation.[4] In Italy, an anticipated result of the new EU competition policy will be a relative reduction of ministerial power within this area. The ministry retains control primarily as regards Council decision-making, whereas in policy implementation the authority increasingly prevails.

The establishment of the AGCM is a comparatively recent development when considered alongside similar cases in a range of other EU states. The administrative revolution of the 1990s in Italy provided the context which combined with specific Commission pressures to professionalize regulation policy. Thus, the AGCM appears both as an institutional product of a change in national administrative approach and as a well-adapted response to EU demands. A driving factor in the process was, however, the national political will to reform.

Among various pressures behind the strengthening of the AGCM, influence from the EU level is of particular pertinence to my research. The dynamic effect of EU activism in this field is fairly straightforward. The compulsory application of EU directives – as well as added regulation policies – pushes national governments to delegate implementation to an autonomous and specialized authority. The AGCM, being assigned this specific task, is provided with relatively little room to manoeuvre: collaboration and respect of communitarian policy is mandatory. At the national level, the distribution of power and authority in relation to the government is clearly stated in the statute of the authority. A relatively clear distribution of roles has thus been secured, maintaining the ministerial 'last word' in political decision-making.

In light of the new framework of competition law, attempts at strengthening relations with the European Commission could be a successful strategy for the Italian Antitrust Authority. In the longer term this relationship could also work to carve out a stronger position for the AGCM within the domestic arena. However, the driving forces behind enhanced cooperation are complex. Rather than an overt strategy on the part of the authority to bypass ministerial influence, it seems more accurate to speak of a response to EU pressures of harmonization, in pursuit of institutional leverage. Notably, the AGCM may apply EU regulation to support its position, referring to the obligations laid down by a Europeanized system of competition policy.

Discussion and conclusions

Is the Commission challenging the internal consistency of national governments by connecting up national agencies (Egeberg, chapters 1 and 3)?

Does Europeanization influence institutional dynamics within the Italian public administration? And is it possible to assess the influence of environmental determinism, of institutional choice, and of autonomy (Olsen 1992)? As shown above, both the competition and environment fields highlight a three-level relation between the communitarian institutions, the Italian government and the Italian independent institutions. At first glance, EU influence on Italian public administration could be interpreted as *the* driving factor behind organizational change. The networked administration put in place by the EU in the environmental field and the EU directives on competition policy exemplify this influence. A plausible consequence of strengthening ties between communitarian and Italian independent institutions could be less consistency within the Italian government.

Behind the scenes, however, the reality appears a bit different. The Antitrust Authority was provided with formal autonomy. However, even if its statute guarantees a strong degree of independence, we cannot yet affirm empirically that its relationship with the DG Competition works exclusively without government interference. Political decisions remain within the ministerial domain; nothing seems to indicate a change in this respect. The new European competition policy opens prospects for the creation of a network of fully independent national institutions which could enhance the hypothesized 'bypass' phenomenon. This is in the development phase; whether results will conform to our expectations – or, to the contrary, a re-nationalization of competition policies occurs – is not obvious at present.

The Italian Environment Agency was established only a few years ago as part of a general administrative reorganization in which the creation of technically independent institutions was a stated aim. European influence on organizational design in this field is considerable – yet, if analysed, the network approach appears deeply rooted in the old system of Italian regional and provincial institutions. With regard to APAT, discerning the influence of communitarian pressures from those emanating from within the public administration is difficult. The impact of the EU on the relations/relationship between APAT and the Environment Ministry is low. The activities of APAT are deeply influenced by EU directives, yet ministerial relations are equally prominent. At the structural level, organizational characteristics of APAT have been decided within the national domain, although partly designed to meet the demands of EU environmental policy.

The limited EU impact on institutional features of the Italian public administration does not challenge the fact that changes have indeed taken place. Thus, though a major structural reorientation in Italy cannot be confirmed, a move towards institutional decentralization and autono-mization is undeniable. Following from this development, some indica-tions point towards transnational administrative coalitions. Still, a consistent bypass of national ministries is not supported by my research. In the cases considered, EU pressure is a recurring factor with regard to competition as well as environmental policies. In the environmental field, controversies between EEA and the DG Environment add another element of complexity to the analysis.

In conclusion, one cannot unequivocally argue the case for a decline in national government coherence. In the environmental domain, EIONET, EEA and the national agency all have technical mandates, while APAT – with the exception of managerial independence – seems to be under the control of the Environment Ministry as regards so-called 'political' issues. In the case of competition policy, the strong leadership of DG Competition underpins the mandatory independence of the Italian Antitrust Authority. The regulatory nature of this field makes more likely the existence of a reliable and independent connection between AGCM and the European Commission, with the former remaining, however, within the framework of ministerial influence.

Acknowledgements

I'm grateful to Professor Morten Egeberg for his helpful support and his extended comments on a previous version of this chapter. I also thank Professor Johan P. Olsen, Dr Ulf Sverdrup and Dr Åse Gornitzka for their many useful comments. The research was carried out during my stay at ARENA, UiO as guest researcher from February 2004 to June 2004. Financial support from ARENA, UiO and Cergas, Bocconi University is gratefully acknowledged.

Notes

1. *Organizational* autonomy refers primarily to independence in staff and per-sonnel management rules. Autonomy in a *financial* and *accountancy* sense is incomplete, as authorities receive state funding, yet autonomy is considerable compared with the previous financial direction of these institutions.
2. This personnel is co-nominated by the presidents of each of the two chambers of parliament.
3. The practices and powers of EU competition policy emanate mainly from Articles 81 and 82 in the Treaty of European Union (ratified 1992).
4. This consultation may take different forms. In France, notably, it is the resort ministry that is ultimately responsible in competition issues – hence, the inde-pendent authority remains essentially non-independent.

Sources

During the research, interviews were conducted with functionaries of APAT (Agenzia per la Protezione dell'Ambiente e per i Servizi Tecnici) – International Relation Office; AGCM (Autorita' Garante della Concorrenza e del Mercato) – International Relation Office; and Ministry for the Environment of Italy.

AGCM: http://www.agcm.it.

APAT: http://www.apat.it/site.

SINANET: http://www.sinanet.apat.it/rete.

UE, DG Competition: http://europa.eu.int/comm/competition/index_ it.html.

12
Conclusion
Morten Egeberg

We have in this book argued that the EU does not only add considerably to already existing patterns of multilevel governance taking place in and around a huge number of international governmental organizations (IGOs), but that it in addition makes a *unique* difference to executive organization and politics in Europe. The uniqueness first of all relates to the existence of the European Commission which is the only multipurpose executive body at the international level that is organizationally separated from councils of ministers. Since this institution also in practice has the potential to act relatively independently as an executive, this means that the executive branch of EU member states has got a new and higher layer of executive organization to relate to. Second, we have argued that the peculiar functional division of labour that exists between the Commission and the Council triggers unique centrifugal forces at the very heart of national governments. The Commission is in need of expertise for drafting new policy proposals and it depends on reliable partners for ensuring that EU decisions are properly implemented at the national level. Both seem to be found among national (regulatory) agencies that over the last years increasingly have been organized at arm's length from their respective ministries. Thus, we might see a genuine multilevel Union administration emerging. Such developments indicate what we will denote as a profound transformation of executive politics within the EU, and, as shown, within the European Economic Area (EEA) as well.

The supranational executive

It is far from unusual to portray the European Commission as being permeated by national interests at all levels. I have argued in this book, however, that the Commission in fact seems to have enhanced its autonomy vis-à-vis national governments over the years. (Whether the Commission has become more or less successful in promoting its interests in various arenas is another story.) A more independent Commission has been observed by looking at its organizational and recruitment procedures over time and at how it actually makes decisions at different points in time (Egeberg, chapters 3 and 4). For example, rather than having to rely heavily on personnel seconded from member state administrations, today most posts are permanent and life-long careers are quite common. National clusters of officials, which might be conducive to national interest representation, are less likely to develop since rules require multinational staffing both vertically (in the chain of command) and horizontally (within units). As regards the appointment of top officials, the Commission services have gradually enhanced their control. New procedures for such appointments seem so far to have contributed further to reducing the amount of interference by governments or commissioners in such processes. The new rules of procedure have introduced several objective criteria for candidate selection, and provided more organizational capacity in the services for dealing with top appointments. Although commissioners are to take the final decision, our study shows that they normally seem to accept the shortlist of candidates presented to them by the services. It seems to be deemed inappropriate to ignore the proposed list and also as highly risky to do so (Egeberg, Chapter 3). At the political level, commissioners' cabinets also have to be multinationally composed thus diluting their previous role as exclusive access points and enclaves for particular nationalities. The president of the Commission has also been empowered by treaty reform as regards the distribution of portfolios, both at the inception of a new College and during its term of office.

The directorate general (DG) to which officials and commissioners are affiliated stands out as a particularly important key for understanding their actual decision-making behaviour (Egeberg, chapters 3 and 4). Had these departments reflected the territorial composition of the EU (for example, one DG for each country), this could have meant the internalization of intergovernmental patterns of decision-making at the Commission. However, instead, the sectoral and functional principles prevail, meaning that attention tends to be focused primarily along sectoral and functional lines of conflict rather than geographical ones. We have seen that the 'portfolio role' seems to be the one most frequently evoked in the College, meaning that commissioners tend to champion the interests that are inherently linked to their respective briefs. This is not to say, though, that nationality does not matter: we know, for example, that officials may facilitate access to the Commission for their compatriots and that commissioners may take on what we have called a 'country role' as regards issues that might become of particular significance for their country of origin. These instances occur, however, relatively rarely (Egeberg, chapters 3 and 4). In that respect, commissioners are probably not very different from national ministers who might also be particularly aware of the concerns of their home constituency.

The College has increasingly been composed of political heavyweights and one might assume they are carrying with them more clear-cut party-political identities. And the European Parliament (EP) has not only the right to dismiss the College as a collective but has also got a stronger role as regards the composition of the College and in daily policy-making vis-à-vis the Commission (Egeberg, chapters 3 and 4). Although the 'party political role' is currently the least frequently evoked role at College meetings, party politicization of the College of Commissioners may in some situations complement or even displace cleavages along sectoral and national lines. Thus, in sum, this collection has revealed that the Commission has become increasingly 'normalized' in the sense that it at present embodies many of the organizational and behavioural patterns that are highly typical of executives as we know them from national settings.

Committees and agency networks

The first indication that national administrations might be playing two different roles, one as the traditional 'servant' of national ministers and one as a part of a Union administration (for example by being a contributor to policy formulation in the Commission), appeared in our studies of EU-level committees. Thus, national officials attending Commission expert committees, Council working parties and comitology committees clearly differ from each other (although they may be the same individuals) as regards the weight they assign to the role of being a national government representative at the EU level. While those participating in Council and comitology committees most typically perceive of themselves as representing their respective governments, those on Commission groups tend to assume more multi-faceted and expert-oriented roles (Egeberg, Schaefer and Trondal, Chapter 5). Members of Commission expert groups are also considerably less subject to instruction and coordination by foreign ministries or other central authorities than those on Council and comitology committees. The more modest role that nationality plays in the Commission setting is also clearly expressed by the fact that translation and interpretation facilities are much less available here than in Council committees (Egeberg, Schaefer and Trondal, Chapter 5). Since language tends to go together with national identity, a similar reduction to the use of only a very few languages is more difficult to foresee in the Council.

Policy area-specific networks consisting of national agencies and the Commission or an EU-level agency as a kind of hub can, in comparison with Commission expert committees, be interpreted as a step further in the development of a genuine multilevel Union administration. Both as regards policy formulation and implementation, the Commission is certainly in need of stable institutional partners and not only individual experts. Those partners might be found among national agencies that, due to, inter alia, 'New Public Management' reforms (sometimes in the form of EU directives), have been established at arm's length from ministries in order to apply regulatory statutes in an impartial manner.

We have in this volume presented studies of five different policy fields which all show some signs of national agencies serving two masters. In the areas of competition (Støle, Chapter 6; Barbieri, Chapter 11), telecom (Nørgård, Chapter 10), food safety (Ugland and Veggeland, Chapter 9), environment (Martens, Chapter 8; Barbieri, Chapter 11) and statistics (Sverdrup, Chapter 7) national agencies no doubt constitute parts of national governments in a generally traditional way. As integral parts of national governments, national agencies assist their respective ministries at Council and comitology meetings. Also, when EU directives are to be transposed into national legislation, national regulatory authorities often do much of the preparatory work with which they are familiar from other legislative processes. However, at the same time, national agencies are involved in European networks in which the Commission or an EU-level agency often makes up the hub. At the stage of practising transposed legislation, national agencies may operate in close cooperation with their respective directorates in the Commission and their respective sister agencies in other member states. As a consequence, national regulatory authorities may end up having to defend decisions that are at odds with the policies of their own governments. Arguably, such agency–ministry conflicts also occur quite independently of the EU; they are indeed the result of 'agencification' itself. What is probably new is that the national agency in a way acts 'on behalf of' a *second* master or centre, or at least, 'on behalf of' a transnational network of agencies in which the EU executive may constitute a node.

As in the telecom sector (Nørgård, Chapter 10), the Commission may itself have initiated the creation of such a network. However, the EU executive has also successfully entered already existing networks and gradually taken over the coordinating functions, as seems to be the case for the implementation network of pollution authorities (Martens,

Chapter 8). Just as national ministries might be perceived by experts as a potential threat to their independence, the Commission, in its role as a 'second master', might be looked upon in a similar way (Ugland and Veggeland, Chapter 9). In addition to playing a crucial role at the implementation stage, agency networks may also contribute in the policy formulation phase at the Commission.

According to the policy sector-studies presented in this book, ministries are informed about the network activities of their respective agencies. Ministries usually abstain from steering network activities, however, for example by appointing and instructing participants. Such interference seems to be deemed inappropriate, at least by the agency personnel themselves. Two of our case studies can be seen as critical to the argument in the sense that they both deal with agencies in member states (Denmark and Italy) that are known for certain strong hierarchical features. Arguably, 'double-hattedness' proves to be more than a mere theoretical construction if national agencies even under these circumstances are 'captured' or 'absorbed' by transnational networks of the kind we have described above. On this point, Nørgård's study (Chapter 10) clearly shows that the Danish telecom agency operates in network activities on its own without much interference from the ministry. This room for manoeuvre is, however, based on a considerable amount of trust between the two institutions concerned. In the Italian case (Barbieri, Chapter 11), however, trust does not seem to exist to the same extent. Even if the Italian environment agency is allowed to participate on its own in the European Environment Agency's network (EIONET), its representatives are appointed and mandated by the ministry. Close supervision, at least as regards political issues, also seems to be a matter of routine as regards the Italian competition authority's network involvement. However, notwithstanding this, DG Competition's strong leadership role in this area seems to strengthen the agency's actual autonomy from its ministry.

An organizational account of changing patterns of executive politics

The most crucial step in our story is probably the innovative establishment of an executive body separated from the ministers' council. However, a genuine organizational or institutional approach has probably little to offer as regards the coming about of the key institution dealt with, namely the European Commission and its predecessors. This formative event is probably best explained by the quite exceptional window of opportunity provided by the WWII catastrophe, a window that clever entrepreneurs could exploit (Egeberg, chapters 1 and 2). We believe that organizational theory has something to offer primarily when certain institutional and organizational arrangements are already in place.

This is so because the organizational setting provides goals and role expectations as well as mechanisms – such as cognitive frames, sanctions, rewards and norms of appropriateness – that may ensure compliance with these expectations. Thus, in order to understand and explain patterns of executive politics – such as Commission autonomization, sectorization, party politicization and 'capture' of national agencies – we have emphasized organizational and institutional factors such as various procedures, ways of specialization, demography and culture. Such independent variables have been considered at two levels: the EU level and the national level.

Starting with the Commission itself, it appears that when this body was first established with certain organizational resources, the new executive triggered an institutional dynamics that gradually demarcated the new body in relation to the Council. It has been shown that this was partly done over time by installing several procedures for organization and staffing that served to encapsulate such processes within the Commission itself, and, as regards recruitment, even within the administrative part of it. In addition, as shown, sectoral and functional specialization seems to have largely *displaced* territorial politics at the Commission (Egeberg, chapters 3 and 4). Given the historical background, the struggle for institutional integrity has primarily been fought against the Council and member governments. The institutional dynamics between the Commission and the EP as well as the changed demography of the College points in the direction of a more party politicized Commission.

The functional specialization between the Council and the Commission, which is rather peculiar at the international level, is thought to trigger the centrifugal forces within national governments that lead to 'double-hatted' agencies (Egeberg, Chapter 2). However, the institutional architecture at the EU level may be a necessary but not a sufficient condition for the emergence of the type of multilevel administrative relationships that we have described in this book. In addition, such a development has been seen as highly contingent upon particular organizational and institutional features at the national level as well. In general, we expect national governments that are clearly vertically specialized into ministries on the one hand and agencies on the other to be more conducive to 'agency capture' by the Commission than governments that are vertically integrated. Our two 'critical cases', Denmark and, in particular Italy, provide some support for this assumption.

The existence of 'double-hatted' national agencies could be one significant indication of important changes in the European order: integrated polities have in common that the executive at the centre possesses or disposes over agencies at the level beneath that are at least partly decoupled from the political core at that same level. Thus, we might see an emerging multilevel genuine *Union* administration and a concurrent transformation of executive politics in Europe. In this respect, it has been emphasized that the EU is characterized at the international level by a *unique* organizational division of labour between a political executive (the Commission) and the ministers' council which then tends to trigger *unique* centrifugal forces within the apparatuses of national governments. Do these observations then suffer from a *sui generis* problem in the sense that powerful theoretical arguments cannot be generated? We do not think so: the general insight that might be drawn from this book is that political systems that acquire similar institutional and organizational features to those of the EU at the system and sub-system level would probably have a larger propensity than others to develop similar patterns of executive politics as well.

Bibliography

Almer, J. and M. Rotkirch (2004) *European Governance – an Overview of the Commission's Agenda for Reform*, Stockholm: Swedish Institute for European Policy Studies.

Alonso, W. and P. Starr (eds) (1983) *The Politics of Numbers*, New York: Russell Sage Foundation.

Andersen, S.S. (1997) *Case-studier og generalisering. Forskningsstrategi og design*, Bergen: Fagbokforlaget.

Andersen, S.S. (2003) 'On a clear day you can see the EU. Case study methodology in EU research', ARENA Working Paper 16/03, Oslo: ARENA.

Andersen, S.S. and K.A. Eliassen (2001) 'Informal processes: lobbying, actor strategies, coalitions and dependencies', in S.S. Andersen and K.A. Eliassen (eds) *Making Policy in Europe*, London: Sage.

Anderson, B. (1983) *Imagined Communities: Reflections on the Origin and Spread of Nationalism*, London: Verso.

Ansell, C. (2000) 'The networked polity: regional development in western Europe', *Governance* 13: 303–33.

Arnull, A. (2003) 'The Community courts', in M. Cini (ed.) *European Union Politics*, Oxford: Oxford University Press.

Aspinwall, M. and G. Schneider (2001) 'Institutional research on the European Union: mapping the field', in G. Schneider and M. Aspinwall (eds) *The Rules of Integration. Institutionalist Approaches to the Study of Europe*, Manchester: Manchester University Press.

Augier, M. and J.G. March (2001) 'Remembering Herbert A. Simon (1916–2001)', *Public Administration Review* 61: 396–402.

Batora, J. (2005) 'Does the European Union transform the institution of diplomacy?', *Journal of European Public Policy* 12: 44–66.

Bauer, M. (2002) 'The EU "Partnership Principle": still a sustainable governance device across multiple administrative arenas?', *Public Administration* 80: 769–89.

Becker, H.S. (1992) 'Cases, causes, conjunctures, stories, and imagery', in C.C. Ragin and H.S. Becker (eds) *What is a Case? Exploring the Foundations of Social Inquiry*, Cambridge, MA: Winthrop Publishers.

Benz, A. and J. Bogumil (2002) 'Civil servants in a federal system: the case of Germany', Paper, FernUniversität Hagen: Institute of Political Science.

Blakemore, M. and L. McKeever (2001) 'Users of official European statistical data – investigating information needs', *Journal of Librarianship and Information Science* 33 (2): 59–67.

Boje, P. and M. Kallestrup (2004) *Marked, Erhvervsliv og Stat – Dansk Konkurrencelovgivning og det Store Erhvervsliv*, Aarhus: Aarhus Universitetsforlag.

Boyle, M. (2000) 'Euro-regionalism and struggles over scale of governance: the politics of Ireland's regionalisation approach to Structural Fund allocations 2000–2006', *Political Geography* 19: 737–69.

Börzel, T. (1998) 'Organizing Babylon – on the different conceptions of policy networks', *Public Administration* 76: 253–73.

Börzel, T. (2001) 'Non-compliance in the European Union: pathology or statistical artifact?', *Journal of European Public Policy* 8: 803–24.

Börzel, T. and T. Risse (2000) 'When Europe hits home: Europeanization and domestic change', EUI Working Papers, Robert Schuman Centre for Advanced Studies, RSC No. 2000/56.

Bulmer, S. (1994) 'The governance of the European Union: a new institutional approach', *Journal of Public Policy* 13: 351–80.

Bulmer, S. and C. Lequesne (2002) 'New perspectives on EU–member state relationship', *Research in question* No. 4 – Centre d'études et de recherches internationals, Paris: Science Po.

Bulmer, S. and C. Lequesne (eds) (2005) *The Member States of the European Union*, Oxford: Oxford University Press.

Burgess, M. (2004) 'Federalism', in A. Wiener and T. Diez (eds) *European Integration Theory*, Oxford: Oxford University Press.

Bursens, P. (2002) 'Why Denmark and Belgium have different implementation records: on transposition laggards and leaders in the EU', *Scandinavian Political Studies* 25: 173–95.

Cameron, F. and D. Spence (2004) 'The Commission-Council tandem in the foreign policy arena', in D. Dimitrakopoulos (ed.) *The Changing European Commission*, Manchester: Manchester University Press.

Capano, G. (2003) 'Administrative traditions and policy change: when policy paradigms matter. The case of Italian administrative reform during the 1990s', *Public Administration* 81: 781–99.

Chambers, G.R. (1999) 'The BSE crisis and the European Parliament', in C. Joerges and E. Vos (eds) *EU Committees: Social Regulation, Law and Politics*, Oxford, Portland: Hart Publishing.

Checkel, J.T. (1998) 'Norms, institutions and national identity in contemporary Europe', ARENA Working paper 16/98, Oslo: ARENA.

Checkel, J.T. (2001) 'Why comply? Social learning and European identity change', *International Organization* 55: 553–88.

Child, J. (1972) 'Organizational structure, environment and performance. The role of strategic choice', *Sociology* 6: 1–22.

Christensen, T. and M. Egeberg (1997) 'Sentraladministrasjonen – en oversikt over trekk ved departementer og direktorater', in T. Christensen and M. Egeberg (eds) *Forvaltningskunnskap*, Oslo: Tano Aschehoug.

Christensen, T. and P. Lægreid (eds) (2001) *New Public Management. The Transformation of Ideas and Practice*, Aldershot: Ashgate.

Christiansen, T. (1997) 'Tensions of European governance: politicized bureaucracy and multiple accountability in the European Commission', *Journal of European Public Policy* 4: 73–90.

Christiansen, T. and E. Kirchner (2000) *Europe in Change. Committee Governance in the European Union*, Manchester: Manchester University Press.

Cini, M. (1996) *The European Commission. Leadership, Organisation and Culture in the EU Administration*, Manchester: Manchester University Press.

Cini, M. (2000) 'Administrative culture in the European Commission: the case of competition and environment', in N. Nugent (ed.) *At the Heart of the Union. Studies of the European Commission*, Basingstoke: Macmillan Press.

Cini, M. (2003a) 'Implementation', in M. Cini (ed.) *European Union Politics*, Oxford: Oxford University Press.

Cini, M. (2003b) 'Intergovernmentalism', in M. Cini (ed.) *European Union Politics*, Oxford: Oxford University Press.

Cini, M. and L. McGowan (1998) *Competition Policy in the European Union*, New York: St Martin's Press.

Codex Alimentarius Commission (2001) *Report of the Sixteenth Session of the Codex Committee on General Principles*, Paris, France, 23–27 April 2001, Codex Alimentarius Commission, ALINORM 01/33A.

Codex Alimentarius Commission (2003) *Report*, Twenty-sixth Session, FAO Headquarters, Rome, 30 June–7 July 2003, Codex Alimentarius Commission, ALINORM 03/41.

COM (2002) 718 final: Communication from the Commission. The operating framework for the Regulatory Agencies.

COM (2000) 788 final: Externalization of the Management of Community Programmes – including presentation of a framework regulation for a new type of executive agency.

Coombes, D. (1970) *Politics and Bureaucracy in the European Community*, London: George Allen and Unwin.

Coser, L.A. (1956) *The Functions of Social Conflicts*, New York: The Free Press.

Cram, L. (1994) 'The European Commission as a multi-organization: social policy and IT policy in the EU', *Journal of European Public Policy* 1: 195–217.

Cross, S. (2003) 'Campaigner rounds on Eurostat "rip-off"', *European Voice*, 25 September.

Dehousse, R. (1997a) 'European integration and the nation-state', in M. Rhodes, P. Heywood and V. Wright (eds) *Developments in West European Politics*, London: Macmillan.

Dehousse, R. (1997b) 'Regulation by networks in the European Community: the role of European agencies', *Journal of European Public Policy* 4: 246–61.

Dehousse, R. (2002) 'Misfits: EU law and the transformation of European governance', in C. Joerges and R. Dehousse (eds) *Good Governance in Europe's Integrated Market*, Oxford: Oxford University Press.

De Michelis, A. (1997) 'How European statistics are rising to the challenges of economic globalization', *Sigma* 1: 47–51.

De Michelis, A. and A. Chantrine (2003) *Memoirs of Eurostat – Fifty Years Serving Europe*, Luxembourg: European Communities.

Desrosières, A. (1998) *The Politics of Large Numbers – a History of Statistical Reasoning*, Cambridge, MA: Harvard University Press.

Di Maggio, P. and W.W. Powell (1983) 'The iron cage revisited: institutional isomorphism and collective rationality in organizational fields', *American Sociological Review* 48: 147–60.

Dimitrakopoulos, D. (ed.) (2004) *The Changing European Commission*, Manchester: Manchester University Press.

Dinan, D. (2004) *Europe Recast. A History of European Union*, Basingstoke: Palgrave Macmillan.

Directive 2002/19/EC of the European Parliament and of the Council of 7 March 2002 on access to, and interconnection of electronic communications networks and associated facilities (Access Directive), *Official Journal of the European Communities*, 24 April 2002.

Directive 2002/20/EC of the European Parliament and of the Council of 7 March 2002 on the authorisation of electronic communications networks and services.

Directive 2002/21/EC of the European Parliament and of the Council of 7 March 2002 on a common regulatory framework for electronic communications networks and services.

Directive 2002/22/EC of the European Parliament and of the Council of 7 March 2002 on universal service and users' rights to electronic communications networks and services (Universal Service Directive), *Official Journal of the European Communities*, 24 April 2002.

Donnelly, M. and E. Ritchie (1994) 'The college of commissioners and their *cabinets*', in G. Edwards and D. Spence (eds) *The European Commission*, Harlow: Longman.

Drake, H. (2000) *Jacques Delors. Perspectives on a European Leader*, London: Routledge.

Duchêne, F. (1994) *Jean Monnet. The First Statesman of Interdependence*, New York: W.W. Norton.

Duncan, A. (2001) 'The history of IMPEL', the IMPEL homepage: http://europa.eu.int/comm/environment/impel.

Eberlein, B. and G. Grande (2005) 'Beyond delegation: transnational regulatory regimes and the EU regulatory state', *Journal of European Public Policy* 12: 89–112.

The Economist (2002) 'A dearth of data at the ECB', 20 April.

Egan, M.P. (2001) *Constructing a European Market: Standards, Regulation and Governance*, Oxford: Oxford University Press.

Egeberg, M. (1989) 'Mot instrumentelle modeller i statsvitenskapen', in M. Egeberg (ed.) *Institusjonspolitikk og forvaltningsutvikling. Bidrag til en anvendt statsvitenskap*, Oslo: TANO.

Egeberg, M. (1996) 'Organization and nationality in the European Commission services', *Public Administration* 74: 721–35.

Egeberg, M. (1999) 'Transcending intergovernmentalism? Identity and role perceptions of national officials in EU decision-making', *Journal of European Public Policy* 6: 456–74.

Egeberg, M. (2000) 'Mot en europeisk union? Den organisatoriske dimensjonen', *Nordisk Administrativt Tidsskrift* 81: 297–305.

Egeberg, M. (2001) 'How federal? The organisational dimension of integration in the EU (and elsewhere)', *Journal of European Public Policy* 8: 728–46.

Egeberg, M. (2003a) 'How bureaucratic structure matters: an organizational perspective', in B.G. Peters and J. Pierre (eds) *Handbook of Public Administration*, London: Sage.

Egeberg, M. (2003b) 'The European Commission', in M. Cini (ed.) *European Union Politics*, Oxford: Oxford University Press.

Egeberg, M. (2004) 'An organisational approach to European integration: outline of a complementary perspective', *European Journal of Political Research* 43: 199–219.

Egeberg, M. (2005) 'The EU and the Nordic countries: organizing domestic diversity', in S. Bulmer and C. Lequesne (eds) *The Member States of the European Union*, Oxford: Oxford University Press.

Egeberg, M. and H. Sætren (1999) 'Identities in complex organizations: a study of ministerial bureaucrats', in M. Egeberg and P. Lægreid (eds) *Organizing Political Institutions. Essays for Johan P. Olsen*, Oslo: Scandinavian University Press.

Egeberg, M. and J. Trondal (1999) 'Differentiated integration in Europe: the case of the EEA country Norway', *Journal of Common Market Studies* 37: 133–42.

Ehlermann, C.D. (2000) 'The modernization of EC antitrust policy. A legal and cultural revolution', Florence: EUI Working Paper, No. 17.

Elgie, R. (2003) 'Governance traditions and narratives of public sector reform in contemporary France', *Public Administration* 81: 141–62.

Elster, J. (1986) *The Multiple Self*, Cambridge: Cambridge University Press.

Elster, J. (1998) 'Deliberation and constitution making', in J. Elster (ed.) *Deliberative Democracy*, Oxford: Oxford University Press.

Eriksen, E.O. and J.E. Fossum (eds) (2000) *Democracy in the European Union. Integration through Deliberation?* London: Routledge.

Eriksen, E.O., J.E. Fossum and A.J. Menéndez (eds) (2004) *Developing a Constitution for Europe*, London: Routledge.

EU Commission (2000) 'The results of the public consultation on the 1999 communications review and orientations for the New Regulatory Framework', *Communication forms the Commission*, COM (2000) 239.

EU Commission (2002a) 'Commission Decision of 29 July 2002, establishing the European Regulators Group for Electronic Communications Networks and Services (2002/627/EC)', *Official Journal of the European Communities*, 30 July 2002.

EU Commission (2002b) 'Commission guidelines on market analysis and the assessment of significant market power under the Community Regulatory Framework for Electronic Communities Networks and Services (2002/c 165/03)', *Official Journal of the European Communities*, 11 July 2002.

European Commission (2000a) *White Paper on Food Safety*, COM (1999) 719 final.

European Commission (2000b) *Communication from the Commission on the Precautionary Principle*, COM (2000) 1.

European Communities (2002) 'Regulation (EC) No. 178/2002 of the European Parliament and of the Council of 28 January 2002 laying down the general principles and requirements of food law, establishing the European Food Safety Authority and laying down procedures in matters of food safety', *Official Journal of the European Communities, Official Journal L 031, 01/02/2002 P. 0001–0024*.

European Communities (2003) 'Council Decision of 17 November 2003 on the accession of the European Community to the Codex Alimentarius Commission', *Official Journal of the European Union L 309/14*, 26 November 2003.

European Communities (2004) 'Regulation (EC) No 882/2004 of the European Parliament and of the Council on official controls performed to ensure the verification of compliance with feed and food law, animal health and welfare rules', *Official Journal of the European Union, L 165*, Vol. 47, 30 April 2004.

European Council (2000) *Presidency Conclusions*, Nice European Council Meeting, 7–9 December 2000.

European Food Safety Authority (2005) European Food Safety Authority Website: http://www.efsa.eu.int/.

European Parliament (1997) *Report on Alleged Contraventions or Maladministration in the Implementation of Community Law in Relation to BSE, without Prejudice to the Jurisdiction of the Community and National Courts*, Temporary Committee of Inquiry Brussels: European Parliament, 07.02.97.

European Parliament (2000) 'EU Parliament first reading of proposal for a European Parliament and Council directive on a common regulatory framework for electronic communications networks and services', *Minutes* (COM 2000), 393-c5-0428/2000–2000/0184(COD).

Eurostat (1995) *Yearbook*, Luxembourg: European Communities.

Everson, M., G. Majone, L. Metcalfe and A. Schout (eds) (1999) 'The role of specialised agencies in decentralising EU governance', Report presented to the Commission, Maastricht: European Institute of Public Administration.

FAO/WHO (1999) *Understanding the Codex Alimentarius*, Rome: Food and Agriculture Organization of the United Nations and World Health Organization.

Feldman, M.S. and J.G. March (1988) 'Information in organizations as signal and symbol', in J.G. March (ed.) *Organizations and Decisions*, Oxford: Blackwell.

Fouilleux, E., A. Smith and J. de Maillard (2002) 'Council working groups: their role in the production of European problems and policies', in G.F. Schaefer (ed.) *Governance by Committee. The Role of Committees in European Policy-making and Policy Implementation*, Maastricht: EIPA.

Franklin, D. (2003) 'Why its data is dodgy too', *European Voice* 9 (39), 20 November.

From, J. and P. Stava (1993) 'Implementation of Community law' in S. Andersen and K. Eliassen (eds) *Making Policy in Europe*, London: Sage.

Glatzel, D. (1999) 'Greater clarity for excessive deficit procedure', *Sigma* 2: 31–3.

Goetz, K.H. (2001) 'European integration and national executives: a cause in search of an effect', in K.H. Goetz and S. Hix (eds) *Europeanised Politics? European Integration and National Political Systems*, London: Frank Cass.

Goldsmith, P. and C. Lanz (2001) 'Maybe definitely – definitely maybe? EC competition law – is the time ripe for reform?', Eipascope No. 2: http://www.eipascope.nl.

Golub, J. (1999) 'In the shadow of the vote? Decision-making in the European Community', *International Organization* 53: 733–64.

Gornitzka, Å. (2005) 'Networking administration in areas of national sensitivity. The Commission and European higher education', Paper prepared for the Connex conference in Oslo, 27–28 May 2005.

Goyder, D.G. (2003) *EC Competition Law*, Oxford: Oxford University Press.

Graver, H.P. (2002) 'National implementation of EU law and the shaping of European administrative policy', ARENA Working Paper 17/02, Oslo: ARENA.

Gulick, L. (1937) 'Notes on the theory of organization. With special reference to government', in L. Gulick and L. Urwick (eds) *Papers on the Science of Administration*, New York: Institute of Public Administration, Columbia University.

Haas, E. (1958/2004) *The Uniting of Europe: Political, Social and Economic Forces, 1950–57*, Stanford: Stanford University Press (1958); Notre Dame, Indiana: University of Notre Dame Press (2004).

Hallstein, W. (1962) *United Europe. Challenge and Opportunity*, Cambridge, MA: Harvard University Press.

Hayes-Renshaw, F. and H. Wallace (1997) *The Council of Ministers*, New York: St Martin's Press.

Hayward, J. and A. Menon (eds) *Governing Europe*, Oxford: Oxford University Press.

Heritier, A., D. Kerwer, C. Knill, D. Lehmkuhl, M. Teutsch and A.-C. Douillet (2001) *Differential Europe. The European Union Impact on National Policymaking*, Lanham, MD: Rowman & Littlefield.

Hine, D. (1993) *Governing Italy. The Politics of Bargained Pluralism*, Oxford: Oxford University Press.

Hix, S. (1998) 'Elections, parties and institutional design: a comparative perspective on European Union democracy', *West European Politics* 21: 19–52.

Hix, S. (2001) 'Legislative behaviour and party competition in the European Parliament: an application of nominate to the EU', *Journal of Common Market Studies* 39: 663–88.

Hoffman, S. (1995): 'Introduction', in S. Hoffman (ed.) *The European Sisyphus. Essays on Europe 1964–94*, Boulder, CO: Westview.

Holland, W. and E. Mossialos (eds) (1999) *Public Health Policies in the European Union*, Aldershot: Ashgate.

Holsti, K.J. (2004) *Taming the Sovereigns. Institutional Change in International Politics*, Cambridge: Cambridge University Press.

Hood, C. (1991) 'A public management for all seasons?' *Public Administration* 69: 3–19.

Hooghe, L. (1999) 'Supranational activists or intergovernmental agents? Explaining the orientations of senior Commission officials towards European integration', *Comparative Political Studies* 32: 435–53.

Hooghe, L. (2000) 'A house with differing views: the European Commission and cohesion policy', in N. Nugent (ed.) *At the Heart of the Union. Studies of the European Commission*, Basingstoke: Macmillan Press.

Hooghe, L. (2001) *The European Commission and the Integration of Europe. Images of Governance*, Cambridge: Cambridge University Press.

Hooghe, L. and G. Marks (2001) *Multi-level Governance and European Integration*, Lanham, MD: Rowman and Littlefield.

Hopwood, A. and P. Miller (eds) (1994) *Accounting as a Social and Institutional Practice*, London: Cambridge University Press.

IMPEL Multi annual work program at IMPEL's homepage: http://europa.eu.int/comm/environment/impel/workprog.htm#multiannual.

Jachtenfuchs, M. (2001) 'The governance approach to European integration', *Journal of Common Market Studies* 39: 245–64.

Jachtenfuchs, M. and B. Kohler-Koch (2004) 'Governance and institutional development', in A. Wiener and T. Diez (eds) *European Integration Theory*, Oxford: Oxford University Press.

Jacobsson, B., P. Lægreid and O.K. Pedersen (2003) *Europeanisation and Transnational States. Comparing Nordic Central Governments*, London: Routledge.

Jeffery, C. (2000) 'Sub-national mobilization and the European integration: Does it make any difference?' *Journal of Common Market Studies* 38: 1–23.

Joana, J. and A. Smith (2004) 'The politics of collegiality: the non-portfolio dimension', in A. Smith (ed.) *Politics and the European Commission*, London: Routledge.

Joerges, C. and J. Neyer (1997) 'Transforming strategic interaction into deliberative problem solving: European comitology in the foodstuffs sector', *Journal of European Public Policy* 4: 609–25.

Johansson, K.M. (2005) 'The European Commission and the growing significance of party politics', Paper prepared for the Connex conference in Oslo, 27–28 May 2005.

Jordan, A. (1999) 'The implementation of EU environmental policy: a policy problem without a political solution', *Environment and Planning C: Government and Policy* 17: 69–90.

Jordan, A. (ed.) (2002) *Environmental Policy in the European Union*, London: Earthscan.

Kadelbach, S. (2002) 'European administrative law and the law of a Europeanized administration', in R. Dehousse and C. Joerges (eds) *Good Governance in Europe's Integrated Market*, Oxford: Oxford University Press.

Kahn, J. (1997) *Budgeting Democracy – State Building and Citizenship in America 1890–1928*, Ithaca, NY: Cornell University Press.

Kassim, H. (2003) 'The European administration: between Europeanization and domestication', in J. Hayward and A. Menon (eds) *Governing Europe*, Oxford: Oxford University Press.

Kassim, H. and A. Menon (2004) 'European integration since the 1990s: member states and the European Commission', ARENA Working Paper 6/04, Oslo: ARENA.

Kassim, H. and V. Wright (1991) 'The role of national administrations in the decision-making processes of the European Community', *Rivista Trimestrale di Diritto Pubblico* 41: 832–50.

Kassim, H., B.G. Peters and V. Wright (eds) (2000) *The National Co-ordination of EU Policy. The Domestic Level*, Oxford: Oxford University Press.

Kaufman, H. (1976) *Are Government Organizations Immortal?* Washington, DC: Brookings.

Kelemen, R.D. (2004) *The Rules of Federalism. Institutions and Regulatory Politics in the EU and Beyond*, Cambridge, MA: Harvard University Press.

Kerremans, B. (1996) 'Do institutions make a difference? Non-institutionalism, neo-institutionalism, and the logic of common decision-making in the European Union', *Governance* 9: 217–40.

Kickert, W.J.M. and T. Beck Jørgensen (1995) 'Introduction: managerial reform trends in Western Europe', *International Review of Administrative Sciences* 61: 499–510.

Kimberly, J.R., R.H. Miles et al. (1980) *The Organizational Life Cycle*, San Francisco: Jossey-Bass.

Knill, C. (1998) 'European policies: the impact of national administrative traditions', *Journal of Public Policy* 18: 1–28.

Knill, C. (2001) *The Europeanisation of National Administrations. Patterns of Institutional Change and Persistence*, Cambridge: Cambridge University Press.

Kohler-Koch, B. (1996a) 'Catching up with change. The transformation of governance in the European Union', *Journal of European Public Policy* 3: 359–80.

Kohler-Koch, B. (1996b) 'The strength of weakness: the transformation of governance in the EU', in S. Gustavsson and L. Lewin (eds) *The Future of the Nation-state. Essays on Cultural Pluralism and Political Integration*, London: Routledge.

Kohler-Koch, B. (1997) 'Organized interests in European integration: the evolution of a new type of governance', in H. Wallace and A.R. Young (eds) *Participation and Policy-making in the European Union*, Oxford: Clarendon Press.

Kohler-Koch, B. (1999) 'The evolution and transformation of European governance', in B. Kohler-Koch and R. Eising (eds) *The Transformation of Governance in the European Union*, London: Routledge.

Kohler-Koch, B. (2002) 'European network and ideas: Changing national policies?' *European Integration online Papers (EIOP)* 6 (6).

Kohler-Koch, B. and R. Eising (eds) (1999) *The Transformation of Governance in the European Union*, London: Routledge.

Konkurrencestyrelsen (2003) *Konkurrenceredegørelse 2003*, Chapter 9: http://www.ks.dk/publikationer/konkurrenceredegoerelsen/kr2003/.

Kreher, A. (1997) 'Agencies in the European Community – a step towards administrative integration in Europe', *Journal of European Public Policy* 4: 225–45.

Lægreid, P. and J.P. Olsen (1984) 'Top civil servants in Norway: key players on different teams?', in E.N. Suleiman (ed.) *Bureaucrats and Policy-making*, New York: Holmes and Meier.

Laffan, B. (1998) 'The European Union: a distinctive model of internationaliza- X tion', *Journal of European Public Policy* 5: 235–53.

Laudati, L. (1996) 'The European Commission as regulator: the uncertain pursuit of the competitive market', in G. Majone (ed.) *Regulating Europe*, London: Routledge.

Lequesne, C. (2000) 'The European Commission: a balancing act between autonomy and dependence', in K. Neunreither and A. Wiener (eds) *European Integration after Amsterdam. Institutional Dynamics and Prospects for Democracy*, Oxford: Oxford University Press.

Lewis, J. (1998) 'Is the "hard bargaining" image of the Council misleading? The committee of permanent representatives and the local elections directive', *Journal of Common Market Studies* 36: 479–504.

Lewis, J. (2000) 'The methods of community in EU decision-making and administrative rivalry in the Council's infrastructure', *Journal of European Public Policy* 7: 261–89.

Lewis, J. (2002) 'National interests: Coreper', in J. Peterson and M. Shackleton (eds) *The Institutions of the European Union*, Oxford: Oxford University Press.

Leyland, P. and D. Donati (2001) 'Executive accountability and the changing face of government: UK and Italy compared', *European Public Law* 7: 217–57.

Lipset, S.M. and S. Rokkan (1967) 'Cleavage structures, party systems, and voter alignments: an introduction', in S.M. Lipset and S. Rokkan (eds) *Party Systems and Voter Alignments*, New York: The Free Press.

Lipsky, M. (1980) *Street-level Bureaucracy: Dilemmas of the Individual in Public Services*, New York: Russell Sage Foundation.

Lowi, T.J. (1964) 'American business, public policy, case studies, and political theory', *World Politics* 16: 677–715.

Ludlow, P. (2004) 'The Barroso Commission: a tale of lost innocence', *Briefing Note No 3.4/5*, Brussels: EuroComment.

MacMullen, A. (2000) 'European commissioners: national routes to a European elite', in N. Nugent (ed.) *At the Heart of the Union. Studies of the European Commission*, Basingstoke: Macmillan Press.

Mair, P. (2004) 'Review essay: the Europeanization dimension', *Journal of European Public Policy* 11: 337–48.

Majone, G. (1991) 'Cross-national sources of regulatory policy-making in Europe and the United States', *Journal of Public Policy* 11: 79–106.

Majone, G. (1996) *Regulating Europe*, London: Routledge.

Majone, G. (1997) 'The new European agencies: regulation by information', *Journal of European Public Policy* 4: 262–75.

Majone, G. (2000) 'The credibility crisis of Community regulation', *Journal of Common Market Studies* 38: 273–302.

Majone, G. (2002) 'The European Commission: the limits of centralization and the perils of parliamentarization', *Governance* 15: 375–92.

March, J.G. (1987) 'Ambiguity and accounting: the elusive link between information and decision-making', *Accounting, Organizations and Society* 12: 153–68.

March, J.G. (1999) 'A learning perspective on the network dynamics of institutional integration', in M. Egeberg and P. Lægreid (eds) *Organizing Political Institutions. Essays for Johan P. Olsen*, Oslo: Scandinavian University Press.

March, J.G. and J.P. Olsen (1976) *Ambiguity and Choice in Organizations*, Bergen: Universitetsforlaget.

March, J.G. and J.P. Olsen (1989) *Rediscovering Institutions. The Organizational Basis of Politics*, New York: The Free Press.

March, J.G. and J.P. Olsen (1995) *Democratic Governance*, New York: The Free Press.

March, J.G. and J.P. Olsen (2006) 'Elaborating the "New Institutionalism"', ARENA Working Paper 11/05, Oslo: ARENA. Forthcoming in R.A.W. Rhodes, S. Binder and B. Rockman (eds) *The Oxford Handbook of Political Institutions*, Oxford: Oxford University Press.

March, J.G. and G. Sevon (1988) 'Gossip, information and decision-making', in J.G. March (ed.) *Organizations and Decisions*, Oxford: Blackwell.

Marks, G. (1993) 'Structural policy and multi-level governance in the EC', in J. Klausen and L. Tilly (eds) *Processes of European Integration, 1880–1995: States, Markets and Citizenship*, Boulder, CO: Rowman & Littlefield.

Marks, G. and M.R. Steenbergen (eds) (2004) *European Integration and Political Conflict*, Cambridge: Cambridge University Press.

Marks, G., L. Hooghe and K. Blank (1996) 'European integration from the 1980s: state-centric v. multi-level governance', *Journal of Common Market Studies* 34: 341–77.

Mattila, M. (2004) 'Contested decisions: Empirical analysis of voting in the European Union Council of Ministers', *European Journal of Political Research* 43: 29–50.

Mattila, M. and J.-E. Lane (2001) 'Why unanimity in the Council? A roll call analysis of Council voting', *European Union Politics* 2: 31–52.

Maurer, A. and T. Larsson (2002) 'Democratic legitimacy in EU politics – no way out for committees', in G.F. Schaefer (ed.) *Governance by Committee. The Role of Committees in European Policy-making and Policy Implementation*, Maastricht: EIPA.

Mazey, S. and J. Richardson (1996) 'The logic of organisation. Interest groups', in J. Richardson (ed.) *European Union: Power and Policy-making*, London: Routledge.

Mbaye, Heather (2001) 'Why national states comply with supranational law: explaining implementation infringements in the European Union, 1972–1993', *European Union Politics* 2: 259–82.

McGowan, F. (2000) 'Competition policy', in H. Wallace and W. Wallace (eds) *Policy-making in the European Union*, Oxford: Oxford University Press.

McNamara, K.R. (2001) 'Where do rules come from? The creation of the European Central Bank', in A. Stone Sweet, W. Sandholtz and N. Fligstein (eds) *The Institutionalization of Europe*, Oxford: Oxford University Press.

Meier, K.J. and L.G. Nigro (1976) 'Representative bureaucracy and policy preferences: a study in the attitudes of federal executives', *Public Administration Review* 36: 458–69.

Mendrinou, M. (1996) 'Non-compliance and the European Commission's role in integration', *Journal of European Public Policy* 3: 1–22.

Menon, A. (2003) 'Member states and international institutions: institutionalizing intergovernmentalism in the European Union, *Comparative European Politics* 1: 171–201.

Meyer, J.W. and B. Rowan (1977) 'Institutionalized organizations: formal structure as myth and ceremony', *American Journal of Sociology* 83: 340–63.

Michelmann, H.J. (1978) 'Multinational staffing and organizational functioning in the Commission of the European Communities', *International Organization* 32: 477–96.

Mittag, J. and W. Wessels (2003) 'The "One" and the "Fifteen"? The member states between procedural adaptation and structural revolution', in W. Wessels, A. Maurer and J. Mittag (eds) *Fifteen into One? The European Union and its Member States*, Manchester: Manchester University Press.

Moravcsik, A. (1993) 'Preferences and power in the European Community: a liberal intergovernmentalist approach', *Journal of Common Market Studies* 31: 473–524.

Moravcsik, A. (1998) *The Choice for Europe. Social Purpose and State Power from Messina to Maastricht*, London: UCL Press.

Morbidelli, G. (2000) 'Le autorità indipendenti: introduzione ad una lettura comparata', *Diritto Pubblico Comparato ed Europeo* 3.

Mörth, U. (2000) 'Competing frames in the European Commission – the case of the defence industry and equipment issue', *Journal of European Public Policy* 7: 173–89.

Nedergaard, P. (2001) *Organiseringen av Den Europæiske Union*, Copenhagen: Handelshøjskolens Forlag.

Neuhold, C. (2001) 'The "legislative backbone" keeping the institution upright? The role of European Parliament committees in the EU policy-making process', *European Integration online Papers (EIoP)* 5 (10).

Neunreither, K. (1972) 'Transformation of a political role: reconsidering the case of the Commission of the European Communities', *Journal of Common Market Studies* 10: 233–48.

Neyer, J. (1999) 'Justifying comitology: the promise of deliberation', Paper presented to the European Community Studies Association's Sixth Biennial International Conference, Pittsburgh.

Nicolaides, P. (2002) *'Reform of EC competition policy: a significant but risky project'*, Eipascope No. 2: http://www.eipa.nl.

Nørgård, G.H. (2004) 'Forvaltningspolitik i den Europæiske Union og nationalstaterne. Mod et netværk-administrativt system i EU?' Master's thesis, Institute for Political Science, Odense: Odense Universitetsforlag.

Nugent, N. (ed.) (2000) *At the Heart of the Union. Studies of the European Commission*, Basingstoke: Macmillan Press.

Nugent, N. (2001) *The European Commission*, Basingstoke: Palgrave.

Nugent, N. (2003) *The Government and Politics of the European Union*, Basingstoke: Palgrave.

O'Rourke, R. (1998) *European Food Law*, Bembridge: Palladian Law Publishing.

Olsen, J.P. (1980) 'Governing Norway: segmentation, anticipation, and consensus formation', in R. Rose and E.N. Suleiman (eds) *Presidents and Prime Ministers*, Washington, DC: American Enterprise Institute.

Olsen, J.P. (1992) 'Analyzing institutional dynamics', *Staatswissenschaften und Staatspraxis* 3: 247–71.

Olsen, J.P. (1995) 'Europeanization and nation state dynamics', ARENA Working Paper 9/95, Oslo: ARENA.

Olsen, J.P. (1997) 'European challenges to the nation state', in B. Steunenberg and F. van Vught (eds) *Political Institutions and Public Policy*, Dordrecht: Kluwer Academic Publishers.

Olsen, J.P. (2001) 'Organizing European institutions of governance: a prelude to an institutional account of political integration', in H. Wallace (ed.) *Whose Europe? Interlocking Dimensions of Integration*, London: Macmillan.

Olsen, J.P. (2002a) 'Reforming European institutions of governance', *Journal of Common Market Studies* 40: 581–602.

Olsen, J.P. (2002b) 'The many faces of Europeanization', *Journal of Common Market Studies* 40: 921–52.

Olsen, J.P. (2003) 'Towards a European administrative space?' *Journal of European Public Policy* 10: 506–31.

Olsen, J.P. (2004) 'Citizens, public administration and the search for theoretical foundations. The 2003 John Gaus Lecture', *Political Science and Politics* 37: 69–79.

Page, E.C. (1997) *People Who Run Europe*, Oxford: Clarendon Press.

Patriarca, S. (1996) *Numbers and Nationhood: Writing Statistics in Nineteenth-century Italy*, London: Cambridge University Press.

Pedersen, T. (2000) 'Denmark', in H. Kassim, B.G. Peters and V. Wright (eds) *The National Coordination of EU Policy. The Domestic Level*, Oxford: Oxford University Press.

Peters, B.G. (1992) 'Bureaucratic politics and institutions of the European Community', in A. Sbragia (ed.) *Euro-politics. Institutions and Policy-making in the 'New' European Community*, Washington, DC: The Brookings Institution.

Peters, B.G. (1997) 'Policy transfers between governments: the case of administrative reforms', *West European Politics* 20: 71–88.

Peters, B.G. (2000) 'The Commission and implementation in the EU: is there an implementation deficit and why?', in N. Nugent (ed.) *At the Heart of the Union: Studies of the European Commission*, Basingstoke: Palgrave.

Peterson, J. (1999) 'The Santer era: the European Commission in normative, historical and theoretical perspective', *Journal of European Public Policy* 6: 46–65.

Peterson, J. (2002) 'The college of commissioners', in J. Peterson and M. Shackleton (eds) *The Institutions of the European Union*, Oxford: Oxford University Press.

Peterson, J. (2004) 'The Prodi Commission: fresh start or free fall?', in D. Dimitrakopoulos (ed.) *The Changing European Commission*, Manchester: Manchester University Press.

Peterson, R.L. (1971) 'Personnel decisions and the independence of the Commission of the European Communities', *Journal of Common Market Studies* 10: 117–37.

Pfeffer, J. (1982) *Organizations and Organization Theory*, Boston: Pitman.

Pierson, P. (1996) 'The path to European integration: a historical institutionalist analysis', *Comparative Political Studies* 29: 123–63.

Pollack, M.A. (2004) 'The new institutionalisms and European integration', in A. Wiener and T. Diez (eds) *European Integration Theory*, Oxford: Oxford University Press.

Porter, T.M. (1995) *Trust in Numbers – the Pursuit of Objectivity in Science and Public Life*, Princeton, NJ: Princeton University Press.

Power, M. (1994) 'The audit society', in A. Hopwood and P. Miller (eds) *Accounting as a Social and Institutional Practice*, London: Cambridge University Press.

Prodi, R. (2000) 'Europe and global governance', speech given at the Second COMECE Congress, Brussels, 31 March 2000.

Raunio, T. (2002) 'Political interests: the EP's party groups', in J. Peterson and M. Shackleton (eds) *The Institutions of the European Union*, Oxford: Oxford University Press.

Reinalda, B. and B. Verbeek (eds) (2004) *Decision Making within International Organizations*, London: Routledge.

Risse, T. (2002a) 'An emerging European identity? What we know and how to make sense of it', in *Europe Transformed? The European Union and Collective Identity Change*, ARENA/IDNET International Policy Conference, 11 October.

Risse, T. (2002b) 'Transnational actors and world politics', in W. Carlsnaes, T. Risse and B.A. Simmons (eds) *Handbook of International Relations*, London: Sage.

Romanov, A. (1981) *Case Studies of Organizational Change: a Review*, Stanford, CA: Stanford University Press.

Ross, E. (1920) *The Principles of Sociology*, New York: Century.

Ross, G. (1995) *Jacques Delors and European Integration*, Cambridge: Polity Press.

Rouban, L. (2003), 'Politicization of the civil service', in B.G. Peters and J. Pierre (eds) *Handbook of Public Administration*, London: Sage.

Sandholtz, W. and A. Stone Sweet (eds) (1998) *European Integration and Supranational Governance*, Oxford: Oxford University Press.

Sangolt, L. (1997) 'Counting and governing', Doctoral dissertation, Department of Administration and Organization Theory, University of Bergen, Norway.

Sangolt, L. (2004) 'Statistics, democracy and trust', Paper presented at the conference Politics and knowledge: democratizing knowledge in times of the expert, Bergen.

Sbragia, A. (1999) 'Environmental policy. Economic constraints and external pressures in policy-making in the European Union', in H. Wallace and W. Wallace (eds) *Policy-making in the European Union*, Oxford: Oxford University Press.

Schaefer, G.F. (ed.) (2002) *Governance by Committee. The Role of Committees in European Policy-making and Policy Implementation*, Maastricht: EIPA.

Schaefer, G.F., N. Flatz and M. Gotthard (2002) 'How do comitology committees work: an insider perspective', in G.F. Schaefer (ed.) *Governance by Committee. The Role of Committees in European Policy-making and Policy Implementation*, Maastricht: EIPA.

Schattschneider, E. E. (1975) *The Semisovereign People: a Realist's View of Democracy in America*, New York: Holt, Rinehart & Winston.

Schimmelfennig, F. (2004) 'Liberal intergovernmentalism', in A. Wiener and T. Diez (eds) *European Integration Theory*, Oxford: Oxford University Press.

Schmitter, P.C. (1970) 'A revised theory of regional integration', *International Organization* 24: 836–68.

Schneider, G. and M. Aspinwall (eds) (2001) *The Rules of Integration. Institutionalist Approaches to the Study of Europe*, Manchester: Manchester University Press.

Schout, A. and F. Claessens (1999) 'The European network for the Implementation and Enforcement of Environmental Law (IMPEL) – the strengths and weaknesses of an informal network', in M. Everson, G. Majone, L. Metcalfe and A. Schout (eds) *The Role of Specialised Agencies in Decentralising EU Governance*, Report presented to the Commission, Maastricht: European Institute of Public Administration.

Schroeder, P.W. (1994) *The Transformation of European Politics 1763–1848*, Oxford: Oxford University Press.

Scott, W.R. (1981) *Organizations. Rational, Natural, and Open Systems*, Englewood Cliffs, NJ: Prentice-Hall.

Searing, D.D. (1994) *Westminster's World. Understanding Political Roles*, Cambridge, MA: Harvard University Press.

Selden, S.C. (1997) *The Promise of Representative Bureaucracy. Diversity and Responsiveness in a Government Agency*, Armonk: M.E. Sharpe.

Selznick, P. (1957) *Leadership in Administration. A Sociological Interpretation*, Berkeley: University of California Press.

Shapiro, M. (1997) 'The problems of independent agencies in the United States and the European Union', *Journal of European Public Policy* 4: 276–91.

Sigma (1995) 'A more independent Eurostat', *Sigma. The Bulletin of European Statistics*, Winter: 37–8.

Simon, H.A. (1957/1965) *Administrative Behavior*, New York: Macmillan (1957); New York: The Free Press (1965).

Singer, J.D. and M. Wallace (1970) 'Intergovernmental organization and the preservation of peace, 1816–1964: some bivariate relationships', *International Organization* 24: 520–47.

Skogstad, G. (2001) 'The WTO and food safety regulatory policy innovation in the European Union', *Journal of Common Market Studies* 39: 485–505.

Smith, A. (2003) 'Why European commissioners matter', *Journal of Common Market Studies* 41: 137–55.

Smith, A. (ed.) (2005) *Politics and the European Commission*, London: Routledge.

Sørensen, E. and J. Torfing (2004) 'Making governance networks democratic', Working Paper 2004:1, Centre for Democratic Network Governance, Roskilde University.

SOU (1996) *Ett år med EU. Svenska statstjänstemäns erfarenheter av arbetet i EU*, Stockholm.

Spence, D. (1994) 'Structure, functions and procedures in the Commission', in G. Edwards and D. Spence (eds) *The European Commission*, Harlow: Longman.

Statskonsult (1999) *Norsk deltakelse i EU-komiteer. En oversikt over trekk ved forvaltningens deltakelse i komiteer og ekspertgrupper under Europakommisjonen*, Oslo.

Statskontoret (2003) 'Förvaltningssamverkan inom EU', Report 29/2003, Stockholm: Statskontoret.

Stiglitz, J.E. (2003) *The Roaring Nineties – A New History of the World's Most Prosperous Decade*, New York: W.W. Norton & Company.

Strøby Jensen, C. (2003) 'Neo-functionalism', in M. Cini (ed.) *European Union Politics*, Oxford: Oxford University Press.

Sverdrup, U. (2002) 'An institutional perspective on treaty reform: contextualizing the Amsterdam and Nice Treaties', *Journal of European Public Policy* 9: 120–40.

Sverdrup, U. (2003a) 'Compliance and styles of conflict management in Europe', ARENA Working Paper 8/03, Oslo: ARENA.

Sverdrup, U. (2003b) 'De-nationalizing public administration policy?' manuscript, Oslo: ARENA.

Sverdrup, U. (2004) 'Compliance and conflict management in the European Union: Nordic exceptionalism', *Scandinavian Political Studies* 27: 23–43.

Tallberg, J. (1999) *Making States Comply. The European Commission, the European Court of Justice and the Enforcement of the Internal Market*, Lund: Studentlitteratur.

Taylor, A.J.P. (1945/2001) *The Course of German History. A Survey of the Development of German History since 1815*, London: Routledge.

Taylor, A.J.P. (1990) *The Habsburg Monarchy 1809–1918*, London: Penguin Books.

Thatcher, M. and A. Stone Sweet (2001) 'Theory and practice of delegation to non-majoritarian institutions', *West European Politics* 25: 1–22.

Thomson, R., J. Boerefijn and F. Stokman (2004) 'Actor alignments in European decision making', *European Journal of Political Research* 43: 237–61.

Tilly, C. (1975) 'Reflections on the history of European state-making', in C. Tilly (ed.) *The Formation of National States in Western Europe*, Princeton, NJ: Princeton University Press.

Tranøy, B.S. and Ø. Østerud (2001) *Den fragmenterte staten*, Oslo: Gyldendal Akademisk.

Trondal, J. (2000) 'Multiple institutional embeddedness in Europe. The case of Danish, Norwegian and Swedish government officials', *Scandinavian Political Studies* 23: 311–41.

Trondal, J. (2001) Administrative integration across levels of governance. Integration through participation in EU committees, Doctoral dissertation, ARENA Report 7/01, Oslo: ARENA.

Trondal, J. (2002) 'Beyond the EU membership–non-membership dichotomy? Supranational identities among national EU decision-makers', *Journal of European Public Policy* 9: 468–87.

Trondal, J. (2006) 'Governing at the frontier of the European Commission. The case of seconded national experts', *West European Politics* 29: 147–60.

Trondal, J. and F. Veggeland (2003) 'Access, voice and loyalty. The representation of domestic civil servants in EU committees', *Journal of European Public Policy* 10: 59–77.

Trondal, J., M. Marcussen and F. Veggeland (2005) 'Re-discovering international executive institutions', *Comparative European Politics* 3: 232–58.

Tuerk, A. and G.F. Schaefer (2002) 'Legislation and implementation: theoretical considerations and empirical findings', in G.F. Schaefer (ed.) *Governance by Committee. The Role of Committees in European Policy-making and Policy Implementation*, Maastricht: EIPA.

Ucarer, E.M. (2003) 'Justice and home affairs', in M. Cini (ed.) *European Union Politics*, Oxford: Oxford University Press.

Ugland, T. (2002) *Policy Re-categorization and Integration – Europeanization of Nordic Alcohol Control Policies*, Oslo: ARENA Report 3/02.

Ugland, T. (2003) 'Adaptation and integration through policy re-categorization', *Journal of Public Policy* 23: 157–70.

Ugland, T. and F. Veggeland (2004) 'Towards an integrated approach? Food inspection reforms in Canada and the European Union (EU)', *Policy and Society* 23 (4): 104–24.

Ugland, T. and F. Veggeland (2006) 'Experiments in food safety policy integration in the European Union', *Journal of Common Market Studies* (forthcoming).

Veggeland, F. (2000) 'Eksterne sjokk og institusjonell endring: Kugalskap-saken og reformer i EU', *Nordiske Organisasjons-Studier* 2: 29–63.

Veggeland, F. and S.O. Borgen (2005) 'Negotiating international food standards: the World Trade Organization's impact on the Codex Alimentarius Commission', *Governance* 18: 675–708.

Verdun, A. (2003) 'Economic and Monetary Union', in M. Cini (ed.) *European Union Politics*, Oxford: Oxford University Press.

Vos, E. (1999) 'EU committees: the evolution of unforeseen institutional actors in European product regulation', in C. Joerges and E. Vos (eds) *EU Committees: Social Regulation, Law and Politics*, Oxford, Portland: Hart Publishing.

Vos, E. (2000) 'EU food safety regulation in the aftermath of the BSE crisis', *Journal of Consumer Policy* 23: 227–55.

Weale, A. (1999) 'European environmental policy by stealth: the dysfunctionality of functionalism?', *Environment and planning C: Government and Policy* 17 (Feb.): 37–52.

Wessels, W. (1998) 'Comitology: fusion in action. Politico-administrative trends in the EU system', *Journal of European Public Policy* 5: 209–34.

Wessels, W. and D. Rometsch (1996) 'Conclusion: European Union and national institutions', in W. Wessels and D. Rometsch (eds) *The European Union and Member States. Towards Institutional Fusion?*, Manchester: Manchester University Press.

Winter, S. (2003) 'Implementation perspectives: status and reconsideration', in B.G. Peters and J. Pierre (eds) *Handbook of Public Administration*, London: Sage.

Working Party on Official Statistics in the UK, chaired by P.G. Moore (1991) 'Official statistics: counting with confidence', *Journal of the Royal Statistical Society* 154: 23–44.

WTO (2000a) *Communication from the European Commission on the Precautionary Principle*, Committee on Sanitary and Phytosanitary Measures, G/SPS/GEN/168.

WTO (2000b) *Summary of the Meeting held on 15–16 March 2000*, Note by the Secretariat, Committee on Sanitary and Phytosanitary Measures, G/SPS/R/18.

Yataganas, X. (2001) 'Delegation of regulatory authority in the European Union. The relevance of the American model of independent agencies', Jean Monnet Working Paper 3/01, New York University School of Law.

Yin, R.K. (1989) *Case Study Research. Design and Methods*, London: Sage.

Zito, A. (2002) 'Task expansion: a theoretical overview', in A. Jordan (ed.) *Environmental Policy in the European Union*, London: Earthscan.

Index